Violence, Prejudice and Sexuality

Routledge Advances in Criminology

Violence, Prejudice and Sexuality

Stephen Tomsen

Routledge
Taylor & Francis Group
New York   London

First published 2009
by Routledge
270 Madison Ave, New York, NY 10016

Simultaneously published in the UK
by Routledge
2 Park Square, Milton Park, Abingdon, Oxon OX14 4RN

Routledge is an imprint of the Taylor & Francis Group, an informa business

© 2009 Taylor & Francis

Typeset in Sabon by IBT Global.
Printed and bound in the United States of America on acid-free paper by IBT Global.

Library of Congress Cataloging-in-Publication Data
Tomsen, Stephen.
Violence, prejudice and sexuality / by Stephen Tomsen.
    p. cm. — (Routledge advances in criminology ; 6)
Includes bibliographical references and index.
1. Gays—Crimes against. 2. Homophobia. 3. Hate crimes. I. Title.
HV6250.4.H66T67 2009
364.15086'64—dc22   2008040047

ISBN10: 0-415-95655-2 (hbk)
ISBN10: 0-203-88290-3 (ebk)

ISBN13: 978-0-415-95655-0 (hbk)
ISBN13: 978-0-203-88290-0 (ebk)

Contents

Foreword

This book has the ingredients of a thriller. It has sex and crime. It has decisions with life-and-death stakes, hidden identities, doubt in high places, courtroom drama, ambushes in the dark and brutal murder.

Indeed, some of the killings described here are so violent that they suggest a state of war. That there might be some kind of war going on in the perpetrators' minds, at least, is strongly suggested by the unfolding evidence.

But this book is not entertainment. It is something much more important: social science, original and carefully researched, dealing with very troubling issues of contemporary life.

In this generation questions about sexuality, and the social relations that affect sexual conduct and experience, have become much more central in the social sciences. We no longer think of sexuality just as an undercurrent in the psyche, or a matter of elementary biology. We recognise that issues about bodily interaction, emotional attachment, and the role of sexuality in the making of identities and the drawing of boundaries, are important features of our social world.

We also recognise that sexuality is often not romantic. While sexualised relationships involve beauty and love, they can also involve hostility and violence. Sexual disgust and antagonism, as well as desire, can be the conduits for social tensions that arise from many sources—class inequalities, population movements and ethnic antagonisms among them.

Social science has also been generating new ways of thinking about such antagonisms, about personal and collective violence, and about crime. The gendered character of crime has come into focus. We now have ways of understanding the links between social marginalisation or inequality and violence that keep social structure in view, without arguing away the agency of marginalised people or the intentionality of violence.

Violence, Prejudice and Sexuality is written at a place where these advances meet. It gives us a highly sophisticated analysis, backed by empirical research, of prejudice and violence against lesbians and gay men, and how this violence is handled by the public institutions responsible for order and law.

Social science comes in multiple forms, and this is a multifaceted study. This book has a strong sense of history, not just of the communities immediately affected by anti-homosexual violence, but also of the larger culture in which ideas about sexuality and identity are embedded. It gives an exceptionally clear account of the way our society's commonsense distinction between heterosexuals and homosexuals came into being.

This requires a study of the discursive construction of identities, the ways it is possible to think about who we are, and the central role sexuality now plays in that process. However, the author also recognises that discourses don't float free. He has a strong sense of the material inequalities that shape lives and create dilemmas that can lead to violence. He affirms the material force of physical bodies and the power of the unconscious. Notably, too, he explores the role of institutions, such as courts and police. These institutions have their own ideologies of gender and sexuality that shape the way they deploy state power.

Sexuality and violence both involve face-to-face interactions between people. Stephen Tomsen has a real talent for portraying personal relationships, both long-standing and fleeting, and their crises. Violence is not a fixed condition; it is something that happens, at a particular time and place. The book gives vivid pictures of the way interactions, on the street or in the home, can move towards violence, given certain circumstances. And it sometimes makes telling contrasts with interactions that don't move towards violence.

To understand this range of questions, the author brings together a wide range of data, including international research on prejudice and violence, and an intriguing local study of the audience at the Sydney Gay and Lesbian Mardi Gras parade. At the core, however, is his harrowing examination of homophobic killings in New South Wales over two decades, using detailed legal records as well as press and other sources. With great care, Tomsen teases out the main patterns in these killings and tests the available theories against them. As well as exploring the motives of different groups of perpetrators, this gives a unique, and disturbing, picture of the legal and police system at work.

An important part of the social role of social science is its capacity for critique. This book is notable for its thoughtful critique of mainstream assumptions about these issues. Its examination of court proceedings, for instance, dissects the assumptions about identity, gender and social marginality made by judges and juries, and sometimes intelligently appealed to by defence counsel.

The book also weighs critically the concepts that have been offered by gay theorists and activists in attempts to understand prejudice and violence. Among the main contributions of the book is its careful examination of the ideas of 'homophobia' and 'hate crime', and the limitations of these formulae for understanding what actually happens on the ground.

Yet the book is more than data plus critique. It has a substantive interpretation to offer, and a surprising one—certainly one that runs against the trend of much recent deconstructive theory about sexuality and identity, which only emphasises their discursive form.

The thread that links many of the problems that the book discusses is the politics of masculinity—the gendered social hierarchies among men, the tensions around the construction of masculinity in situations of poverty, the fragility of claims to respect and—anachronistic as it may sound—male honour. Homophobic violence falls within a spectrum of other forms of masculinised violence. Nor is masculinity just an issue about the marginalised young men who are the authors of many of these violent acts. It is also an issue about gay/homosexual men, about police, about judges, indeed about the gender order as a whole.

There have been debates about the concept of 'hegemonic masculinity'. This book provides a notable demonstration of the power of this concept, which always implies a struggle for position in which authority in the gender order is at stake. The dire consequences of challenges, violations of gender order and conflicting claims for respect, within a context of disputed hegemony, are all too clear to see.

Most popular thinking about sexual difference is, as the author observes, categorical and essentialist. It assumes people can be divided into a few clear-cut groups and that the divisions between them are based on some fixed, essential feature of their bodies or minds.

That is certainly the most popular image of gender. A pop psychology book along these lines that suggests men and women are like beings from different planets has sold *thirty million* copies. It is also the most popular way of thinking about sexuality: There are straights and there are gays, completely distinct groups, each with their own fixed character. This way of thinking has certain attractions for lesbian and gay communities. It provides an answer to prejudice, a ground for claims about human rights and—though it is beyond the concerns of this book—it helps to define lesbians and gay men as a legitimate market segment and thus assimilates them into the world of corporate capitalism.

The author rightly rejects this doctrine, agreeing with the critique of essentialism that has been widespread in post-structuralist thought in the last generation. He has much to say about the way the heterosexual/homosexual division operates in contemporary culture. But he goes beyond the usual terrain of this argument, as he does not simply replace 'natural' categories with the idea of discursively constructed subjectivities.

In one of its most challenging moves, *Violence, Prejudice and Sexuality* also explores the ambiguous motives that link people across categories and make the reassertion of boundaries sometimes a matter of great urgency. While rejecting the mechanical argument that homophobes are just repressed homosexuals, the author is alert to the complexities of sexual pleasure and desire that underpin, and sometimes undermine, claims to social identity and masculine honour.

Thus Tomsen offers—and I think it is an important advance in this field—what might be called a consistently *situational* analysis of prejudice and homophobic violence. He offers a credible solution to the paradox of mass heterosexual support for the lesbian and gay Mardi Gras, in a culture that remains heteronormative and produces anti-homosexual violence. Looking at the killings, he offers credible accounts of the processes that lead up to the different types of violence, and thus gives an explanation of the exceptional brutality that many of them involve.

Looking at the police and gay community, he observes the changing character of gay community life, the different relations of homosexually active people to the 'community', the changing strategies of policing as the criminalisation of most homosexual acts was ended and police were called on to address problems of safety. Looking at the courts, he traces the recent emergence of the 'homosexual panic' defence—with an unexpected look back at the origins of this concept in the writings of a nearly forgotten early twentieth-century psychiatrist.

Conceptually, the book shows that researchers and activists must hold on to a gender analysis, which gives them a grip on problems of masculinity, while also acknowledging the relative autonomy of sexuality. In some theoretical writing, gender and sexuality are conflated, while in other writing they are sharply separated. *Violence, Prejudice and Sexuality* shows the value of getting these concepts to work together.

Through all of these analyses, the author draws a picture of human interaction in changing, fraught situations that has the ingredients of a thriller, as I remarked at the start, but has the shape of a tragedy.

The drawing of a line between heterosexual and homosexual bodies, identities and life courses, though it has deeper historical roots, was mainly an accomplishment of the twentieth century, so far as rich Anglophone countries are concerned. It wasn't an isolated development, but fed into the remaking of gender orders also being reshaped by war, industrialisation and mass culture. In particular it fed into the social construction of masculinities, creating both a threat and a form of abjection against which normative masculinities were henceforward defined.

But since men's sexual lives have always involved a great deal of same-sex activity, in a variety of forms, the emerging social definition of normative masculinity as exclusively heterosexual created a series of tensions. The figure of the closeted middle-class homosexual man was one expression of this; bashings of presumed homosexual men by police, and by groups of working-class youth, was another; explosions of violence around male prostitution was yet another.

The emergence of a visible gay and lesbian community in the late twentieth century was a stunning success for liberationist and identity politics. But as Tomsen makes clear, this did not resolve the tensions that had generated homophobic violence. It certainly reconfigured them—dramatically so, in the changing role of police and the appearance of a kind of normative gay masculinity and normative lesbian and gay citizenship. But it also created newly visible targets for the rage of marginalised youth. With the commercial sex scene expanding and becoming legitimised, it also multiplied the situations where severe violence in private spaces might be triggered.

Where we take this new understanding, in terms of preventing violence and responding to prejudice, has yet to be seen. I am certain, however, that action on these problems will be guided by the sustained research and theoretical work that has gone into this book, and has taken our understanding to a new level. Some of this text is so frightening it is hard to read, and must have been even harder to research and write. We owe Stephen Tomsen a debt of gratitude, and I hope his work will have a wide influence.

Raewyn Connell
University Professor
University of Sydney

Preface

There is a great paradox in contemporary ideas about human sexuality. Modern research has produced abundant evidence that sexual desire is very diverse, is shaped by culture and changes over time. But popular media, and many expert discourses in medicine and law, cling to the nineteenth-century belief that sexuality can be pigeonholed, that there are just a few fundamentally fixed types of people and natural sexual desires. Such a belief, that one's sexuality is preordained and closed, means that sexual prejudice can likewise appear as natural and hence justified in its protection of a basic, majority identity.

The binary model of sexuality has very serious social consequences. It grants a normal and often esteemed status to 'heterosexuals' and their desires. Yet it can be devastating and even fatal for people left outside this category. This is abundantly clear in the case of violence directed against sexual minorities, including 'homosexual' men. The investigation of this signals how essentialist categories of sexuality and gender are enforced by harassment and violence. This is the backdrop to questions about why men launch assaults on sexual minorities, why these attacks are so vicious and frequently irrational, what are the identities of perpetrators and their victims, and why such violence has some acceptance or is even condoned in fields such as law, psychiatry, the media and popular opinion. These are the key questions that motivated writing this book.

This book springs also from social science debates regarding models of understanding human sexuality and gender, and the nature and extent of 'hate' violence and prejudice in contemporary societies. It moves between discussion of the theoretical and research literatures on these themes and an analysis from the author's own original research to draw out the contradictory nature of both sexual identity and violence and the significance of viewing both fields as linked domains.

The major empirical source for this work was research on anti-homosexual homicides that took place in one Australian state from the 1980s. This comprised a close examination of these crimes as 'masculine' offences and reflections on shifts in the criminal justice responses to homosexuality and this violence. These shifts occurred against the backdrop of an emerging activism that was part of a new global social-movement mobilisation against sexual prejudice and related violence. Further sources of information were a national study of hostility at public gay and lesbian celebrations and a survey examining gay and lesbian experiences of safety at such events. These research strands were then complemented by focus groups that examined the contradictions of mainstream understandings of sexual deviance and irrational and bodily experienced feelings of threat and disgust in relation to sexual matters.

Throughout the text, this book demonstrates the nexus between essentialist views of sexuality and an increasingly problematic understanding of 'homophobia' as a wholly irrational and minority pathology. In so doing, it interrogates the everyday forms of this prejudice grounded in collective gendered identity, and it makes an important contribution to current and future discussions of the nature of social prejudice and its ties to legal rulings, collective beliefs and mainstream culture. Hatred, harassment and violence directed against sexual groups are contradictory and varied phenomena. Categorical fixed notions of identity and narrow pathologised views of prejudice should be discarded in order to appreciate this complexity. This work insists that violence and many other crimes directed at gay men, lesbians and transsexuals are not wholly distinct from other forms of masculine violence. They are widespread but shifting and collective social phenomena built on the artificial contrast between images and understandings of a sexual mainstream and subordinate others.

Acknowledgments

A large number of organisations and individuals assisted with this work and the research it is based on. Firstly, I acknowledge Raewyn Connell, Gail Mason, Les Moran and Betsy Stanko for their help and conversations regarding this subject and its social and political significance. Over 15 years, many researchers and scholars have given feedback on presentations of parts of this research at national and international conferences and seminars on criminal justice, hate crime, law, gender and sexuality including Amsterdam (1997), San Francisco (1999), Sydney (1999), Paris (2004), London (2004), Leeds (2005) and Keele (2006). This was added to by the insights from my time as a visiting fellow in Law, Gender and Sexuality at the Universities of Westminster and Keele in 2006.

The staff of the New South Wales Supreme Court, Director of Public Prosecutions, Court Reporting Service, the Coroner's Court, New South Wales Police and the Australian Institute of Criminology are all owed a debt. So too are employees and volunteers from ACON's Lesbian and Gay Anti-Violence Project in Sydney. Individual thanks are given to David Buchanan, Greg Coles, Justice Michael Kirby, Jan Nelson, Justice Megan Latham, Prita Supomo, Sue Thompson and Greg Coles. Staff within the Netherlands Ministry of Justice and the University of Amsterdam Homodok Archive facilitated my work as a visiting researcher in 1997 and 2005.

Funds for the research on anti-homosexual homicides were granted as an Australian Criminology Research Council Grant in 1995–1996 and later funding came from the University of Newcastle. The study of sexual prejudice and safety at gay and lesbian events was funded by the Australian Research Council (2003–2006). Help and research assistance for this came from Louise Askew, Allen George, Patti Johnson, Kevin Markwell, Michelle Mansfield, Paul Stolk and Erin Taylor. Permission for the reproduction of artwork was given by the Art Gallery of New South Wales and Gilbert and George Ltd. Special thanks to ACON's Anti-Violence Project in Sydney for their permission to use the posters from their 'Violence can Happen. Just be Aware' campaign. Richard Lever gave detailed advice through the editing process. Lastly, I want to thank Patrick Tanner for many years of encouragement, partnership and personal support.

1 Understanding Sexual Diversity

INTRODUCTION

A truly remarkable feature of contemporary human societies is that a wide level of same-sex desire and activity exists alongside constant censure and often severe punishment of individuals who act on this desire. The thin legal nets of premodern states, caught, prosecuted and inflicted draconian penalties on a narrow band of criminal offenders. Yet seeing the ongoing social response to same-sex practice, it is difficult to imagine another matter that has been so commonly engaged in and yet so loathed and punished. Sexuality is a ready-made sphere for the inducement of a collective anxiety about identity that is socially divisive. This now drives a ubiquitous shaping or 'governance' of the modern self that gives great significance to and is fuelled by prejudice and violence. Anti-homosexual prejudice and attacks are premised on the presumed existence of a clear and meaningful divide between a sexually normal majority and a deviant minority. This divide is a chimera. Sexual desire has important links to human unconscious drives and to the differences between male and female bodies, but all human sexuality is a highly variable and culturally divergent matter. Recognising this is the first challenge of understanding sexual prejudice and related violence.[1]

ESSENTIALISM AND SEXUAL DIVERSITY

Human sexuality has been understood as the sphere of life reflecting erotic desires and preferences. Many aspects of this are shaped by people's gender identities, such as the common gap that exists between the desire for casual sex by many men and the desire for romantic love among many women. The notion that males are masculine and active and females are feminine and passive appears as a natural complement to heterosexual relations. Yet gender is generally understood as the many social aspects of being masculine or feminine, and sexuality as the erotic realm of life. These are not identical to each other and sexuality should not just be discussed in the sole context of gender difference.

The most significant commonsense view about human sexuality that pervades contemporary societies has often been referred to as *essentialism*. More broadly, this refers to an understanding of different social phenomena via an aspect of these that is assumed to be an innate, ongoing and core characteristic. In the sexual sphere, this constitutes the notion that sexual desire, acts and identities are the outcome of biological forces rather than historical and social factors.[2] For example, much comment on sexuality refers to its innate and predetermined qualities based in bodily differences, hormones or unconscious instincts and drives that remain the same across different periods and cultures. The science that underpins this has an established tradition that is ongoing and well resourced. Various strands of research on this subject are founded on the idea that human sexual actions reflect biological drives which are ever present, though often constrained, in all societies (Weeks, 2003). These drives are understood to be of primary importance for the majority of men and women who are 'naturally' inclined towards exclusive opposite-sex relations in their adult sex lives.

As homosexual behaviour subverts the straightforward link between gender and sexual desire and practice that essentialism assumes, it is a particularly problematic phenomenon. In fact, it is revealing that is has been regarded as more problematic than a range of other sexual aberrations that are quite antisocial in their consequences but still fit the heterosexual mould. Developing an explanation for same-sex desire and acts has been the central goal of many studies of sexuality in which homosexuality is conceived as a biological malfunction which repeatedly occurs in a minority of people. There has now been more than a century of ongoing scientific inquiry in the modern West that has been preoccupied with the body shapes, hormone levels, brain functions and inherited gene structures of homosexual men and women (Terry, 1999).

Overall, this research has been remarkably unsuccessful in finding the 'essential cause' of heterosexual or homosexual behaviour. And it is also often accompanied by accounts of animal sexual behaviour, natural heterosexual male urges and men's polygamy, which offer a transparent excuse for male philandering and sexual aggression (Dowsett, 1996b). Paradoxically, some of these accounts of natural male promiscuity and female faithfulness now even suggest that the pursuit of casual sex among contemporary subcultures of urban gay/homosexual men[3] is an example of unbridled male sexual desire without the constraints imposed by heterosexual monogamy (LeVay, 1993).

Like essentialist popular understandings of human sexuality, this research work has not abated. But it is now more frequently challenged by the gradual late twentieth-century rise to prominence of a contrasting viewpoint that suggested a wide level of variation in human sexual desire and behaviour derived from cross-cultural, anthropological, historical and social research. This is now often referred to as constructionism (Greenberg, 1988; Vance, 1989b; Stein, 1990; Connell & Dowsett, 1992; De Cecco &

Elia, 1993; Bristow, 1997). As a theoretical approach, it has brought on a near revolution in the most recent thinking about sex. Furthermore, it has had a major impact on how many people now understand sexuality in their personal lives and collective identities. Constructionists challenge the notion that human sexuality is the simple outcome of natural or pregiven drives which result in basic consistencies in erotic desire and that sexuality is a fixed facet of an individual's psyche.

By contrast, they share in common the view that sexuality is socially varied and fluid, rather than uniform across cultures and history. Against the idea of an all-powerful natural drive that always expresses itself in a similar way, a range of sociologists and sex researchers have come to insist that sex and all sexual identities are defined, shaped and even produced by the effects of social and cultural forces. In the mid-1980s a leading British scholar of the history of sexuality powerfully expressed this new perspective to his readers:

> we must abandon the idea that we can fruitfully understand the history of sexuality in terms of a dichotomy of pressure and release, repression and liberation. Sexuality is not a head of steam that must be capped lest it destroy us; nor is it a life force we must release to save our civilization. Instead we must learn to see that sexuality is something which society reproduces in complex ways. It is a result of diverse social practices that give meaning to human activities, of social definitions and self-definition, of struggles between those who have power to define and regulate, and those who resist. Sexuality is not given, it is a product of negotiation, struggle and human agency. (Weeks, 1986: 25)

A few luminaries have occupied an ambiguous intellectual place in this essentialist–constructionist debate and are claimed by the rival camps. The essentialist approach often invokes Freud as an authority for the naturalness of certain sexuality—particularly heterosexuality—and the idea that human sexuality is built around a single repressed erotic drive. Nevertheless, a full reading of Freud's own account of the human unconscious and phases of sexual development suggests that in many of his writings he regarded the sexual potential of all people as fluid and open (Freud, 1977). People are born with a 'polymorphous perversity' that is shaped and redirected by cultural requirements. These requirements and social expectations are the backdrop to phases of psychosexual development that begin in infancy. They all leave their imprint on each sexual adult such that heterosexual 'genital' (or what is commonly called 'normal') sexuality is the melded result of each individual passing through psychic phases with various 'perverted' interests and it is the final aggregate of these in the psyche of each person.

The constructionist approach confirms the many studies of human sexuality that show a wide cultural variation between sexual desire, acts and identities, and the unstable nature of ideas of what is masculine, feminine, heterosexual or homosexual in these three fields of desire, acts and identity. In the 1940s and 1950s Alfred Kinsey and his colleagues conducted groundbreaking large-scale surveys of human sexual activity in the United States. They found a high frequency of homosexual activity in the broader population (46 per cent of males and 28 per cent of females admitted to homosexual experience or arousal at some time in adult life), and a high frequency of premarital sex and extramarital sexual liaisons (Kinsey et al., 1948). From these studies, Kinsey came to realise the difficulty of clearly categorising people via such terms as 'homosexual' and 'heterosexual'. He suggested these categories were adjectives describing behaviour, rather than nouns for truly different types of people. Accordingly, he then described the shifting sexual activities in a person's life as happening along a continuum (expressed on a scale of 1 to 6 with bisexuals in the middle). The results of this research work were regarded as scandalous. Kinsey and his Institute of Sex Research were accused of deliberately seeking to undermine the morality of postwar American life. Despite this conservative hostility, new studies produced further revelations by bearing out these important findings about the mutable and diverse forms of human sexuality.

A general case for the constructionist approach has been reinforced by growing social science evidence of diverse sexual practice and identities. The ongoing evidence of this has been amassed by a further range of sociologists, anthropologists and sex researchers (McKintosh, 1968; Plummer, 1975; Herdt, 1981; Dowsett, 1996a; Manderson & Jolly, 1997). A key contemporary statement of this sort came from researchers in the symbolic interactionist tradition studying the generation of social meanings in the ongoing forms of interaction between groups of people. These focused on interaction in different forms of sexual conduct to emphasise the idea of social 'scripts'. In the 1970s and 1980s Gagnon and Simon stressed the importance of socially learned sexual 'scripts' in all lives. All people have a complex understanding of sexual identity and related behaviour that is socially circulated and learnt and reflects the evolving culture they live in (Gagnon & Simon, 1973; Gagnon, 1977). This is a major part of each individual's social development. What is male or female sexuality, and what different identities and practices mean in different social contexts, is quite varied and always evolving. Yet we all acquire much of the collective social knowledge about this.

In particular, this approach draws out the wide extent of same-sex activity among men who do not identify as homosexual or gay. Recent sociological studies of sexuality have grown greatly, especially due to funding for research assessing HIV and other contemporary sexual health risks. These studies describe the diversity of different sexual activities that are engaged in by people who elect to call themselves 'heterosexual' or 'normal'. There is a high frequency of same-sex contacts and diverse sexual activities among designated heterosexuals. Cross-cultural and anthropological research on sexuality also suggests the significance of homosexual activity in contexts that do not signal an abnormal social identity. Distinctions are drawn between forms of acts that may or may not impact on identity. In some cases this has even been practised as a rite of passage for younger males entering the adult world. Even more commonly, some cultures only believe that assuming a passive role in homosexual activity between men has any link to a deviant identity.

Most interestingly, there is evidence about cultures with more than two key sexual identities. Anthropologists have conducted research in cultures that do not appear to reproduce the overarching modern Western distinction between two sexualities built on the matter of opposite-sex attraction. In many parts of contemporary South America like Brazil, men can move easily between what we call heterosexual and homosexual activity if they maintain an active role in sexual activity (Parker, 1991). Sexual relations with a gay/homosexual male or transsexual/transgender (M>F) partner need not undermine a heterosexual or masculine social identity. The merging of traditional and new ideas of sexual identity can produce even more complex variation. Research suggests that in contemporary Thailand, there are a surprising number of different types of sexual identity for males and females (Jackson, 1996; Jackson & Sullivan, 1999a). Six different sexualities for men and three for women mostly vary according to the gender of a person's sexual partner, the actual sexual role assumed in sexual activities and the levels of masculine or feminine social presentation that a person bears.

This growing research knowledge about the complex ways that traditional and modern Western notions of sexual identity have become intermingled in the contemporary process of sexual globalisation further cautions us about reproducing essentialist models of natural sexualities (Altman, 2001). Furthermore, we should not believe that Western views of sexuality are superior or more evolved and a template that the rest of the world will necessarily move towards.

HISTORY, SEXOLOGY AND SOCIAL DISCIPLINE

The evidence in favour of constructionism has also been added to by historians studying past forms of sexuality which prevailed in antiquity, medieval and early modern Europe, and the rapid rise of newly formed identities in the late nineteenth and early twentieth centuries (Weeks, 1985, 2003; Dollimore, 1991). It is this latter period of early industrialism, beginning with the first accounts of the homosexual and then ending with descriptions of the heterosexual as distinctive sexual types, which is deemed as especially critical by most commentators (Weeks, 1991; Halperin, 1990; Segal, 1994; Katz, 1995). Studies of the nineteenth-century creation of distinctive sexual identities, and the resulting split between the homosexual and heterosexual, comprise a further contribution to studies of same-sex activity that may not be connected with homosexual identity. This historical work also suggests evidence about this fluidity, and instructs us that a very different understanding of sexuality has emerged in the modern West, most notably the distinctive use of sexuality as a key term of social identity (Phillips & Reay, 2002).

The historical background for this change is linked to the influence of the rise of expert and scientific discourse about sexual normality and deviance in the late 1800s, and its eventual adoption as part of the popular consciousness about sexuality that most people in the contemporary industrial nations hold. In the classical world, sexuality was regarded as a matter of taste, like preferences in food or drink (Halperin, 1989). In the medieval era, uncontrolled passion and engaging in prohibited sexual practices indicated a state of sinfulness which could be corrected by prayer.

But from the late 1800s' rise of the human sciences and related expert and scientific accounts of sexuality, the industrial societies viewed sexuality as reflecting a core component or a key term of individual identity. From this time, sexuality became strongly linked to forms of social power and key definitions of deviance, normal identity and the boundaries of acceptable behaviour. This power was exerted by new groups of doctors and experts, and everyday people who over time became more and more conscious of how certain acts or desires suggested these acceptable and dangerous categories of people. And then people regulated their own sexual activity accordingly.

A development in the forms of social control in industrialised nations with an intensification of social power in the 1800s and 1900s, and its apparent centralisation by state agencies, was also behind these changes. This shift has intrigued historians and sociologists from a range of different intellectual positions. Before the rise of industrial capitalism in Western Europe in the 1800s, power in society was much less developed. Despite the savage penalties that existed for a wide range of crimes, the criminal justice arm of the state was undeveloped with only a weak chance of detecting offenders (Hay et al., 1977). In the 1800s some key developments reflected new forms of the exercising of power and control over people. These included the development of full-time policing, a shift away from public corporal punishment and the rise of imprisonment as a regular means of social discipline. Furthermore, punishment assumed a new form of being aimed at changing the actual nature of deviants and offenders. Ideas about rehabilitation and reform took hold in prisons and early welfare systems in the late 1800s in direct contradiction to the classic liberal notion of a free and reasoning individual choosing behaviour that was right or wrong (Garland, 1985).

A new range of experts and scientists became involved in this process of reform by describing, studying and treating many new types of deviant or criminal. Different deviants and criminals were then regarded as distinct from each other and from the mainstream citizenry. In criminology, Lombroso classified criminals by an elaborate taxonomy of physical characteristics and founded the positivist school. This period witnessed the locking up and control of a wide range of different sorts of people in institutions including prisons. It has been referred to as a time of 'great incarcerations' with many people coerced into prisons, juvenile borstals, asylums, workhouses, military barracks and hospitals (Cohen, 1985).

Alongside these eruptions, in the 1860s and following decades the new discipline called 'sexology' began to document human sexual types. Scientific figures including Ulrichs, Krafft-Ebing, Ellis, Hirschfeld, Forel and Freud generated detailed descriptions of an exotic range of sexual deviants. The term 'homosexuality' was first used in 1869 by Karl Maria Kertbeny and entered the English language soon after (Weeks, 1991; Halperin, 1989). Homosexual activity was previously associated with the sinful practice of sodomy (which may or may not be committed with a same-sex partner).

But in this period the emphasis on 'sin' was replaced by study of the 'homosexual' as an entire species of sexual deviant in need of serious study, treatment and correction. This creation of the homosexual as a category of deviant person was the precursor to campaigns directed at homosexuals. These decades were also characterised by the appearance of nascent urban homosexual subcultures, fresh pressures towards sexual conformity within the confines of marriage and the family, and elements of moral panic that resulted in harsher legal sanctions against male homosexuality (Lauritsen & Thorstad, 1974; Katz, 1976; D'Emilio, 1983; Weeks, 1985; Mort, 1987). It was homosexual desire which from this time became the key motif of sexual dissidence in the modern world (Dollimore, 1991).

Paradoxically, the creation of a deviant homosexual category by study, treatment and legal punishment eventually served to create a new awareness of difference and the possibilities of collective resistance towards the deviant label that emerged in gay and lesbian subcultures and politics. Most importantly, the creation of homosexuals in the discourse of sexology made possible the logical opposite of a homosexual species. Critical work on the history of heterosexuality grew in the 1990s (Segal, 1994; Katz, 1995). Katz provocatively suggested that the 'invention' of this esteemed identity in its modern sense began only in the 1920s. From then the term 'heterosexual' became more widely used. At first, this term described men and women who were sexual-pleasure seekers regardless of whether or not procreation was the intended outcome, and it often meant bisexuality. It eventually took on its contemporary meaning as describing someone who has an overwhelmingly erotic focus on people from the opposite gender. This new sexual species then became the ideal that people seeking classification as sexually normal had to aspire to.

IDENTITY AND SEXUAL LIBERATION

In the last two decades, the critical understanding of sexuality has been filtered through the major contribution of a gay French social theorist. This was an uncompromising repudiation of the claims of essentialism concerned with the creation and regulation of forms of sexuality within expert discourse. Michel Foucault described the social effects of the new nineteenth-century human sciences (such as biology, psychology, sexology and criminology) as intricately linked to an increased regulation and discipline of widening categories of people rather than humanitarian enlightenment (Smart, 2002). He studied the relationship of expert knowledge and power in his accounts of historical shifts in the definition of madness, criminality and sexuality in Western industrial society. A key aspect of the new form of power operating through expert discourses concerned the 'psychiatrization of perverse pleasure' (Foucault, 1978: 105). This meant recasting the sodomite from an individual engaged in a sinful sexual practice, into the homosexual, as a disturbed species whose sickness marked them out from the rest of society and required detailed study and treatment (Foucault, 1978).

As well as the intensified power of new closed institutions, this suggested that in the wider society in the industrial era there had been a greater surveillance concerned with the control of whole populations by state bureaucracies using new expert knowledge. The rise of demography and the serious gathering of statistics on health, fertility and crime levels all made possible a use of these forms of knowledge to examine and regulate larger groups of people. Bio-power involved surveillance of large groups of people who were thought of as a material resource for the reproduction of a healthy population and modern sexuality was a vital part of this (Dreyfus & Rabinow, 1982; Smart, 2002). In addition to defining and regulating sexual perversion (especially homosexuality) other key aspects of this change were greater medical control over women's bodies, further control of children's sexuality (especially masturbation) and a concern with ensuring 'procreative sex' among couples (Foucault, 1978: 105).

For Foucault, power is ubiquitous in human relations and not just concentrated in the economy and the state. Relations of power produce identities rather than merely repressing them by prohibition, the imposition of force on people or the effects of false ideologies. Thus, the establishment of personal identity often involves the production and shaping of identities via education and rehabilitation. In late industrialism this reshaping of personal identity in power relations has taken more subtle forms. People themselves are involved in the intricate aspects of self-regulation and attempts to mould who they are. This process of 'governmentality' affects all citizens in liberal society, not just institutionalised deviants. It appears as a more general process of people's own involvement in self-regulation with active participation in being governed (Burchell et al., 1991; Rose, 1999).

Foucault's analysis of homosexuality, discourse and power can also be seen in the light of its critical implications for ideas about sexuality that prevailed in the 1960s and 1970s. In these decades new social movements, particularly feminism and Gay Liberation, challenged dominant and expert ideas about sexuality. A phase of more public rebellion by a variety of groups rendered deviant began. In Gay Liberation, homosexual men and women struggled against what many radicals understood as the 'repression' of a predetermined sexual minority. The sexual liberation of the 1960s and 1970s argued for new 'freedom' from the restraints of sexual morality, especially the morality that was thought to prevail in the Victorian era that peaked in the late 1800s. Foucault was very sympathetic to this opposition directed against conservative sexual morality and political activity opposing the regulation of groups rendered deviant. Yet in key ways he disagreed with aspects of this analysis of the relation between sexuality and social power and the possibilities of any true sexual liberation.

This view is also significant for its rejection of the 'repressive hypothesis' that was notably offered by the libertarian Freudian thinkers who had a profound effect on the first generation of post–Stonewall Gay Liberationist writers and sex radicals in the 1960s and 1970s. This is the idea that sexual identity (either normal or deviant) is the result of the repression of sexual drives in a puritanical anti-sex culture. The 'repressive hypothesis' suggested the view of power as mere prohibition, and this had been rejected in the emphasis on how power is exercised in the positive creation of deviant identities. Modern sexuality reflects the positive and productive nature of power and new 'normal' and 'deviant' identities are created in relations of power with expert knowledge. Sexual deviants were not simply repressed by morality; they were instead created as new social types by expert discourses about sexuality. No sexual identities can be wholly liberated from power, and power in sexuality can only be resisted and subverted in an ongoing and shifting struggle.

In particular, Foucault's account rejects the view that industrial society was generally silent about sexuality. This society was characterised by a major growth of discourse about sexuality, and its sexual taboos and prohibitions expressed this. Instead of repressing sex, the 1800s and then the 1900s were periods characterised by a deep obsessiveness with sex. Western culture came to be saturated with a fascination over human sexuality, the different categories of sexuality that existed and how these determined each person's basic nature:

> The society that emerged in the nineteenth century—bourgeois, capitalist, or industrial society, call it what you will—did not confront sex with a fundamental refusal of recognition. On the contrary, it put into operation an entire machinery for producing true discourses concerning it. Not only did it speak of sex and compel everyone to do so; it also set out to formulate the uniform truth of sex. (Foucault, 1978: 69)

This major social change was accompanied by the spread of the 'confessional' discourse or mode of speaking about sex as the Christian confessional had been transposed to professionalised contexts exploring and assessing the sexuality of individuals (Foucault, 1978: 61). Experts soliciting such confessions and seeking to discover the inner truth of sexuality were drawn from medicine, psychology, psychoanalysis and sexology. In this vein, these have been understood as including recent 'sex doctors' such as Masters and Johnson as well as a plethora of new media commentators on sexual matters (Plummer, 1995).

QUEER

An accentuated relation between sexuality and extended forms of power and the resulting new consciousness of dividing people into two major sexual groupings around the criterion of the biological sex of sexual partners was specific to the modern West. Awareness of this reinforced the claims of constructionism and the rejection of closed categories in relation to the study of human sexuality. It rejects the sexual liberationist view of a need to release natural repressed sexuality by, for example, declaring a 'true identity' for homosexuals or more sexual experimentation for heterosexuals. Boosted by Foucault's writing, this implies that the contemporary imposition of social power around issues of sexuality is not exercised by a straightforward repression of sexual drives that should be allowed to freely determine identity. This occurs far more complexly in the discursive production of different sorts of identities, including the deviant labelling and even the rebellious self-acclamation of new categories such as the 'leather queen', the 'lipstick dyke' or the controversial 'boy-lover' (Spargo, 1999).

The implications of these new insights spread at the same time as misgivings about the direction of gay and lesbian politics in the 1970s and 1980s. Gay Liberation originally suggested the open sexual potential of all people (Altman, 1972). Some forms of lesbian-feminism continued in this tradition by suggesting that all women had a lesbian potential that could be attained in relations between women (Stein, 1992). But political and legal victories in the West came with a degree of new social respectability for urban middle-class lesbians and gay men. Especially in the United States, these were often focused on the protection of minority rights without seeking to challenge the heterosexual label that applied to the majority of the population in society (Epstein, 1987). This drive for minority protection ran in tandem with the expansion of limited gay and lesbian urban enclaves.

A curious political paradox arose from strands of essentialism in views about human sexuality. A fully constructionist view sat uneasily with the view of natural and inevitable sexual identities that most people believed in, as well as the emphasis on gay and lesbian identities that were recast as a source of pride by activists. Recent clashes between conservative Christians and gay and lesbian groups have often become a matter of conservatives stressing free choice in sexual orientation and sexual radicals stressing predetermination (Weeks, 2003). One position stresses that homosexuality results from a sinful moral choice and the other argues that homosexuality refers to a sexual minority that is inevitable or 'natural' and should therefore not be discriminated against or violated. This clash between ideas of free choice and full determinism is a false opposition if it is appreciated that human sexuality is neither wholly predetermined nor a fully open choice. Actual sexual desire (at both conscious and unconscious levels) is varied in each individual, and sexual practices will move and alter throughout a person's own life history (Stein, 1999).

In the 1980s and 1990s activists found that the essentialist stress on minority group status had left them unprepared for the shock of the HIV/ AIDS crisis and a new tide of official, media and widespread homophobia that accompanied it. More radical impulses in sexual politics grew out of AIDS politics to confront homophobia in the media and politics in Western nations. Moreover, this overlapped with some internal dissatisfaction with the sexually conservative turn in mainstream feminism. Notably, Californian feminist lesbian sex-radicals began to advocate the pursuit of more overtly sexualised behaviour among lesbians (Rubin, 1993; Segal, 1994). The resulting clash between sex-radical and more anti-sex feminists became known as the feminist 'sex wars' (Vance, 1989a).

These insights and developments were the backdrop to much of the more recent accounts of sexuality offered by perspectives that strongly reinforced the constructionist approach. These stressed the artificiality of the homo/ hetero dyad which took hold in the late nineteenth century. From that time, sex became a master category for defining the self and the likely direction of any life. This shift has been marked by a nearly universal preoccupation of each person with the biological sex (and to a lesser though now growing extent, the age) of their sexual partners. It had been suggested that theoretical and discursive deconstruction is the most effective means of overcoming the tight sexual ordering of modernity (Butler, 1990; Gamson, 1995; Stein, 1992; Jagose, 1996).

The dissatisfaction with mainstream gay and lesbian thinking about sexuality and the influence of Foucault's views merged in the early 1990s, to result in what has been termed as 'queer theory'. A queer perspective was critical of aspects of newly respectable gay and lesbian identities and suggested that such identities were often regarded as rigid categories (Warner, 1993). It also sought to further challenge the boundaries of sexuality in the modern West around the great distinction between heterosexuality and homosexuality. People principally classify a person's sexuality according to the sex of each sexual partner, yet from a queer perspective it is possible to imagine sexual subcultures where people classify each other by such means as particular sexual practices, a preference for an active or passive role, attraction to a younger or older partner, an interest in sadomasochistic or fetishistic sexual practices and so on.

This implied a shared positioning with others who are not gay or lesbian and may identify with other sexual/gender categories. 'Queer' advocated the inclusion of other sexual 'deviants' in queer subcultures and politics and a transcending of sexual and subcultural boundaries through resistance by an ongoing subversion of classification of identities with a sense of playfulness, performance and irony in sexual identities. Queer politics celebrated difference in cases where the categories drawn around whether or not people are same-sex or opposite-sex attracted become irrelevant or nonsensical (Seidman, 1997). It attracted a variety of people on the margins of conventional sexual and gender identities like transgenders, sex workers and leather and SM and BD enthusiasts.

This signalled the unsettling effects of these people's activities and identities, by referring to the mixed reception that these groups have among lesbian and gay communities that (just like the heterosexually identifying majority) impose and police appropriate identity boundaries. For example, some gay men and lesbians have objected to, and continue to object to, the presence of bisexuals, transgenders or sexually unconventional heterosexuals at a range of events and venues. A particularly cogent example of this was the late 1990s action to exclude certain groups from full membership of the Sydney Gay and Lesbian Mardi Gras and requiring new applicants to nominate a particular sexual identity in written form (Maddison & Scalmer, 2006).[4]

Internationally some hostility to the deconstruction of minority sexual identities has surfaced in multifaceted debates over the meaning and political efficacy of the term 'queer' (Gamson, 1995; Jagose, 1996; Seidman, 1997). A few voices decried an alleged marginalisation of lesbians in queer discourse (Jeffreys, 2004) or they questioned the originality of its transgressive claims (Altman, 1998). More telling criticism also regretted the obscurantism of much queer theory, and it asked about the wider political relevance in one model of sexual activism generated in the United States. Queer radicalism may have less direct relevance in the social democratic scenarios of other Western nations, and its meaning for new gay and lesbian consciousness in developing societies and the former Communist Eastern Europe is uncertain (Ballard, 1992; Duyvendak, 1996; Altman, 2001).

A qualified defence gave a very plausible account of the origins of confrontational queer politics in the dual impact of the AIDS crisis and the intolerance of Atlantic political elites in the Reagan–Thatcher years (Watney, 1994). Also, these new views suggest valuable insights into homophobia and its consequences. The contemporary primacy of the division between homosexuality and heterosexuality and its relation to the prohibition on overt expressions of male homosexual desire have become the focus of recent post-Foucauldian scholarly interest. This has thrown some light on the nature of male anti-homosexual violence and official responses to it. Most importantly, Sedgwick has analysed modern literary representations of men and male desire to powerfully argue that the homo/hetero divide, and an underlying anxiety about homosexuality, is central to contemporary understandings of masculinity, and that wider cultural analysis must now fully 'incorporate a critical analysis of modern homo/heterosexual definition' (1994: 1).

If legal text and talk can be seen as narrative discourse (Brooks, 1996) this observation gestured towards the timeliness of a critical analysis of the role of the law and courtroom findings in regulating and affirming this dichotomy and the positioning of a homosexual 'minority' in cases of anti-homosexual assault and killing. It also left important clues about the etiology of the motives for such violence in ubiquitous—rather than rare or highly disturbed—elements of the heterosexual male psyche. The intense policing of this sexual divide in expert discourses and commentaries and in the myriad aspects of the everyday social interaction between men, runs in tandem with an ongoing homoerotic economy among straight-identified men which is an 'open secret' central to the social order of modernity (Sedgwick, 1994: 22).

THE UNCONSCIOUS AND THE BODY

The evident links between this violence, conventional forms of male identity and the socially widespread anxiety about homosexuality described by Sedgwick compel further exploration of the psychodynamics of heterosexuality and conventional masculinity and a revisiting of some older theories of sexuality and the male unconscious. This contemporary interest partly follows the pathway signposted by an earlier radical reworking of Freud which saw widespread homosexual desire as evidence that heterosexuality is not a universal human phenomenon and argued that 'anti-homosexual repression is itself an indirect manifestation of homosexual desire' (Hocquenghem, 1978: 41). In recent decades, Freud's theories and the entire psychoanalytic approach to understanding human sexuality and gender have been the terrain of much debate among gay and lesbian writers (Lane, 1997; Weeks, 2003).

Most notably, this approach has also fallen in and out of favour with generations of feminists. These included those who saw little promise in a theory which so closely equated feminine psychology (and perhaps also female complaints about a patriarchal world) with hysteria and envy. Others launched a feminist revision of Freud and an interest in theories of the role of language in the unconscious, which attempted to explain the origins of male power over women in psychoanalytic terms and rejected notions of the immutability of the Oedipus complex and 'innate' instincts (Mitchell, 1974; Chodorow, 1994; Buhle, 1998). A different theoretical path was assumed by feminists moving away from a focus on the human unconscious to explore the importance of historical and social understandings of male and female corporeality in accounts of power and violence (Grosz & Probyn, 1995; Allwood, 1998).

At first glance, a Freudian account appears to hold even less promise for a historically and socially critical analysis of the mostly deviant positions that have been allocated to homosexual practice in different cultures. Homosexuality (alongside a range of 'perverse' sexual interests) is equated with an immature, narcissistic and 'pregenital' formation of the mind which is less developed than adult heterosexuality. Among Freud's conservative professional heirs this distinction was often taken as implying a moral hierarchy of desire and practice. Pro-Freudian Gay Liberationists referred instead to the occasional voicing of sexually liberal views by the father of psychoanalysis. Moreover, his model of the unconscious and the innate and openly perverse potential of all humans, which is only overcome by an elaborate apparatus of 'civilised' cultural repression, seemed to confirm the view that the intense study and control of sexual minorities since the late nineteenth century was linked to the highly valued place of the procreative family in early capitalist industrialisation (D'Emilio, 1983). This family model, and the 'surplus repression' (Marcuse, 1966) of desire among the general population that accompanied it, had become an unnecessary sexual straightjacket in contemporary post-industrial conditions (see Connell, 1995a).

This last reading of Freud has been thrown into considerable doubt by constructionist, Foucauldian and queer critiques of the essentialism and hydraulic model of human sexuality that often lurks behind such notions of repression (Bristow, 1997; Weeks, 2003). This model, suggesting the unhealthy outcomes of the repression of desire, claims an explanatory power which disregards matters of history and culture; in particular simplifying understanding of the socially varied patterns of homosexual identity and the sorts of individuals and institutions who have been most hostile to them. Importantly for understandings of violence, this also has ties with the very problematic notion that a serious hostility to homosexuals is a consequence of an aberrant condition reflecting the repression of homosexual urges.

The particular dangers of the uncritical and privileged use of such terms as 'instinct' and 'repression' in discussions of sexuality must be acknowledged. Equally, the significant differences between early formulations which took more account of history and culture and therefore most easily fit the contemporary stress on the regulation and production of sexualities, and the fully conservative tone of his final writings, may justify drawing a distinction between the early and late Freud. Nevertheless, contemporary gay, lesbian and feminist intellectuals find promise in a use of psychoanalysis to explain such phenomena as the ambiguous depictions of sexuality in contemporary popular media and film, and a similar qualified deployment of psychoanalysis could explain and critique aspects of the oppression and violence directed at homosexuals. Most importantly of all, the associated model of 'normal' sexual development quite radically suggests the artificiality and narrowness of the homo/hetero divide which is so often falsely viewed as a chasm between different sexual species.

Lastly, it should be noted that a psychoanalytic approach to sexuality is not incompatible with notions of the regulation and productivity of desire which seek to move beyond essentialist categories (Dollimore, 1991; Chodorow, 1994; Lane, 1997; Bristow, 1997). This does not have to be reduced to the simple view that 'gay-bashers' are themselves always homosexual, as in the clumsiness of many courtroom accounts of 'homosexual panic' and violence. Instead, it suggests that unconscious elements of male same-sex desire pattern the interaction and relations between all men, and that these have a heightened significance in the contemporary circumstances of sudden change and public friction about gender relations and male power, bodies and identity.[5]

THE PERSISTENCE OF ESSENTIALISM

Evidence for sexual constructionism has by no means meant a complete shift in scientific research about sexuality or its political understanding. The essentialist model of 'natural' or 'instinctive' drives still prevails in most popular discourse about sexuality and sexual identity, including discussions of homosexuality, and it has a dominant place in the human sciences (LeVay & Valente, 2002; Stein, 1999). Essentialism lurks behind much contemporary medical and biological research on HIV/AIDS which has again turned homosexual bodies into a new focus of legitimate scientific inquiry (Bland & Doan, 1998). The most controversial of all contemporary research in this tradition concerns an American study of the supposedly distinctive characteristics of the 'gay brain' (LeVay, 1993).

Furthermore, the deconstructionist queer approach with its stress on the restrictiveness of all sexual categories and ongoing acknowledgment of the differences inside sexual categories sits uneasily alongside an ongoing emphasis on positive gay and lesbian identities that have only been recast as a source of pride with enormous personal pain and collective struggle. 'Pride' is now the most globally popular term used to name gay and lesbian rallies and festivals (Johnston, 2005). For many gay men and lesbians who have acclaimed formerly deviant sexual labels, the critique of identity can seem like a patronising charge of false consciousness. To a suspicious few, the apparent refusal of such labels seems like a fresh pattern of self-denial. Sedgwick's late-twentieth-century words about the assumed role of intellectuals in critiquing identities are worth heeding here:

> To alienate conclusively, definitionally, from anyone on any theoretical ground the authority to describe and name their own sexual desire is a terribly consequential seizure. In this century, in which sexuality has been made expressive of the essence of both identity and knowledge, it may represent the most intimate violence possible. (1994: 26)

These words were penned in a pro-queer vein, yet they could critically apply to any discourse that makes a personal commitment to a gay or lesbian identity appear restrictive. Most importantly of all, many activists and commentators feel troubled with any theory or strategy that appears to undermine the possibilities of effective social-movement mobilisation around relatively fixed notions of identity.

Researchers have found that human sexuality is not a simple reflection of biological forces and instinct. It is fluid and takes varied forms across history and cultures. By contrast, contemporary gay and lesbian politics frequently incorporate elements of a commonsense essentialism in viewpoints that stress a fundamental dichotomy between heterosexuals and homosexuals. This view has appeared in revisionist discussions of gay and lesbian identity among social-movement activists and may currently be reproduced by patterns of sexual globalisation. In particular, this sort of approach to understanding gay identity and oppression has a more obvious fit with political demands built on liberal models of justice and minority rights.

Most importantly, for issues of violence and official and law enforcement responses to these, this view now dovetails with the new citizen status that has been attained by gay men and lesbians in a growing number of liberal states. At face value, this relatively fixed understanding of identity also seems to be ready-made for the most effective mobilisation against violence, harassment and discrimination. As will be demonstrated in the discussion that follows, an important pattern of political symbolism in which heterosexuals are recast as 'perpetrators' and homosexuals as 'victims' has emerged in official discourse and everyday understanding about these issues.

2 'Homophobia' and the Social Context of Sexual Prejudice

HOMOPHOBIA, GENDER, AND BODIES

A common view among gay and lesbian lobbyists and media is that it is 'homophobia' that motivates and shapes harassment and violence directed against homosexual men, lesbians, transsexuals and bisexuals. Although this term was originally meant to label an actual mental illness resulting in an exceptional hatred or fear of homosexuals, in recent decades its social-movement appropriation has described a commonplace dislike of homosexuals and/or an opposition to their political claims directed towards attaining equality and full citizenship rights in democratic systems. Thus, much of its currency and appeal seems to be due to its apparently successful inversion of a historical injustice. It raises a charge of illness against heterosexuals by groups who themselves formerly suffered under labels of perversion and sickness. In a simplistic but immediate way, the term appears to draw up clear battle-lines and reverse the onus of social prejudice and the suspicion of illness onto heterosexuals themselves. Additionally, it has often highlighted acts of discrimination, harassment and violence which might otherwise be dismissed by authorities as routine, trivial and as inevitable responses to sexual nonconformity.

The first use of 'homophobia' reflected the impact of Gay Liberationist efforts to lift homosexuality out of its deviant position in medicine and professional psychology. An American psychotherapist named George Weinberg (1972) offered a liberal challenge to the orthodox sickness model of homosexuality, insisting that mental health problems among homosexual men and lesbians were a consequence of the social stigmatising of, and hostility directed at, homosexuality. He insisted that he had uncovered a new phobia marked by 'the dread of being in close quarters with homosexuals' which experts had overlooked by virtue of their anti-homosexual prejudice (1972: 4).

In the three decades since its first use by Weinberg, 'homophobia' has had a widespread but confusing usage. Both the original and most subsequent interpretations suggest a conservative Freudian model of fixed human sexual desires and identities. Weinberg's account of homophobia as a psychological disturbance that afflicts sexually repressed individuals was innovative, but it needlessly pathologised prejudiced individuals as 'homophobes' and was tied to the essentialist model of identity. Much ambiguity followed Weinberg's own suggestion that a key clinical symptom of homophobia was a marked 'fear of being homosexual oneself' (1972: 11). This observation led to a misleading view that all homophobes are themselves repressed homosexuals, so that homophobia itself became pathologised and resurfaced as a disturbed minority condition. Also, this set down the paving stones for the development of a sickness model of anti-homosexual prejudice. This was less complex than Weinberg's own views concerning a socially extensive though irrational form of bigotry held by unexceptional individuals.[1]

Some commentators now speak of the widespread and varied dislike of homosexuals as narrowly comprising a pathological condition that afflicts a disturbed minority who cannot accept their own homosexual urges (Kantor, 1998). At its worst, this bowdlerizing of Freudian insights runs along a well-worn short cut to the trivialisation of violence against homosexuals as an internal minority problem which echoes throughout 'homosexual panic' discourse in recent debates about the causes of anti-homosexual assaults and killings. Furthermore, the model is essentialist as it suggests people have true identities that are destined to be either heterosexual or homosexual. It is just the socially imposed denial of homosexuality that leads to homophobia.

Scholarly and political critiques of Weinberg's understanding of anti-homosexual sentiment and behaviour ensued in the following decades. Notably Greg Herek observed that it is problematic for a series of inter-related reasons. Psychological research does not confirm the view that these sentiments are usually like a clinical phobia and many anti-homosexual individuals do not display physiologically typical 'phobic' reactions to homosexuality. Far from being a mental phobia that is unpleasant and troubling for sufferers, anti-homosexual sentiment is often highly rational and rewarding and it enhances the social esteem of those who display it. Furthermore, the term often suggests that such sentiments are to be understood as an individual entity rather than being derived from social group relations and the wider culture which every 'homophobic' person inhabits (Herek, 1984, 1992).

Feminist critics have alleged that this term ignores gender and pays insufficient attention to the disadvantaged situation of lesbians that is linked to the sexism incurred by all women in patriarchal societies (Kitzinger, 1987). Many activists came to prefer the term 'heterosexism' because it offered a structural dimension and suggested parallels with other forms of disadvantage linked to prejudice. Herek (1992) shared this position and distinguished between cultural heterosexism (based in such institutions as social customs, religion and law) and psychological heterosexism (the attitude and behaviour of individuals). In later work, he favoured analysis of harassment and violence as instances of 'sexual prejudice' (Herek, 2000). Still others have preferred the use of 'heteronormativity' (stressing language, representations and discourse) (Adam, 1998).

These are not merely esoteric debates without importance beyond the academy. A backdrop of political doubt—among lesbians, gay men, bisexuals and transsexuals—about the real value of coalitionist strategies in fighting prejudice and related violence dovetails with differences about the descriptive terminology and theoretical models used to explain the prejudice and hostility that often meet overt same-sex desire and non-heterosexual identities. Problematically for any analysis of violence, the situation of distinct groups can be unevenly addressed, being either privileged or marginalised by the use of such different conceptual frameworks. Most notably, a major feminist understanding of the causes and patterns of violence in patriarchal societies which has been developed by researchers and theorists in the last three decades, leads to uncertainty as to whether there is any resemblance between violence directed at homosexual men and violence directed at lesbians.

This understanding insists on gender primacy and maintains that violence against all women has an intrinsic link with the male–female divisions of patriarchy. The explanatory models feminism has developed to account for the patterns of violence towards women tend to position systems of gender inequality as the dominant rationale for men's use of violence (Scutt, 1991; Hester et al., 1996). Sexuality may then become synonymous with heterosexuality and signifies male power over women without consideration of how it represents the privileged half of a hetero/homo dyad (MacKinnon, 1983; Jeffreys, 1990). Moreover, some feminist literature takes anti-lesbian violence as its primary concern and regards homophobia as a 'weapon' of sexism or patriarchy (Robson, 1992; Pharr, 1988; von Schulthess, 1992). The logical end point of this suggests that anti-lesbian violence fully epitomises the victimisation of women in patriarchal culture and its significance necessitates a return to the separatist political responses that peaked in the 1970s and 1980s (see Jeffreys, 1990; Stein, 1992; O'Sullivan, 1997). Seen through this single lens, this violence appears to have little or no relationship to the experience of other minority groups such as gay men, bisexuals and transsexual or transgendered people.

Along these lines, the oppression of lesbians has been understood as a form of 'double disadvantage' incurred by their dual experience as homosexual women: Though it is problematic how this general understanding of disadvantage situates the large number of lesbians who have developed an effective social distance from the domestic exploitation and physical dangers of intimacy with men. The oppression of gay-identified men is also difficult to fully comprehend. In some models they are described as disadvantaged by sexual prejudice but always advantaged on gender grounds. This situation is blurred by recent influential accounts of the many ways in which gay men are denied the privileges that attach to dominant forms of masculinity (Connell, 1992, 1995b). In fact, gay men occupy a very contradictory position in societies which ascribe full status and power to heterosexualised masculinity. In particular, evidence about the exceptional vulnerability of gay and homosexual men to acts of serious physical assault and murder appears to defy a commonsense structural understanding of various levels of group oppression.[2]

Violence against lesbians has been seen as different to violence against gay men because issues of gender are believed to have a less obvious relation to anti-gay violence. The danger is that these claims about the primacy of gender may be reduced to a one-sided, deterministic or essentialist understanding of difference, where gender is a source of difference that always trumps 'homophobia' and in so doing erodes the potential of coalitionist movements and organisations working to counter harassment and violence. While the problem of violence has provided a rallying point between lesbians and gay men in recent decades, the attempt to explain and counter this violence as a question of 'homophobia' has been marked by incomplete calls to recognise the ways in which it is gendered.

The orthodox feminist understanding contrasts with an approach that may heavily privilege homophobia as a causal explanation of violence, and gender becomes merely another variable in understanding the mixed results of prejudice or 'hatred' on victims (Herek & Berrill, 1992). Attacks on gay men, lesbians and other sexual minorities all importantly reflect the imposition of gender norms and the various modes of society's policing of sex/gender identities. An insistence on a gendered analysis must now also look closely at the gendered identities of the individuals and groups expounding hostility and perpetrating violence against sexual minorities.

Much contemporary gay and lesbian activism grounds its quest for social justice in the assumed existence of discrete gay and lesbian identities and self-contained systems of sexual oppression. Similarly, research on violence towards lesbians and gay men demonstrates a tendency to look at the problem through singular categories of identity and relations of power. While there are excellent understandings of the way that violence towards women is gendered and an understanding of the way in which violence towards lesbians and gay men is homophobic, there is still little detailed knowledge of the way in which this violence is intimately shaped by regimes of gender and specifically by social forms of masculinity (Tomsen & Mason, 2001).

Considerations of gender in this field need not imply a position that cannot recognise anti-homosexual violence as significant in itself or that would attach fundamental privilege to anti-patriarchal politics. An important strand of recent theory and commentary on sexuality has insisted that homosexual oppression is not reducible to gender issues alone and cannot be simply 'read off' from the patriarchal characteristics of societies (Rubin, 1993; Sedgwick, 1994). This assertion of the analytical autonomy and irreducibility of regimes of sexuality is one of the defining characteristics of queer theory and related perspectives. With a wide backdrop of debate about the qualities of different expressions of sexual prejudice, a growing number of scholars and researchers have given ground to the persistent popular use of 'homophobia'. And this may also yet be redeemed by calls for its retention and development among constructionist and queer analyses of sexuality (see Adam, 1998).

These positions link the understanding of prejudice and violence to notions of 'sex panic' by emphasising the significance of homophobia to modern Western notions of male heterosexuality and the common irrationality that shapes much thought, talk and action around gender and sexuality. In this way 'homophobia' is not meant as an extreme mental condition, but it does instead reflect aspects of the tense proximity of homosexuality and heterosexuality in everyday ideas and social practice (Dollimore, 1991). Ordinarily, this goes socially unnoticed but it becomes obvious during such periods as the widespread public anxiety set off by false notions about HIV risk in the 1980s or mooted reforms in the 1990s allowing the admission of homosexual men and lesbians in the United States military (Butler, 1997; Adam, 1998). Scholarship has broadly connected this approach with histories of moral panic inscribed in institutional settings and dominant religious, literary, medical and legal discourses (Wickberg, 2000).

One further strand of feminist theory usefully suggests another dimension to understanding responses to male and female homosexuality, although it also may incline towards essentialism in understanding male/female difference. Queer commentators such as Dollimore (1991) have signalled the still limited usefulness of much 'difference feminism' that reifies generalised divisions between males and females to an extended understanding of homophobia or the power hierarchies that permeate relations between groups of men. It is obvious that this theoretical approach needs to be extended by evidence about variation in sexuality and gender and the social significance of homophobia. Corporeal feminism suggests that the cultural characterisation of women's bodies and bodily fluids as unhygienic or polluting has a long history in Western societies (Grosz, 1994). But in addition to this, it can be argued that the cultural understanding of the human body as naturally heterosexual and of non-heterosexual desire as a bodily threat or fault is reflected in constructs of gay men and lesbians as unclean groups of social outsiders. These bodily reactions are not part of any rational ideation process though they importantly inform unconscious anxieties and fears among many people.

Bodies are endowed with dirtiness when they disrupt the expected social order (Douglas, 1969). The frequency with which lesbians are characterised as dirty may be a product of a sense of disorder generated by the bringing together of seeping female bodies. The common insults used to vilify lesbians concern the concept of cleanliness (Mason, 2001b). Similarly, gay/homosexual men have been characterised as unhygienic with transgressive sexual practices that represent not just a danger to the physical and mental health of an individual but also to the body politic. This is an implication that has come to the fore in recent HIV/AIDS discourse and an extensive public dread of male-to-male anal sexual activity (Bersani, 1988). Most importantly, much serious violence against gay men suggests the cultural imagining of men's bodies as unbroken and powerful, protected from penetration and any emasculating desire (Tomsen & Mason, 2001). Critical research on homophobia and sexual prejudice can demonstrate the intersection of somatic and unconscious elements, as well as the fundamental but individually and collectively varied concern with these images of male bodies.

THE CONTRADICTIONS OF SEXUAL PREJUDICE

The implications of research confirming the variation of sexual identity has mostly failed to spill over into the wide body of theory and research that now exists in relation to sexual prejudice and anti-gay/anti-lesbian violence. Much understanding is attuned to the diversities of individual prejudice but does not examine the many social and contextual factors that may suspend or block negative reactions towards homosexuality and the contradictory ways that prejudice shapes social actions. In addition to its links with gender panic, the notion of 'homophobia' can be updated with a less reductionist and more dynamic understanding of everyday and contradictory aspects of sexual prejudice among both intolerant and more tolerant people.

Evidence of the shifting nature of homophobia is also apparent from the results of the growing literature on sexual attitudes that assess individual variation. Although this reinforces the view of researchers of violence that anti-homosexual perspectives are commonplace, it also notes that views are mixed and that bias need not translate into significant threat (Kite, 2002). This signals that prejudice may be contradictory, left concealed or suspended even in groups, locations and cultures that have been characterised as broadly homophobic. Explanations for the suspension of homophobia usually concern the concealment of sexual identity and positive levels of friendship in social interactions (Herek & Capitanio, 1996). These play an important role, but there has been less researcher exploration of situational variation and the contradictory ways that prejudice shapes social actions.

Material from the author's interviews with people attending gay and lesbian public events, and from focus groups concerning views about sexual difference and diversity, draws out the limits of tolerance and also the ongoing but evolving influence of essentialist ideas about sexual categories among the general public. Public gay and lesbian celebrations offer a unique opportunity to learn about contemporary views of homosexuality as in a spectacular way these celebrate queer sexualities and non-hegemonic gender identities that in most social circumstances are stigmatised and draw hostile or even violent reactions (Johnston, 2005). These events generally assume the form of street parades with visible, explicit and unconventional displays of sexuality. Despite national histories of legal and cultural censure of overt homosexuality (Willet, 1997), such events have become more public and are growing in number.

The idea of 'gay pride' made manifest through street marches and other public events arose in the United States as a means of commemorating the Stonewall Riots of 1969, which have come to occupy an important, if somewhat romanticised, place in the symbolic landscape of Gay Liberation. Initially an American metropolitan concept, the Pride March and its variations have been adopted in a number of European cities (which ironically have narratives of the liberation of sexual minorities that predate Stonewall) and to Australia, Aotearoa/New Zealand and some South-East Asian nations (Waitt & Markwell, 2006). Indeed, according to the International Association of Lesbian, Gay and Transgendered Pride Coordinators Inc. (Interpride), more than 148 separate Pride events were scheduled in 2005, involving 19 nations.

Pride events are thus emblematic of special events that are based on the collective, public celebration of particular expressions of gay and lesbian identity and community. The Pride March idea transposed from the US metropolitan context has helped give shape to the various gay festivals that have emerged in Australia. But, as argued by Johnston (2001, 2005), discourses of protest and resistance that characterise the North American examples are reconfigured somewhat in the Australian (and Aotearoa/New Zealand) context, whereby some events, notably Sydney Gay and Lesbian Mardi Gras, Perth Pride and the HERO Parade in Auckland, New Zealand, are 'constructed around ideas of performance and entertainment, as well as protest' (Johnston, 2001: 190).

The growing scale and general popularity of these 'Pride' events in national and urban settings around the globe is particularly significant to understandings of sexual identity, safety and violence. These parades and related street parties often appear to have the key ingredients of a serious law and order problem, including visible displays of transgressive sexualities, large crowds that include young heterosexual men who may be unsympathetic to homosexuality, wide consumption of alcohol and illicit drugs and a rule-breaking atmosphere of exceptional social licence.

Accordingly, the intricate planning and management of such large events now comprise major local police and security initiatives. They have been conducted against a backdrop of official and media support, indifference or hostility, but the minimal level of overall conflict alongside heterosexual viewing or participation at most of these events appears unexplained against the view that the host societies and cultures are fundamentally 'homophobic'. The widening heterosexual participation at these is a major example of both the contemporary 'queering' of popular culture and the contradictory aspects of sexual prejudice.

In recent decades the Sydney Gay and Lesbian Mardi Gras has been promoted as a cosmopolitan attraction for both local and foreign tourists (Markwell, 2002). The night-time parade is a major international example of a gay and lesbian public event that attracts a very large number of hetero-sexually identified people as supporters and onlookers. Since evolving from a street demonstration in the 1970s, this event has grown substantially (Carbery, 1995). It comprises hundreds of decorated, noisy and brightly lit floats and thousands of parade participants in fancy-dress costumes. These take several hours to pass through key city streets closed off in read-iness for the occasion. Crowds have been estimated by organisers to be between 400,000 and 600,000 in the early to mid-1990s (Carbery, 1995), and 450,000 in 2005 (I. Gould, 'Parade and party return in style', *Sydney Star Observer* 755, 10 March 2005, p. 3). Unlike the majority of the Pride marches of North America and Europe, this event takes place at night and reconfigures the traditional street parade with its flamboyant, subversive theatricality and performance within the tradition of carnival.

Participants include queer businesses, community and counselling ser-vices, HIV services and support groups, police liaison officers, as well as political, legal, health, religious, parents, ethnic, sporting and regional organisations. More provocatively, the parade features Leather/BD and other fetishists, sex workers, transsexuals and drag performers, troops of semi-clothed marching men and women, nudists, 'radical faeries' and protesters with messages against war, police harassment, discrimination and violence and in favour of cannabis law reform. Overall, there is a mix of overtly political statements, community group representation and some visual gags and entries without any obvious gay or lesbian link.

Among onlookers, the most appreciated entries have been the largest, most visually impressive and sexualised of all, such as hundreds of bare-breasted, kissing and fondling Dykes on Bikes and gym-toned Marching Boys in revealing clothing. Typically, there is minimal overt tension with a shared audience purpose of appreciating the spectacle. The large crowd of spectators includes large numbers of gay, lesbian, transsexual and queer people. These are much outnumbered by heterosexual people who come to show their support or to simply enjoy the spectacle that is created. Such a mix of people in large numbers watching nocturnal performances of trans-gressive sexualities would appear to encourage public disorder and expres-sions of homophobia. The mix of spectacle, colour, parody and mocking of authority that characterises this parade takes place against a backdrop of crowding, drinking and rowdiness among thousands of people. Neverthe-less, few conflicts and acts of hostility are officially reported by either the mainstream or gay and lesbian media.

In order to understand the actual levels of hostility and its expression at this event, research on the annual street parade was led by the author between 2004 and 2007. Participant observation provided a rich back-ground sense of the extent of spectacle, crowd patterns, audience mem-bership, participation and usual social relations during each occasion. This had a focus on heterosexual attendance at this event and the ways in which it accommodates the tension of visible homosexuality with ideals of celebration and carnival. In addition to these observations, three pairs of interviewers (comprising two heterosexual females, a heterosexual female and male, and two gay males) conducted short 'vox pop' interviews among the crowds that gathered before and during each parade. One hundred and five interviews were conducted with 157 participants (solo, couples or in small groups) across different sections of the parade route. General questions concerned attendance and knowledge of the event, the importance of its gay and lesbian character, other gay and lesbian community links and commitment to sexual rights. Interviewees were further asked about the particular attractions of the event and its enjoyment, their reactions to sexual display and whether such behaviour was appropriate for public viewing and would be acceptable in other social circumstances.

Almost all interviewees identified as heterosexual. Just over half (54 per cent) were female. Most were aged in their 20s (57 per cent) or 30s (13 per cent), though 15 per cent were over 50 years old. Thirty-six per cent of interviewees were solo and most others in couples (40 per cent) or small groups. A mix of city locals, visitors and tourists was evident, and most onlookers were groups of heterosexual young men and women who travelled from suburban or regional locations to witness the event. Care was taken to interview a wide spread of people that reflected crowd diversity. Consequently, interviewees were drawn from a mix of social classes, groups and localities. Therefore these included many people from blue-collar/working-class and ethnic groups that have been regarded as potentially more intolerant of sexual diversity (Kelley, 2001; Davies, 2004).

The interview material signalled the carnivalesque appeal of this event to a broad range of people and the contingent and shifting nature of homophobia and sexual prejudice. Some were passionate event supporters who were well informed about the nature of the event and some had a family member or close friend in the parade. Yet overall many of the interviewees had very little or confused knowledge about the parade. A majority made comments or gestures that indicated they were either gay-friendly or tolerant while they attended. This majority raised no objections to the parade, saw an educative purpose or suggested only that is was 'a bit startling' but acceptable. Most people voiced their overall support for the event. This often happened against a backdrop of essentialist views about sexuality:

> It's just expressing who they are . . . it's their life. (Female, 40s, from Western Sydney, 2005)

> It's human nature. It's perfectly natural. (Teenage girl from North Shore, 2005)

This essentialism often ran parallel with a reference to liberal discourse regarding sexual rights that stressed such terms as freedom, choice and diversity. This was most evident from the more articulate and middle-class interviewees, although sexual rights were usually conceived as specific minority rights.

Most remarkably of all, just over a quarter were either negative or ambivalent or stated reservations about the event. These people variously objected to overt displays of sexuality and even the gay and lesbian nature of the event. Many of this ambivalent/semi-tolerant group felt that the characteristics of the event challenged everyday norms of decency, decorum or 'privacy' and should only be allowed as exceptional. Therefore, this was strong evidence that a regular and mixed group of crowd members with limited tolerance and mixed sentiments are still keen to attend and enjoy this occasion.

Only 3 per cent of interviewees made statements that were negative about homosexuality and very few thought of the event in extreme terms. A few religious protesters annually denounced the parade as depraved and contrary to Biblical teachings but they attracted very little interest from crowd members. Curiously, two teenage males openly told interviewers that they were 'hoping to see some gay bashings' (2005 interviews). Although it indicated a measure of real hostility, this view was then moderated by comments that suggested some enjoyment in watching a large spectacle.

Given the wide extent of ambivalent views about this event and its gay and lesbian character among the crowd that gathers to watch it, the annual attraction and pleasure that this offers to onlookers needs explanation. A large number stressed their attendance was shaped around the expectation to have a pleasurable experience by witnessing an unusual, 'crazy' and entertaining spectacle. This downplayed the significance of any political themes or the political origins of the event as a street protest. Yet most could recognise that its gay and lesbian genesis and character was a vital transgressive quality and that without this the event would not seem as 'sexual':

> Well, there are mardi gras that aren't gay or lesbian, so it could be something similar. But I think it's a lot funnier, this is a lot funnier, a lot happier than the normal ones. (Male, 60s, from London, 2005)

> I think it gives the parade a flair. I think it makes it probably a little more exciting, maybe more of a statement than a drunk fest I guess. (Male, 30s, from California, 2005)

Among some, this meant an open admission to the sexual pleasure that many heterosexuals find in attendance. These commented that they were present both to witness the sexualised behaviour of gay men and lesbians and for any chance of making sexual contacts with other crowd members:

> Like I don't mind looking at a guy's body. I know they're gay, but it's a good look. (Female, 20s, from Sydney, 2004)

I'd like to see more of the girl-on-the-girl action personally. (Male, 30s, from Lancaster, UK, 2005)

Celebrations such as this parade are a form of collective public protest with many elements associated with carnival that include spectacle, parody, transgression and grotesque bodies (Johnston, 2005; Waitt & Markwell, 2006). In social theory, ritualistic carnivals are characterised by temporary disorder and suspension of normative values and practices among crowds. These occasions of collective festive pleasure are characterised by criticism and mocking of authority alongside creative displays that may give voice to marginalised groups and their ideas in a 'dialogic' exchange (Bakhtin, 1985). Remarkably, aggressive rule-breaking has not yet undermined a mix of transgression and tolerance at this particular event. The norm of intolerance is generally suspended for a collective appreciation of a transgressive sexual spectacle.

The varied erotic and scopic pleasures of this event are both unsettling and desired by observers. The erotic attractions of the difference found in queer locations, events and bodies are reflected in the broad crowd participation (Bell & Binnie, 2004). Displays include forms of theatrical cross-dressing, near nudity, bondage and fetish costumes and highly sexualised posturing. Although this is often confrontational, its overwhelming effect is to further involve heterosexuals in an atmosphere of celebration and partying. This explains some of the puzzle of a large and widely popular occasion that continuously attracts so many people with ambivalent or even hostile attitudes to its form and existence. The proximity of sexual anxiety alongside its psychic attractions was evident in comments from onlookers enjoying the sexual spectacle but wary of the possibility of gay or lesbian bodily advances:

It can be [OK] as long as they keep it to themselves. Meaning, they don't touch the straight people who are uncomfortable . . . it's fine as long as they don't try it on me. (Female, middle-aged, from country town, 2005)

Just lots of colour. Lots of everyone being really happy. Everyone a bit naughty. It's going to be good. So long as no gay guys grab me I'm happy. I mean I can take a few slaps on the arse, but you know, try and kiss me and [they] could be in trouble. (Male, 30s, from Western Australia, 2005)

It appears that the suspension of disgust and prejudice observed here is a trade-off for a pleasurable sexual spectacle and a measure of the displacement of desire onto gay men, lesbians and transsexuals. Holding the interest of a large audience is not always certain. The most popular events appear to be grounded in the right pitch of supportive contemporary sexual liberalism and the image of sexual daring and transgression that challenges traditional constraint. And the mixed fascination that accompanies a suspension of prejudice need not result in any ongoing shift towards more tolerant views. Tolerance as mere indifference to minority groups will not enhance cultural understanding and it can reflect a new configuration of the public/private dichotomy in which any disturbing public sexual deviance is quietly endured but still much resented. The mix of carnival and tolerance achieved at this event may appear rare or unresolved. Despite the positive and even romantic accounts from different social historians and researchers, carnival is often typified by a rule-breaking atmosphere that is masculine, threatening to vulnerable social groups as well as public authorities, and potentially destructive (Free & Hughson, 2003).

Urban 'special events' are also often perceived as safe because they are generally organised and policed, but increases in opportunistic criminal activity and incidents of violence can occur at these (Barker et al., 2003). Event organisers, police and public officials involved in planning and regulation of gay and lesbian events increasingly stress the order and goodwill of these occasions. By contrast, there was anecdotal evidence suggesting that many gay men and lesbians felt significantly unsafe at these and had mixed views about heterosexual participation. It is therefore important to compare the results of the earlier parade interview study with the outcomes of a survey conducted by the author between 2004 and 2005. This was a nationwide Internet-based survey questionnaire conducted to complement the results of the interview study and to obtain further information about the possible real level of suspension of prejudice at these events.[3]

The responses suggested an undercurrent of hostility and forms of incivility and physical attacks that occur in the aftermath of these special events, and particularly following the Sydney Gay and Lesbian Mardi Gras parade, that can elude official notice but generate considerable anxiety among gay and lesbian participants. Just less than 40 per cent of survey respondents attending the parade felt unsafe immediately after the event had taken place (Tomsen & Markwell, 2007). Forty per cent of the entire sample of people attending events had witnessed some form of hostile incident or incidents (Tomsen & Markwell, 2007). In the worst cases, gay men related the details of hands-on street violence and how they were threatened, punched and bashed by apparently heterosexual males in the streets nearby or after this event, and lesbians recorded that heterosexual men approached them suggesting some form of sexual activity and were verbally abusive when their overtures were rejected.

A volatile mix of large numbers of often intoxicated people moving around in all directions and the sudden rupture of the barricades that form a boundary between parade participants and spectators is created immediately after the parade has ended. In this atmosphere a number of people feel threatened and at risk, or have experienced some form of unwanted attention or abuse. The important role of private volunteers acting as parade marshals and police officers in crowd protection must be acknowledged, but safety became a preoccupation of respondents when the parade was over and the crowd dispersed. This view proposed that homophobia is to some extent suspended during the actual performance of the parade, but that a 'return to normal' occurs soon after the parade comes to an end. This abrupt shift in atmosphere, mood and behaviour was described by many respondents, yet its explanation is not clear.

How can this evidence about the apparent suspension of prejudice and post-event harassment and violence be reconciled? During the parade, a relaxed collective attitude towards the breaking of conventional sexual and gender norms reflects shared celebration and pleasure. A key element of this carnival is sexual transgression and a general atmosphere of ribaldry and pleasure triggered by homosexual/queer display. This exceeds ready classification within the binary homo/hetero categories. In this way, the temporary suspension of sexual prejudice in the annual performance also suggests some attainment of what has been called a 'liminal' phase of social ritual involving uncertain status differences and communitarian sentiments among participants (Turner, 1987).

The lower occurrence of overt hostile acts during the parade can be attributed to a number of factors, some of which are structural and some of which are performative. The high level of organisation and vigilance created an atmosphere of legitimacy that deterred the transgression of social norms, in this case of homophobic hostility and violence. Spectators and participants comprise social groups that are bound together by a shared purpose and the general recognition that parades are 'carnivalesque inversions of the everyday' (Ravenscroft & Matteucci, 2003: 1) leads to an acceptance of the transgression of social norms. The carnival is tolerated because it fulfils a social need for entertainment and it will not alter the existing social order. Once the parade ends, the liminality and social licence created by the occasion have different consequences and the social order reverts to its everyday mode of heterosexual hegemony. As crowds disperse, their shared purpose disintegrates, and it is more the case that at this stage overt hostility and violence begin to reappear.

The combined results of this interview study and survey questionnaire caution against any simple interpretation of the extent of sexual prejudice and the danger that it represents in contemporary societies. Although researchers have gathered an expanding body of evidence regarding homophobic prejudice and related harassment and violence in contemporary societies, this prejudice and its pernicious effects are not fixed and static phenomena. Like sexual desire itself, this prejudice is dynamic and either socially reinforced or collectively deconstructed and shifting. This is exemplified by the popularity of some gay and lesbian events, even among many heterosexual people with ambivalent views about such occasions. It is ironic that the actual success of these events signals the same tense proximity between heterosexual and homosexual identities (Dollimore, 1991) that underlies much anti-homosexual sentiment and violence.

TOLERANCE, FEAR AND DISGUST

Further examples of the contradictions of social prejudice and a mix of tolerant and intolerant views can be found in the author's focus group study. This asked people about their broader views regarding gay and lesbian events, venues and spaces, representations of sexuality in the media, personal attitudes to different sexual practices and lifestyles and the apparent causes of different sexual identities. Additionally, interviewees were asked about attitudes to any non-heterosexual work colleagues; the suitability of gay men and lesbians for all forms of work; legal rights in such matters as the age of sexual consent; censorship; protection from discrimination, violence and vilification; and relationship rights and child-rearing issues.

Seventy-two people (43 female and 29 male) were interviewed in eight focus groups conducted from 2004 to late 2005. The bulk were aged in their 20s or 30s, they included people from a broad mix of manual, semi-skilled and professional occupations, and (although all spoke English competently) comprised some mixed ethnic and racial profiles.[4] These groups were held at different city and suburban locations around Sydney and a regional city (Newcastle), with five of them taking place in licensed suburban clubs. Perhaps as a reflection that more strongly prejudiced individuals could avoid participation in a study of attitudes to gay and lesbian issues or even conceal many of their views in an interview context, the overwhelming tone of the majority of responses was in favour of tolerance and support for giving social and legal equality to sexual minority groups.

Nevertheless, this support was given in a partial way. The majority viewed gay and lesbian events and venues as entertaining. In particular, women favoured these as spaces free from male sexual harassment although attendance could result in some 'strange sights' and heterosexuals would 'get called "breeders" and stuff'. Participants had a general acceptance of the increased level of depiction of sexual minorities in local, national and global media including news print, radio, television, film and the Internet (see Burston & Richardson, 1995). At the same time, a regular complaint about this was that these representations had become fashionable and were reaching a saturation point. Some argued that there were too many 'Julian Clarey' and 'Will and Grace' types with a heavy involvement of gay men on lifestyle, personal makeover and home renovation programs such as *Queer Eye for the Straight Guy* that were 'over-egging the pudding' (Dom, 20s, DJ, from Western Sydney).

This ambivalence and discomfort about flamboyant queer characters that were both entertaining and annoying surfaced as an apparent concern about unfair stereotyping. Sometimes this concern for the ignored 'normal' gay men and lesbians was framed in an exaggerated dichotomy between the overrepresented 'podium dancing and designer drugs' lives of some and the 'stock-standard suburban life' of others (Tony, 30s, sales manager, from Northern Beaches). This was an opposition calling up new distinctions between responsible and irresponsible and deviant homosexuals that are also reproduced in gay and lesbian communities and the attribution of blame for violence (see Chapter 8).

Discussions raised mixed views about whether or not sexuality was chosen or predetermined. This did not follow an obvious pattern of greater or less tolerance. But it was notable that one male participant voiced a strong objection to homosexuality on religious grounds and also insisted that it implied a state of sinfulness that could only be cured with spiritual guidance. By contrast with this, and paradoxically, gay male sexual activity was sometimes enviously viewed by men as a consequence of a natural male inclination towards promiscuity that was unfettered in same-sex encounters. Most women are sexually restrained but 'blokes are sort of up for it all the time' (Bill, 50s, community college lecturer, from Wagga) and it is gay men who enjoy the sexual opportunities this presents to them.

The majority accepted queer work colleagues in principle. They thought gay men and lesbians could do most jobs well, though there were reservations about child-care or close supervision of adolescents. Also, most of them adhered to relatively liberal views about sexuality. They favoured notions of legal equality, and saw a need for protection from discrimination, violence and serious forms of verbal abuse. Any reservations about tolerance were often framed around spatial and temporal distinctions and a series of dichotomies drawn between public and private matters, liminal and fixed, urban and suburban, day and night, and special and everyday locations, events and activities. One group readily accepted a sighting of two females sitting on a park bench and kissing as night fell in the inner city as acceptable in a metropolitan place. By contrast, overt sexual behaviour and costumes were inappropriate in suburban or daytime contexts and offensive to see while 'driving to golf on a Sunday morning' (Marco, 30s, lawyer, from Eastern suburbs).

Against this backdrop of general (though obviously circumscribed) tolerance on issues of legal and social rights, a critical shift was evident when discussions turned to matters of the actual possibility of physical contact and same-sex activity. In particular, males voiced a deep uneasiness about homosexual advances that were seen as feminising and unsettling:

> I think you'd be lying, or any straight guy would be lying, if [they said] it doesn't make them feel a bit uncomfortable—it's not their fault, it just does. (Tony)

This unease was also evident in social circumstances where transsexualism raised the possibility of same-sex activity. Some remarks suggested a fine line between cross-dressing being viewed as entertaining and as confronting. In certain contexts where sexual pick-ups were typical it caused sexual confusion, and being touched or sexually objectified was experienced as a very personal threat in such places as

> clubs with blokes that look like Steve Roach [former Australian Rugby League international] dressed as women. I found it intimidating especially with some transvestites picking up the vibes of me being slightly uncomfortable. I remember on one occasion being tapped on the back and turning around and this extremely unattractive transvestite was twinkling her fingers at me and giving me this big smile and obviously revving me up because she could sense the discomfort I was in. (Marco)

By far the greatest sense of offence and dread referred to the fundamental importance of views about hygienic and intact bodies and the actual sexual practices they engage in. Moreover, this irrational, corporeal or even visceral sense of loathing came from people who often gave support for gay men and lesbians in relation to other issues. One woman who lived in the city, worked in theatre and had many gay and lesbian friends related how upset and threatened she had been when a woman in a bar approached her and asked to touch her breasts. Yet the most strident complaints of this sort concerned homosexual men propositioning other men and this form of advance was described as particularly 'invasive' for any man to experience. The threat that male homosexuality (as objectification, bodily touching and even penetration) could imply for the sanctity of the male body also surfaced in one male participant's surprisingly vulnerable disclosure of his fears and projections about being raped and the personal catastrophe this would imply for any heterosexual male:

> I can't think of anything myself more revolting, just to think of myself [having gay sex]. Not some other people who are gay; that's fine. [But] no way in hell is someone going to be doing anything like that to me. If I was to be attacked it would be like going to destruction. [Heterosexuality] just seems more natural. Everybody knows. Your mother and father did it. It is the one thing of the whole gay thing that would just kill me. I really don't like that. Not that anybody would like being raped. (Robert, 30s, police officer, from Southern Suburbs)

The last sentence in this statement appears as a final correction that acknowledges the injury women incur when subjected to rape. Yet it is implied here that a male homosexual attack is far more destructive. The irrational aspect of the fear of violation by sodomy is also suggested here by how the statement was voiced in the focus group context of general discussions about homosexual men. The great bulk of homosexual rapes are perpetrated by heterosexually identified men, and often in such violent masculine institutions as prisons and military barracks (Heilpern, 1998; Sabo et al., 2001). Yet a reflection on homosexual identity and same-sex activity here served to graphically remind this participant about the actual physical possibility of male sexual victimisation.

Further components of this irrational dread and fear of homosexual touching and anal sexual practice included conversational allusions to darkness and smell. Several mentioned that they were repelled by the 'darker side' of male homosexual activities or that homosexual men often wanted to seduce other men 'and they invariably have you thinking that you will come over to the dark side, so to speak' (Lewis, 40s, accounts officer, from Northern Suburbs). The excremental aspect of these fears was evident in references to the significance of smell and revulsion about sex in public toilets (including toilets at dance parties) and specific sexual practices including anal sex and more marginal practices. This mirrored how matters involving the anus and excretion evoke an extreme and near universal sense of disgust (Miller, 1997).[5]

In fact, this loathing of sodomy and disgust about uses of the anal orifice for pleasure was not just another example of a range of matters that offend everyday notions of cleanliness. It sprang instead from the central positioning of this sexual practice and its symbolism of dirt, disease and destruction for collective sexual order and identity. Contemporary panics about HIV/AIDS have been psychically fuelled by a general association of this epidemic with homosexual sodomy (see Bersani, 1988). Furthermore, male heterosexuality is founded in the sublimation of anal desire:

> The anus has no social position except sublimation. The functions of this organ are truly private; they are the site of the formation of the person. (Hocquenghem, 1978: 82)

Some of the women in these groups said they liked gay men as they 'look and smell good' in contrast with heterosexual men who generally have lower standards of grooming. In spite of the positive olfactory attractions of some gay men (which they might consciously induce by careful grooming and scenting), smell was a key point of fear about homosexuality and the animalistic imagery of unconventional sex. One man joked that another could avoid homosexual propositions 'by trying a different aftershave'. Several expressed revulsion about 'bum sex' and any full same-sex intercourse such as the insistence that 'seeing men at it really makes me sick. I really, really hate the thought of two men having sex' (Mel, teens, student, from Newcastle).

Various participants voiced their disgust about sexual cruising and activity in toilets from gay men who were 'skulking the beat, like whores on a beat' (Belinda, 20s, hospitality, from Newcastle). And some of the women also expressed an additional dislike for transsexuals or gay men in women's toilets at mixed venues and parties because 'they don't wash their hands' in a way that reflected the cleanliness/dirt opposition resonating through discussions of homosexuality. A revealing and repeated key phrase in relation to anal sex between men concerned the threat entailed by any subconscious or conscious mental imagery or projections of this activity.

This reflects the often shocking and confusing aspect of the sexual thoughts and depictions that are experienced by all men and women as daydreams—scenarios imagined during the waking state that suggest various forms of wish-fulfilment as sublimated desire (Laplanche & Pontalis, 1973). These seemingly bring to consciousness infantile anxieties induced by the physical proximity of the sexual and waste-removing organs in human bodies and any confusion of purpose between them. People insisted they 'hated the thought of it' or 'tried not to think about it' or that 'you just don't want to think about them having sex' in a way that signalled the surfacing of threatening, hard-to-control and graphic mental awareness of homosexuality, and particularly sodomy, as a deviant corporeal practice.

It is significant that this visceral sense of disgust about homosexuality and associated deviant practices was most apparent in a focus group that included city residents with fairly liberal views about sexual rights. One woman who attended a gay and lesbian dance party felt disturbed by activity in unisex toilets and was also a witness to an episode that itself caused consternation among queer circles in Sydney:

> [In addition to sex in toilets] the other thing I saw is Trough Man. I was describing it to . . . just this morning because it was an extraordinary thing to see. I was offended but I just had to keep looking because I couldn't figure what it was that I was seeing and because it was so outside my thinking. Trough Man was quite a famous person in that culture. He used to get dressed up in the leather gear and I can't remember whether he had one of those things on his face. He used to lie in the trough in the toilet and men used to urinate on him. (Eileen, 40s, actor, from Eastern Suburbs)

In the late 1990s, 'Trough Man' was a dance party regular who would lie prostrate in the metal trough in men's toilets in anticipation of being repeatedly urinated on by a variety of strangers who were either aroused by, indifferent to or repelled by this practice. A sharp exchange of letters in the local gay and lesbian press included both outraged critics and liberal supporters of this activity (George, 2005).

This anecdote about a public display of urolagnia prompted group discussion about a range of other fetishistic practices that were deemed to be highly distasteful. One prominent painting in a local city art gallery was said to be really about 'a gay sexual practice involving a tongue and the anus'. This was an apparent reference to an artwork in the Art Gallery of New South Wales produced by Gilbert and George (Figure 2.1). These are two English gay male artists known for provocative and controversial depictions of young working-class men (including 'skinheads') as sex objects. The homoerotic content of this picture was disturbing enough to be fixed in the memory of this participant, though with some confusion. The artwork's title *Reaming* refers to anal penetration.[6] Yet it was misnamed in this instance as the painting's depiction of a large, curled and phallic tongue placed alongside a young man was taken to refer to oral–anal contact—'rimming'—between men. Another sexual practice that evoked group disgust also signalled a speaker's particular knowledge and focus on such matters. This practice was explained to the more naïve as 'inserting fists into orifices where they were never meant to go'.

Figure 2.1   Gilbert & George, *Reaming*, 1982, 302 x 301 cm, © the artist. Courtesy Jay Jopling/ White Cube (London). Purchased with funds provided by the Art Gallery Society of New South Wales 2000. Collection: Art Gallery of New South Wales.

One participant tried in vain to balance this sense of disgust when he reminded others about all of the drug-fuelled heterosexual activity he had seen in toilets at dance parties, and he also noted that 'any kind of sex is icky and squelchy anyway' (Adrian, 30s, clerk, from Northern Beaches). This was a candid observation, but his failure to convince others of this view signposted the extent to which the group sense of disgust about 'toilet sex' was sharpened in the cases of male same-sex activity or even conflated with homosexuality itself. The overall conclusion was that such sexual activities were far more likely to interest homosexual men. This added to the sense of loathing induced by seeing, imagining or discussing the deployment of male bodies in mutual penetration.

The author's events interviews and survey questionnaire studies confirm that (like sexual identity itself) sexual prejudice is dynamic, situational and can be suspended or suddenly evoked in a range of social circumstances. Yet the fluid nature of human sexuality is even reflected in serious incidents of violence intended to shore up unstable sexual and gender boundaries with a display of traditional prejudice (Tomsen, 2006), as well as occasions of liminality where those same boundaries are momentarily disavowed. This lies at the root of the apparent contradiction between widespread prejudice and the success of positive or even mixed representations of 'minority' sexualities in much popular culture (Doty, 1993; Burston & Richardson, 1995).

The focus group analysis draws out the instability and contradictions of attitudes to sexuality and deviance. The slippery elements of tolerance and prejudice deliver mixed news for the advocates of sexual equality. And sobering examples of this from the earlier interview material suggest the possible coexistence of a conscious support for equality and a measure of sexual tolerance, alongside irrational fears of homosexuality in relation to actual sexual practices that seem less appropriately fitted to male and female anatomy. An acceptance of the view that human sexual desire is fluid and socially and culturally varied can still be held in tandem with the essentialist notion that certain sexual practices are less physically 'natural'. Homophobia is not the sole province of extreme bigots; it also comprises everyday prejudice rooted in unconscious and bodily grounded fears about sexual practice and gender identity.

3   Violence and 'Hate Crime'

VIOLENCE, SEXUALITY AND 'HATE CRIME'

In the last two decades there has been a dramatic international growth in research on violence directed at gay men, lesbians, bisexuals and trans-sexual/transgendered people, along with claims of a marked increase in attacks directed against these groups (Herek & Berrill, 1992; Theron, 1994; Cunneen et al., 1997; Jenness & Broad, 1997; Herek et al., 2002; Moran et al., 2004; Janoff, 2005; Herek, 2007). Surveys of the experience of violence and perceptions of safety were pioneered by researchers from the United States, and soon emulated in Western Europe, Australia, South Africa, Brazil, Canada and Eastern Europe. North American studies in this area include victim surveys conducted by community organisations in the 1980s and the pioneering work of Comstock (1991). Initial research in Australia and Britain was conducted by activist groups and done with the new cooperation of police agencies (Cox, 1990, 1994; Schembri, 1992; Baird et al., 1994; Gay Men and Lesbians against Discrimination [GLAD], 1994; Mason & Palmer, 1996; Sandroussi & Thompson, 1995).

Following this flurry of analysis some American observers even conjectured about a contemporary 'epidemic' of crimes of sexual and racial hatred (Levin & MacDevitt, 1993). A few also suggested that an increase in violence—as a 'second epidemic'—was a consequence of panic regarding the spread of AIDS/HIV (M. Goddard, 'That other epidemic', *Sydney Star Observer*, 15 July 1994, p. 30) and this set off a more open denigration of homosexuals by various church leaders, conservative politicians, medical authorities and media figures in the 1980s. A straightforward causal relationship with harassment and bashings has been difficult to demonstrate. Still these verbal attacks have been viewed as expressions of the same sentiments which have been used to encourage and justify anti-homosexual violence. There has been research evidence of HIV-related violence which suggested a link to panic regarding viral contamination and a view that AIDS was an exclusively 'gay disease' (Schembri, 1995). Yet forms of violence against homosexuals have been common and even officially promoted or tacitly condoned by authoritarian and fundamentalist regimes in countries characterised by a relative complacency about the spread of HIV. Increases in reported levels of harassment and assault may have been related to episodes of AIDS panic, or the greater visibility of expanded urban gay and lesbian subcultures. They were probably also the result of determined efforts towards effective community monitoring.

There may only be speculation about the real level of attacks as in most places these became a focus of recent police attention or research interest and there were considerable flaws in most official records of attacks. In fact, a lack of systematic monitoring has characterised the records of police agencies internationally. The growth in the use of victim surveys by gay and lesbian community groups has often been due to the considerable difficulties faced with studying the official accounts of such attacks. Aspects of crime recording and analysis can still be antiquated and among relevant incidents there is often no indication that these are related to the victim's sexuality. These were failings that police administrations in the United States are now legally compelled to address (Jenness & Grattet, 2001). The ongoing difficulty for researchers studying official records is to consider both the reluctance of homosexual victims to report matters of assault and harassment, and the different and shifting ways that these are recorded. This has made meaningful comparisons across regions and periods of time especially problematic.

Nevertheless, significant and relevant common findings of recent studies include a likely higher rate of criminal victimisation of the homosexual men and lesbians surveyed as compared with heterosexual populations, and relative low rates of reporting which reflected a marked lack of faith in the criminal justice system. Studies revealed that whereas lesbians have been subjected to harassment and violence in public places, the levels of public attacks against gay men are even higher (GLAD, 1994). Attacks in the form of random street violence and actual physical battery are more typical for gay male victims than for lesbians (Mason, 1997). Anti-lesbian attacks occur more often in private contexts with known perpetrators, such as incidents that occur at home or work (Mason, 1997; Schembri, 1992).

Disagreements about 'homophobia', and its perceived conceptual flaws, have dovetailed with contention about an allied term applied to descriptions of anti-homosexual and other forms of violence. 'Hate crime' (or 'bias crime') was a term that evolved in the 1980s and 1990s to refer to victimisation from assaults, abuse, harassment and attacks on property on the basis of a particular minority group identity (Levin, 2007). These incidents were understood as irrational verbal and physical attacks carried out by strangers. Furthermore, they were said to be motivated by an extreme loathing of a group which victims either belonged to or were presumed to belong to. Among community activists and a growing number of researchers, journalists, politicians and policymakers, the term served as a shorthand means of referring to crimes of violence, abuse and harassment and attacks on property motivated by bias against specific social minorities (racial, ethnic, sexual or religious groups). Attacks directed against a range of groups, and which evoked general fear within them, have been commonly described in this way. Such criminal actions were imbued with a tone of symbolic warning meant to more widely intimidate the entire minority group (Tomsen, 2001a). This definition has been succinctly summarised by one commentator as comprising the view that:

> hate crime is also a *message* crime. Essentially the victim is interchangeable. . . .
>
> Therefore the perpetrator, through his or her crime against an individual or small group, is telling a particular wider community that they are different, unwelcome and that any member of that community could be the next victim. As such hate victimisation creates an *in terrorem* effect that extends beyond the individual victim and is projected to all community members creating a sense of group vulnerability and community tension and fear. (Hall, 2005: 69)

Thus in a typical hate crime the perpetrator has been conceived as a stranger to the victim and only concerned with the victim's membership of a hated minority. This definition best fits the scenarios of public attacks on members of distinct racial/ethnic, religious or sexual groups, carried out by extremists with the intention of punishing or constraining the public visibility of that group. Despite the difficulties of monitoring and classifying solved and unsolved crimes, researchers and commentators have mostly agreed that a further vital element is a hateful or biased perpetrator motive causally related to the offending. Victimisation unrelated to bias has not usually been deemed as a genuine 'hate crime'.

Considerable debate surrounds this orthodox definition. Many victims of such crimes know their assailants as acquaintances, neighbours, work colleagues or even family relatives. They are attacked or harassed in a range of community and private settings. Many crimes are carried out by perpetrators with mixed motives and a stress on extremism or specific irrationality is misleading. These incidents may not feature naked hatred. They may reflect awareness of the marginal social status of victims, their reduced likelihood of reporting an offence or being taken as credible by authorities, as well as a perpetrator determination to protect and enforce gendered social identity.[1]

Just as 'homophobia' inverted responsibility for acts of prejudice, 'hate crime' proved popular as it shifted the onus for harassment and violence onto perpetrators. It countered victim-blaming in both public-political discourse and in criminological explanations in which researchers have been known to blame victims for their own situation with narrow analyses of 'victim-precipitated' incidents. Activism and research also ignited a new interest in this field and raised the possibilities of strategic alliance-building among minorities and groups subjected to this form of victimisation.

Along these lines, attacks on minority groups from extreme Right and neo-Nazi organisations in recent decades were described as 'hate crimes' motivated by an irrational xenophobic or homophobic outlook among perpetrators (Hamm, 1993, 1994; Eisenstein, 1996). Ultra-nationalist and neo-Nazi organisations principally opted to harass and assault racial and religious minorities (Greason, 1997). Nevertheless, homosexuals and transsexuals featured regularly as objects of hatred in the rhetoric and the acts of harassment, assault and killing by these groups. Neo-Nazis have perpetrated numerous attacks on homosexuals in various nations, and sometimes this has occurred with only a wavering opposition from state and police authorities.

Despite these terminological advantages, doubts remain about the homogeneity of the attacks experienced by different groups with divergent experiences of being targeted and victimised. This has been despite their shared positioning in the propaganda of extremists. The forms and level of seriousness of these crimes vary inside different time frames, national and local political conjunctures. 'Hate crimes' are not a historically new phenomenon. This is evident in the histories of racial and ethno-religious tension and violence in many nations. This has been signalled most dramatically in such matters as the long history of pogroms and anti-Semitic views in Europe that culminated in the Nazi Holocaust or the racist abuse of slaves, lynchings and contemporary violence directed at African-Americans (Messerschmidt, 1998; Petrosino, 1999; Ferber, 2004). In Australia, recent and past attacks directed against non-whites have been well documented (Human Rights and Equal Opportunity Commission, 1991). Violence against people designated as sodomites, homosexuals and gay, lesbian or queer has been common in a range of societies and periods of history. Histories of state violence directed against lesbians and homosexual men, such as imprisonment in concentration camps and executions in Nazi Germany, or even the abuses carried out under the ostensibly more humane banners of medicine and psychiatry in many nations, stand as reminders that this form of violence is not novel (Plant, 1986; Haeberle, 1989).

The first descriptions of 'hate crime' in the 1980s were related to an increase in attacks against racial, ethnic, religious and sexual minorities that occurred in tandem with a rise of nationalist and racist groups and sentiments in Europe and the United States. Forces of globalisation including further migration and refugee movements reinforced local xenophobias about cultural difference (Eisenstein, 1996). The new visibility of gay and lesbian urban identities disturbed traditional notions of gender and sexual conformity. There was a notable growth of racist, white-supremacist and homophobic subcultures and groups across different industrial nations with many thousands of adherents in this period (Ferber, 2004). The global spread of these has been facilitated by mass use of the Internet and a proliferation of web sites and materials expounding different forms of prejudice.

The attractions of hypermasculine militarism, related insignia and violence cannot be disregarded in explanations of the homophobia, racism and sexism in this constellation of extremist politics and aggression that has seemingly cemented together the notion of 'hate crimes' directed against a variety of victims. The extreme and pathological hatred exhibited by such groups can also be a fool's beacon for researchers exploring the wide extent of prejudice-related attacks carried out by perpetrators with less exaggerated masculine identities in industrialised and developing nations.

The term also implies an individual-offender focus that disregards the societal aspects of the motivating bias. Even advocates of 'hate crime' as a new paradigm in crime research expressed caution about its use and noted it was a problematic term reflecting an individualistic notion of crime causation, prevention and punishment (Cunneen et al., 1997). It thereby lacked a systemic perspective regarding the marginalisation of groups and minorities subjected to violence and harassment on the basis of their shared identity, or the widespread social basis for prejudiced and hateful outlooks. 'Hate crime' flags a focus on exceptional causes of prejudice rather than the everyday nature of such intolerance and its links to the dominant views in a wider culture.

More sophisticated views of social prejudice have been emphasised in a range of research dating from mid-twentieth-century studies of Fascism and racial bias that highlighted the collective nature of this phenomenon in relation to the human unconscious (Young-Bruehl, 1996; Allport, 1999). These led to a more recent focus on the relationships between prejudice and the production of identity in ostensibly objective language, signs and representations that have emphasised social 'difference'. These are 'offered under the guise of value-free descriptions yet smuggle in normative considerations that carry with them the stigma of inferiority' (Rothenberg, 1999: 109). This construction of difference may then readily spill over into strict moral oppositions between blackness–whiteness, citizens–aliens, masculinity–femininity and heterosexuality–homosexuality. Moreover, this 'doing difference' in hate attacks assumes a relational context that is of paramount significance—perpetrators are shoring up dominant elements of their own social identity and the subordinated position of marginalised victims (Perry, 2003).

These are mutable discourses that shift over time and space. The views of perpetrators have been linked to wider ideologies of prejudice and bolstered by the past and recent actions of state and criminal justice agencies. These include past histories of police repression and violence against minorities that foster wider intolerance.[2] In reality, any decline of remnant intolerance and a major break with old official practices can be slow and uncertain. We cannot presuppose an inexorable historical transition to more liberal criminal justice systems offering equal treatment to all minority groups is taking place. Legal systems continue to host official attitudes and practices that foster 'hate crimes'. It is the case that disregarding mainstream attitudes in claims that racist or anti-homosexual crimes are the result of irrational hatred from psychologically dangerous perpetrators will lead to distortion and reductionism in explanations of motive. Perpetrators' motives can appear as either rational, quasi-rational or not. Aspects of these crimes suggest multiple motives and the situational nature of such intolerance. For example, many perpetrators do not express an extreme prejudice against the sexual identity of victims and are driven by other interests and concerns including selection of soft targets for robbery or the protection of gendered status, identity and honour.

In the United States, activism and measures to counter 'hate crime' were advanced by the 1990 federal legislation to monitor these offences, and subsequent state-level reforms that sought to lift the police response to victims. The most politically controversial changes have been laws that prohibit the expression or dissemination of vilification or 'hate speech' inciting or likely to incite acts of violence and harassment, and measures to enhance the penalties imposed if a hate motive is deemed proven. Critics of these changes regard them as a serious infringement of the liberal right to free speech and may even decry the pernicious extension of 'special protections' to minority groups (Jacobs & Potter, 1998).

From the 1970s a progression of national and state laws were enacted to outlaw racial discrimination, violence and vilification in Australia (McNamara, 2002). Controversial provisions regarding sexual vilification were passed in New South Wales in the early 1990s. The debate regarding additional or enhanced penalties has been less developed locally, although there has been argument for and against such laws (Walters, 2005; Morgan, 2002). This lower level of interest may be due to local pressure-group wariness about a heavy reliance on legal measures to regulate social attitudes and any further fostering of law and order politics.[3]

Alongside this disagreement about the threat to civil liberties entailed by anti-vilification provisions and penalty enhancement, debates concern the actual definition of any typical or actual hate crime and which groups of victims this term could reasonably refer to. An emphasis on stranger relations does not ring true for the regular number of real-life situations of racist and anti-homosexual incidents in which victims are known to perpetrators as school and work peers, neighbours, relatives or acquaintances, and so on. A definition stressing attacks by strangers excludes the bulk of violence and abuse directed at women. Many attacks with female victims suggest a misogynist motive. There is no consensus among feminists about the issue, but some insist that much or all anti-female violence is a form of 'hate crime' (Jenness & Grattet, 2001; McPhail, 2002).

The gendered dimension of hate crime offending should also be considered in yet another way. The masculinity of this offending operates at several levels in particular criminal actions. These can range from attacks launched against gay/homosexual men, lesbians and transsexuals who are disciplined for their gender nonconformity, to racist crimes that are partly shaped by elements of sexual desire, jealousy or rivalry and reflect colonialist constructions of male sexual privilege that persist in contemporary cultures. Furthermore, evidence about the everyday qualities of racist abuse and attacks in avowedly tolerant liberal nations suggests some of the specifically gendered nature of insults and racist actions. Female victims from ethnic and racial minorities are frequently said to be 'whores' and minority men are depicted as emasculated or overly masculine and corrupted by predatory sexual desire. Specific actions of racial harassment like the disrobing of veiled Islamic women (see Hage, 1998) are replete with sexual symbolism. These links between racial and sexual prejudice and the gendered actions of perpetrators reflect extant notions of manhood and male identity.

Although 'hate crime' has been mostly understood as comprised of attacks on minority groups by perpetrators with a socially dominant identity (e.g., white or heterosexual), many such attacks are perpetrated by members of minorities or arise as part of the conflicts between them. These can be inflected with detailed prejudices about levels of wealth, business acumen, employment, physical appearance and even cuisine and leisure habits (White, 2002). Wide-ranging discussions about global trends in 'hate crime' also refer to matters that could be as readily described as war crimes, genocide or even as 'crimes against humanity'. The criticisms about what constitutes a 'hate crime' and the efficacy of the term, have pressured observers to broaden the understanding of this form of crime. Nevertheless, there have been serious research and activist reservations about this broadening process based on the belief that the viability of the term will become eroded by such a shift.

HATE CRIME ACTIVISM—A LOCAL EXAMPLE

As noted earlier, it is likely that the rise of urban gay and lesbian subcultures in the last decades of the twentieth century meant a more ready targeting of the victims of street violence. It is also apparent that in most jurisdictions the new official interest in this violence is a result of activist efforts from within this group (Tomsen, 1993; Jenness & Broad, 1997; Moran et al., 2004). Internationally it was community research, protest rallies and other publicity that provided the catalyst for making violence and harassment directed at gay men and lesbians into a public issue. This followed a model that evolved in Europe and the United States (Van den Boogaard, 1987; Comstock, 1991; Herek & Berrill, 1992). In many nations, violence came to loom large as an issue for gay and lesbian organisations and services which dealt with such diverse matters as discrimination and law, education, personal health and counselling, and a range of social and leisure activities.

In Australia these developments and heightened activism were first of all focused on publicising and addressing violence in inner Sydney (see Tomsen,

2001b). The experience of violence became the basis of determined efforts at community building and the promotion of political coalitionism. This partly borrowed on earlier efforts to educate and mobilise gay and bisexual men around the issues of HIV risk, safety and treatment. In the 1990s, incidents of violence and a legal complacency about them resulted in a much greater level of protest, critical public forums and the formation of such lobby groups as the Anti-Violence Project of the Gay and Lesbian Rights Lobby. Violence and safety were pushed into prominence immediately after a serious low point in the political relations between activist lesbians and gay men in Sydney with a gay male focus on the HIV/AIDS crisis and persistence of separatist trends among lesbian feminists. Further conflicts about the inclusion of transsexuals, transgenders and bisexuals in these changes ensued, but overall the issue was heralded for its success in uniting the 'gay and lesbian community'.

In addition to more general rallies against violence, there was an important series of protests against the killings of gay/homosexual and transsexual victims, and often related adoptions of 'homosexual advance' allegations by perpetrators. The most significant moment in specifically lesbian mobilisation on this issue was a rally and placing of a memorial plaque at the location of an anti-lesbian rape that had occurred in Darlinghurst in inner Sydney in 1995.

Initial local activity comprised surveying levels of violence directed at gay men and lesbians, overcoming low levels of reporting, promoting police liaison and raising victim consciousness with an emphasis on caution and safety (Cox, 1990, 1994; Schembri, 1992). Since the mid-1990s there has been more emphasis on wider community advertising and education. This activist and subsequent political and media interest was reproduced in other cities and areas across the nation. As a result of a more nationwide readiness to counter non-fatal violence and harassment, more specific local groups were formed to respond to attacks. These evolved an array of strategies to counter violence and its threat. These included the community monitoring of attacks, closer cooperation with police, politicians and public officials dealing with housing, AIDS, health and discrimination. This was reinforced by publicity and preventive education in the gay and lesbian press with information on safety, risk and rights, and widespread 'anti-homophobia' campaigns in the mainstream media.

The overall scale and rapid growth of these developments appeared to be quite remarkable. Anti-homophobia and hate crime initiatives had a novel concern with redressing the traditionally deviant status of sexual minority groups within the criminal justice system. The official response to anti-homosexual violence reflected a major shift in the overall relationship of homosexual men to the legal system and police. In former times, male homosexuals were regarded as fully deviant and heavily criminalised. They featured regularly in courts as sex perpetrators. Male homosexual activities have been criminalised and punished in most modern legal systems, sometimes with state violence in the form of execution and other severe corporal discipline. Much of the historical under-reporting and under-recording of violence against these groups appeared to be a combined consequence of general social stigma and, in many jurisdictions, substantial levels of complacent or hostile attitudes to victims. Lobbying, rallies and wider education campaigns inverted traditional views by asserting the legitimacy of most victims and the illegitimate moral status of perpetrators.

The strategies adopted to monitor and combat violence reflected unexpected and complex changes in the relationship of lesbians and gay men to the statewide police service. Since major reforms of the police in the 1980s, a concerted attempt to improve public confidence was made with moves against corruption, towards greater professionalism, and also by implementing a policy of community policing. The traditionally poor relations with police due to old-style repressive control deteriorated further after the 1978 Mardi Gras riot and bar raids in the early 1980s. Without resorting to any crudely conspiratorial model of state actions suggesting a deliberate co-opting, it can be observed that from the late 1980s the 'iron fist' was often replaced by a softer, more conciliatory style. NSW police had become markedly more responsive to the demands and needs of articulate, politically organised inner-city homosexuals.

From early changes in the mid-1980s the police department established a full-time gay and lesbian liaison unit, and formed consultative committees dealing with a range of issues, particularly violence. The police response included the introduction of more patrols in gay and lesbian areas, changes to police education and training, and the appointment of gay and lesbian liaison officers at the local station level to assist and communicate with homosexual 'clients'. Advertisements in the gay and lesbian press declared protective initiatives and sought out gay and lesbian recruits, alongside a strong presence at social events like the Mardi Gras parade and the annual Leather Fair. From within, the most important changes were efforts to revise police education and training (denouncing open occupational racism and homophobia), to more accurately record and monitor incidents and to develop trust and official liaisons with the representatives of victim groups. By the mid-1990s the success of this new strategy of consultation was being cited informally among administrators as an ideal international model for progressive police–minority relations.

Homophobia had been a key element of the traditional culture of this occupation (Burke, 1993; Buhrke, 1996; Bernstein & Kostelac, 2002). As recruits to a very masculinist occupation drawn largely from the respectable working class, police officers historically held very rigid notions concerning sexual expression and identity, and had a significant role in the transmission of violent and hostile attitudes about sexual deviance among the general citizenry. Homosexuals were victimised by police in incidents of harassment, blackmail and direct violence. Police malpractice in the form of extortion was often brokered through underworld figures operating illegal gay and lesbian venues (Wotherspoon, 1991). Paradoxically, this hurried the development of nascent urban sexual subcultures from which contemporary homosexual politics drew much of its regional strength.

A far more complex relation of sexuality, policing and the law ensued from this politics and new awareness. A remarkable refiguring of gay men and lesbians in police consciousness took place in little more than a decade between the mid-1980s and mid-1990s. Furthermore, there were other important changes in relation to other arms of the legal system and the state. In these years, gay and lesbian organisations had successes with the positive uses of law and an appeal to the ideals of legality and justice that a previous generation of activists would have deemed impossible. Political mobilisation around violence and its public recognition as an issue by mainstream media and politicians sometimes served as ideological levers to counter reactionary opponents. Official concern about assaults and harassment formed the political backdrop for the watershed 1993 enactment of legislation outlawing 'sexual vilification' in New South Wales. Activists won representation on high level bodies including the Streetwatch Committee (coordinating government department involvement in the prevention of homophobic violence such as school bullying) in the mid-1990s, and a later body reporting on the use of homosexual advance claims in criminal trials. The state Attorney-General's Department appointed its own gay and lesbian policy officer in 1999.

These historical shifts should not be exaggerated. Prejudice against gay and lesbian victims still persists in police agencies. There have been ongoing effects of the traditional homophobia of police even though the public relations arm of the police service has insisted in an unlikely way that 'homophobia' became rare among its officers. Accordingly, dissident voices objected to changes like the presence of gay and lesbian police as an entry marching in the Sydney Gay and Lesbian Mardi Gras parade since 1998.[4] Also, these changes occurred during a period of increased emphasis on law and order and the control and regulation of social groups deemed as engaging in offensive public behaviour. Police actions directed at less respectable homosexual men cruising for public sex outside of the confines of the inner city persisted. From the 1980s these were combined with a use of new technologies of surveillance and changes to the design of public space and its regulation by local councils, businesses and transport authorities (Swivel, 1991).

A localised inner-urban political strength was the most obvious reason for successes in attaining a new status for homosexuals as victims of crime. These changes assumed a very uneven and less progressive pattern elsewhere in Australia (Lesbian and Gay Community Action, 1994; Cherney, 1999). This was due to the comparative weakness of gay and lesbian organisations in other regions and a related lack of political will to alter the marginalisation of these crime victims. Across the globe, it has been 'queer' inner-city locations notable for revival, gentrification and new patterns of consumption (Knopp, 1998) that have been centres of political strength in relation to matters of violence and safety.

Nevertheless, a serious police monitoring and investigation of violence appeared to have resulted in a larger number of cases that involved matters of homosexual victimisation reaching the criminal courts. The advances made in a range of cities and jurisdictions accompanied a greater openness from a small number of legal officials and professionals regarding their own homosexuality. Furthermore, the widening impact of gay men and lesbians in mainstream politics and culture meant a novel consciousness among the judiciary, legal counsel and officials and even jurors, that homosexuality had been claimed as the basis for legal rights and as a legitimate social identity by a significant number of people.

HATRED, IDENTITY POLITICS AND CRITIQUE

Given the key significance of activism and this process of community building in reconfiguring acts of harassment and violence into a public moral issue, some commentators criticised claims regarding a rapid increase in the number of 'hate crimes'. These claims were said to be unfounded due to the subjective nature of the recording of such incidents and the unproven assumptions about hatred as a criminal motivation (Jacobs, 1996; Jacobs & Potter, 1998). The expanded publicity and activism against hate crimes were deemed to be a mere expression of the logic of 'identity politics'. The latter term has often been meant to disparagingly imply group selfishness from such actors as lobbyists who have petitioned state agencies for recognition and resources and to enhance the social status of particular minority groups.

There is a sociological half-truth in these criticisms. It is obvious that the new focus on such crimes reflected shifting power relations with criminal justice systems that resulted from activist measures. But is this an unusual or adverse development in liberal political systems? Social researchers and historians have recognised that the social processes leading to the designation of a range of social acts as major social problems (such as drinking, drug use, family violence and sexual abuse) demand critical analysis of the key role that middle-class opinion leaders and lobby groups can have in these various forms of symbolic crusade (Gusfield, 1963). Along these lines, sociologists have researched and described the various 'collective action frames' that facilitated the social-movement reconfiguration of scattered criminal acts into a more widely recognised social issue (Snow et al., 1986; Jenness & Broad, 1997).

It is difficult to gauge whether racist and homophobic crimes have actually increased in number or severity in recent decades, especially due to a lack of stable long-term monitoring and limited victimisation studies. The recording of such crimes is shaped by the allocation of resources, priorities and work practices in relevant public bureaucracies such as police, human rights and anti-discrimination agencies. Equally, the definitional criteria for classification can prove to be subjective, elastic and shifting. In various nations there has been increased political pressure and official determination to record victimisation on the grounds of race or sexuality. This can, in practice, prove to be patchy and even consciously resisted at the grass-roots level within police bureaucracies (Jenness & Grattet, 2001). Most importantly, violence against homosexual men and lesbians will appear to undergo dramatic rises in more enlightened jurisdictions in which these offences are given greater priority. Matters like the allocation of police resources, as well as the level of political mobilisation of these victim groups will determine this. Sometimes the process of the recognition of new social issues and social problems may take the exaggerated and unjustified form of a full moral panic (Cohen, 1972).

Yet referring to the political processes behind the recent construction of public concern about anti-homosexual violence does not mean these attacks do not exist on a significant scale or merit a serious research focus and official and community response. It is unlikely that many commentators would have the temerity to dismiss concerns about other forms of offending and violence (e.g., domestic violence and child sex assaults) in a similar way as the mere consequence of social panic and political agitation. A sentiment that specific victims and specific types of victimisation are less important than others is reflected in the hostile critique of the effects of 'identity politics' in this sphere. It is therefore worthwhile to turn a critical gaze back onto the implicit and unstated hierarchy of worthy and unworthy public issues and victims that have figured in any selective application of the criticism of anti-violence concern and action. Even among some 'hate crime' lobbyists there has been evidence of a covert hierarchy regarding which sorts of minority victims and which incidents merit the most serious attention (Mason, 2001a).

The most publicly contentious proposals around 'hate crime' have been new laws against vilification and provisions for penalty enhancement, yet the movement against such crime has not been universally driven by the assertion of what has been called 'special protections' in law. In particular, victims have wished to see recording and investigation of these crimes on an equal footing with other incidents. The advocates of such new laws have been frequently alarmed by ongoing problems with a lax police and official response to offending. This laxity has been evident even when these crimes fall into the pre-existing and ordinary range of offences that could be investigated and prosecuted under current laws including criminal assault, trespass, malicious injury and offensive behaviour. Even if they do not generate new types of offending and new laws, these campaigns against 'hate crime' have reasonably prompted a more thorough police and criminal justice response to attacks that have not acquired fresh offence labels.

The liberal state evolved in the 1800s on the model of the neutrality and impartiality of the law and criminal justice system that would rise above social distinctions and inequality. Development of an occupation of paid and independent officers to combat property crime and keep street order in industrial nations appeared to fit this neutral model. The rise of policing eased urban middle-class fears about the poor and 'dangerous classes' in the burgeoning city slums of Western Europe and the United States in the late nineteenth century (Silver, 1967). Repression of labour movement activism and the penetration of police activities into working-class, poor and minority districts both set off overt resistance to these changes in the early and mid-twentieth century (Cohen, 1979).

From the 1960s and 1970s there were further criticisms of police social distance from minority groups (Sarre, 1996). Additionally, a rise of new social movements initiating political actions led to direct conflicts with them. Many movement members were drawn into clashes with police at public rallies, vigils and demonstrations in these decades. More reinforcement of these pressures came from the generation of critical research evidence about the exercise of discretion in police work. This highlighted the limits of a traditional police worldview that has been described as authoritarian, racist and masculine, and the low reporting of offences by victims who had a lack of confidence in police (Chan, 1997).

Traditional patterns of policing had focused on the regulation of public order rather than directly addressing widespread societal violence. The liberal distinction between public and private spheres historically meant the downplaying of violence and abuse in private space or domestic social scenarios. This was a touchstone issue for feminist action against male violence and abuse directed against female partners. Yet a range of other offences that have taken place in public or domestic settings have also been constructed as personal or even trivial matters in a way that reflected the marginal social status of victims, and a history of targeting for criminalisation by typically racist and narrowly masculine police officers.

In these cases, a dual process of over-policing for wrongdoing and under-policing for victimisation constituted oppression by the criminal justice system. This was the common fate of such low status groups as racial minorities, vagrants, homosexuals and sex workers. The high level of intervention due to minor offending and drunkenness among Aboriginal Australians far exceeded responses to victimisation (Cunneen, 2001). For many police, this pattern appeared as the commonsense exercising of discretion to control miscreants offending middle-class morality and public order, and it meant less priority to the least credible of all victims. Nevertheless, the contemporary activist highlighting of this gap and associated publicity about it further eroded liberal claims about equal citizenship and the neutrality and fairness of the police.

This marginalisation of minority groups comprised the historical and social backdrop to lobbying, research and recent reforms in relation to 'hate crimes'. In opposition to this shift, there has been some coalescence of views from conservative, liberal and some Left commentators debunking this trend. These have all been adamant about the threat to personal freedom or a full overlap with repressive law and order campaigns that the new emphasis on 'hate crime' would result in. It is true that the repositioning of minority groups as real or likely victims in criminal justice discourse has been a major social-movement goal reviving coalitionism among gay men, lesbians and groups disenfranchised on the basis of race, ethnicity or disability. This coalitionist potential has seemed especially important in the light of the potentially weakening effects of the postmodern stress on the diversity of post-Left social struggles. The shared experience of bias-driven harassment and violence is something that many groups have conceded they had in common when other sorts of overlap were doubted.

The historical shift towards naming and classifying such violence as 'hate crime' mirrored the proliferation of new research and action that accompanied this process. Nevertheless, offending like the anti-homosexual killings described later in this book was not simply a matter played up by activists, and its complex depiction in discourse has not detracted from its reality as a social phenomenon with serious human costs. An undeveloped observation that the definition of criminal behaviour is historically fluid and that what constitutes deviance or crime reflects social power and pressure group and political relations, may seem banal to anyone familiar with the basic tenets of decades of research on deviance or critical criminology.

Such observations were standard fare in once innovative analyses of the symbolic processes involved in recasting deviance as significant crime (Taylor et al., 1973). Four decades ago, the full emergence of symbolic interactionism in social science stressed the generation of fluid and constructed social meanings in the professional and institutional labelling of deviance. This generally expanded researcher sympathy for marginal and less powerful groups rendered deviant in this process of stigmatisation and criminalisation. In fact, one leading exponent of this approach famously exhorted sociologists to take a firm moral stance in favour of powerless social groups (Becker, 1967). There is a rich historical irony in the more recent appropriation of aspects of this paradigm to selectively emphasise the constructed nature of social problems and discredit claims on legitimate victimhood from socially marginal and subordinated groups winning empowerment to deal with real instances of harassment and violence.[5] The contradictory political elements of such a stance have been lucidly drawn out by one local criminologist in the observation:

> That certain social problems are (apparently) inflated for the purposes of particular lobby groups . . . does need to be recognized. But care has to be taken regarding how to interpret the social processes whereby particular problems become 'public' issues. For instance, there is a danger that critique of the way in which lobbying occurs may inadvertently reproduce the ideology that 'special interest groups' are manipulative and conniving, and that they are out to capture the political agenda for

their own very selective ends. This is a favourite argument of the Right, and one which, along with the phrase 'politically correct', is actively used to de-legitimate the voices and genuine concerns of the less powerful in society. (White, 2000: 359–60)

Recent critical analyses of this activism in relation to hate attacks on sexual minorities have begun to produce a better understanding of the actual processes of hate crime mobilisation, its mixed outcomes and its full consequences for different individuals and groups of people in relation to social identity, respectability, belonging and community (Moran et al., 2004). The responses to prejudice and violence that are discussed in this book demonstrate the vexed ways of understanding the character and fate of victims outside of protective inner-urban subcultures. The currency and symbolic power of key representations of violence and victimhood have important outcomes for general notions of sexual identity both among victims and perpetrators and many more people without the direct experience of attacks. This victimhood is ultimately not a mere matter of public imagery, induced needs and complaint. It has been grounded in the real-life experience of such attacks linked to sexual identity. A growing body of international research has indicated the wide extent of this victimisation linked to the heterosexual and gendered ordering of societies.

4   Researching
   Anti-Homosexual Killings

INTRODUCTION

New research and activism have suggested that the threat and experience of violence linked to sexual identity has been an integral part of the life history of many people from sexual minorities. With justification it is argued that their lives have been shaped, restricted and, for some, ended by it. Furthermore, activists insist that a substantial number of these victims are killed in savage attacks that would invite intense official and media concern if perpetrated against groups with more social status. Until recently, the issue of this form of fatal violence surfaced in the public arena in sensational media accounts of 'deviant' lifestyles and sexual behaviour among victims. Alongside this lurid voyeurism, the great bulk of these homicides with their lesser known victims have been disregarded around the globe. These are cases of victimisation in which the sexual identity and resulting marginal social status of an apparently homosexual victim had a significant relationship to the motives of perpetrators.

Agitation by activist and community groups has resulted in strong evidence that in different times and places, this same projected inferiority of homosexual victims may shape official indifference, lax policing, unjust legal findings and even a disturbing degree of community sympathy for the brutality of perpetrators. These crimes were an occasional theme within the nascent Gay Liberation movement which rose in the United States and other Western nations in the 1970s. Most notably the shooting of San Francisco's councillor Harvey Milk in 1978 and the light sentence that was later imposed on his killer, resulted in the street rioting which became a significant moment in modern homosexual activism (Shilts, 1982). This early homosexual politics was mostly directed towards the limited goal of repealing anti-sodomy provisions in criminal law and it often reflected a one-dimensional view of the criminal justice system as the blunt instrument of heterosexual repression.

A fully fledged response to the violence directed at lesbians and gay men did not arise until this social movement had evolved such that in an expanding number of jurisdictions, eventual victories with decriminalisation campaigns were followed by efforts to enact laws that protect homosexuals, bisexuals and transsexuals from discrimination, harassment and vilification on the grounds of their sexuality. In several nations, this eventual success with law reform grew in tandem with a mobilisation against the threat of HIV/AIDS in the 1980s, the rise of coalitionist efforts between lesbians, transsexuals and gay men, and a modest but significantly increased influence in mainstream politics and the public bureaucracies that deal with such matters as health, law and discrimination (Altman, 1994).

The global response to killings with homosexual and transgender victims in the 1990s has signalled the internationalisation of concern about these crimes and the extensive activism that has emerged around them, especially regarding the wavering pattern of the police and criminal justice reactions to them. In the United States, the best known of these has been the killing of Mathew Shephard in a conservative rural town. In October 1998 Shephard was bashed, bound to a fence and left to die by two men he met in a local bar. In this and most other cases, it has been the stress on hatred as a primary motive among perpetrators that has prevailed in activist pronouncements (Loffreda, 2001; Swigonski et al., 2001).

STUDIES OF ANTI-HOMOSEXUAL KILLINGS

There has been a minor overall focus from mainstream criminologists and researchers in criminal justice agencies on killings related to sexual prejudice. This neglect may not be due to mere oversight as it seems tied to the historical origins of criminology as a research discipline that overwhelmingly studied homosexuality as deviance (Tomsen, 1997c). Accordingly, this victimisation and its patterns have not been studied in depth by researchers. A conventional wisdom among crime researchers is that records for homicides are the most thorough among all categories of violent crime, but homicide research and the official figures rarely mention the sexuality of a perpetrator or victim and in most places the number of these killings remains unknown. For these reasons, the majority of police agencies and criminal justice officials have only a very rudimentary knowledge of such killings; including the historical extent of these and the typical and varying characteristics of fatal incidents.

Although a mobilisation around different killings has proven to be politically galvanising, the new research on violence and sexual prejudice has included a smaller emphasis on anti-homosexual killings. Previous international studies have begun to fill the research void around anti-homosexual killing. In 1980 Miller and Humphreys published a critical overview of the scant and very speculative nature of previous evidence on the subject. They also reported on their own study of 52 homicide cases from the United States and Canada. These were deaths in which the victims not only appear to have been homosexual men, but strong factual evidence or witness testimony suggested that 'the crime related to the victim's homosexual lifestyle' (Miller & Humphreys, 1980: 173). In this sample, killings that followed on from sexual cruising and liaison between men in everyday 'straight' settings (in bars, freeways and public streets) were found to be far more common than fatal gang attacks on homosexual victims; though all forms of these crimes were generally noteworthy for their exceptional brutality:

> Intense rage is present in nearly all homicide cases with homosexual victims. A striking feature of most murders in this sample is their gruesome, often vicious nature. Seldom is a homosexual victim simply shot. He is more apt to be stabbed a dozen or more times, mutilated, and strangled. In a number of instances, the victim was stabbed or mutilated even after being fatally shot. (179)

Most importantly, this study first uncovered a variable pattern of victimisation according to the 'openness' of different homosexual lifestyles. Homicide rates were far higher among what were termed as 'homosexual marginals' who were particularly vulnerable to attacks from male prostitutes and hitchhikers, and 'tend by definition to lack gay identity, engage in furtive sexual encounters, lack skills that facilitate operation in the gay world, and exist on its perimeter' (175). These sexually incompetent victims were viewed as fundamentally 'closeted', and so racked with guilt and fear of discovery that they could not assume a safer and openly homosexual lifestyle.

This stress can be appreciated through its evident link to the early Gay Liberationist challenge to the wide personal unhappiness deriving from socially enforced straight identities. The authors took heterosexual 'moral entrepreneurs' to task for the destructive outcomes of this process, which include a greater vulnerability to violence (182). Nevertheless, they were also oblivious to the resulting conceptual difficulties for distinguishing between sexual identity and desire, and the highly moral overtones of the dichotomy shaped between the 'establishment of gay love relationships and involvement with gay community institutions' (169) and the less fulfilled lives of those who seek out 'clandestine sex with demonstrably dangerous pick-ups in unprotective settings' (182).

The moral lessons about the risks of this sort of sexual activity were even more pronounced in the findings of a study of killings which occurred in Amsterdam in the 1980s (Gemert, 1994). Despite the atmosphere of sexual liberalism which prevailed which prevailed in that city, it was accepted by police officials that a high number of male homicide victims (possibly one in eight) were homosexual men. Data sources were police files on 18 homicides, official personality reports concerning seven known killers and interviews conducted with seven men selected by the researcher as fitting the profile of 'potential victims'. As a group, the homicide victims appeared to have been more open about their homosexual interests than the 'marginals' considered by Miller and Humphreys. Their downfall seemed to be due to their regular level of contact with male sex workers. Killings were typically perpetrated by prostitute boys and young men who attacked older clients during disputes about money or in order to steal from their compromised victims.

Gemert (1994) correctly pointed out the simplicity of viewing these crimes as mere robberies. Elsewhere, his reflections on perpetrators who come from ethnic and religious backgrounds (Arabic, Turkish and Muslim) that place a heavy stress on the defence of heterosexual identity and social honour offer clues about the links between these crimes and the social construction of different masculinities (Gemert, 1991). But his reconstruction of the character weaknesses of victims and killers pathologised both parties without considering the wider social roots of anti-homosexual violence. The end result of this was another instance of victim-blaming. The dramatic title of the published results—'Chicken kills hawk'—conjures up images of predatory homosexual men and vulnerable heterosexual youth. Gemert noted that many victims understood the dangers involved in commercial sex relations but that 'harshness and violence gets people excited' (1994: 157) Despite some tone of sympathy, readers are left with a distinctly negative impression of lonely and pathetic victims:

> Just like the perpetrator, the victim has had bad experiences too. He leads an isolated existence, embittered towards the homosexual world and secretly visiting prostitutes. He would like to have a steady relationship, but he feels that the boys he takes home are not to be trusted and knows that he is not being realistic, thinking they will stay with him. In his situation sex is the main thing left and, accordingly, he is willing to keep on risking his life. (170)

A powerful corrective to this blaming stance was offered by activist surveys of violence against homosexual men, transsexuals and lesbians in Colombia and Brazil (Ordonez, 1995; Mott, 1996). In particular, the second of these provided evidence of the very wide extent and ongoing nature of fatal attacks. This study of legal and press reports for the period between 1963 and 1994 uncovered 1,260 likely killings of homosexuals (comprising 1,239 'gay males and transvestites' and 21 lesbians), and estimated that in reality at least 1,500 homosexuals were probably killed in Brazil in the previous decade (Mott, 1996: 53–4).

This rate appeared to have peaked in the early 1990s with an estimated average of 114 killings per year (Mott, 1996: 54). This peak may have reflected the exacerbated stigma attached to homosexuality due to the spread of AIDS, or a backlash against the rudimentary gains of the Brazilian gay and lesbian movement. It was also considered likely that this form of crime had risen with a general increase in violence (marked by political assassinations, drug wars, massacres of street children and the genocide of indigenous people) during a period of social crisis.

Many crimes were virtual executions 'marked by extensive beating, the use of multiple weapons, bodily mutilations, in particular of the sexual organs, and disfigurement of the face and head' (Mott, 1996: 62). Most significantly, many serious bashings and fatal attacks were perpetrated by right-wing death squads engaged in campaigns of 'human cleansing'. Direct and indirect evidence suggested a high level of routine involvement and complicity with police and military officials from both junior and senior ranks:

> the exaggerated valorization of the conception of honor explain[s] the virulence of homophobia in the military milieu. . . . Police and military forces merit the most urgent intervention by the human rights movement, as they are one of the principal agents for abuse of power, physical violence, and assassinations of homosexuals. (Mott, 1996: 72–3)

This evidence pointed to the strong links existing between the harassment, assault and killing of homosexuals and the practices and culture of state officials and the general society. This victimisation was reinforced by a public awareness of the high level of success that accused perpetrators had in raising the 'legitimate honor defense' to explain the deaths of homosexual victims:

> This argument, which is constantly repeated in newspaper headlines and police reports, represents a strategically used defense well known by sex workers or taught by defense lawyers to sway juries, in the same way that machistas use the 'legitimate honor defense' or 'uncontrolled emotions' when they kill their wives or girlfriends. (Mott, 1996: 75)

This anti-homosexual violence in Brazil was generally validated by the stance of the church, media, politicians and upper echelons of the legal system. A distinguishing feature of such crimes was the comparatively low level of official and international concern that they attracted (Mott, 1996: 55). Many crimes were poorly investigated, and a full or partial exoneration was common in the matters which tend to reach a court hearing. These were typically attacks carried out by poor youths and male prostitutes who often blackmailed or stole from victims and found encouragement for this in the anti-gay ideology of the whole society. Many cases involved evidence of an explicitly anti-homosexual motive, but this is often a powerful factor underlying cases where it is more indirect:

> Gays are killed because a macho ideology teaches that homosexuals in general are weak, timid, and easy to blackmail. Armed robbery

is a frequent motive for murder, and the imagined physical or social weakness of veados [homosexuals] encourages such crimes. (Mott, 1996: 74)

The most important features of this study were the connections drawn between anti-homosexual prejudice, violence and 'machismo' and between the individual actions of killers and the practices and beliefs of state authorities. For other researchers, this clearly signalled the need for more analysis that further interrogated the relationship of such crimes to different masculinities.

The international research of homicides with gay/homosexual victims was further added to by a British study of court records relating to the 77 deaths of male victims that arose from 'gay sex encounters' during a 25-year period (Bartlett, 2007: 574). The crimes studied were fatal assaults resulting from a one-on-one conflict in a private setting, and often in a victim's own residence. These perpetrators were found to be significantly younger than their victims, a high proportion had previously been in borstals or state care, and at the time of the offence most were on welfare benefits or unemployed (Bartlett, 2007). It is uncertain what number of fatal incidents involved actual same-sex activity, but the focus here was on interactions in which casual sexual activity, or some possibility of a victim's hope for it, were a common feature.

In this study, the promise of a non-essentialist analysis that would unpack the 'simple division between gay victim and non-gay perpetrator' (Bartlett, 2007: 582) remained unfulfilled. Problems with the classification of sexual identity were acknowledged with regret about a lack of compelling evidence of the 'nuanced self-perception of the *gay* perpetrators' [emphasis added] (582). Although 'no assumptions should be drawn about the sexual orientation of the perpetrators' (583), around half of the perpetrators were 'gay' with this meaning 'having had sex with another man previously, without payment' (584). Accordingly, the backdrop to the interpretations of these research results concerning 'gay sexual homicide' was that pleasurable engagement in same-sex activity in itself is proof of gay identity.

Different forms of violence with homosexual victims, such as collective stranger violence or more private assaults occurring between male acquaintances and intimates, necessitate recognition of the distinct dynamics of these crimes. But an unintentionally orthodox and restrictive notion of 'hate crime' was implied by a framework in which these killings were seen as fully distinct from the 'homophobic hate crimes' that are understood as public group attacks. The generative importance of the attainment or struggle for masculinity in violent practices as a 'communal activity' (Bartlett, 2007: 594) by men in such public hate crimes was also conceded, but this was not extended to more private crimes. The analysis concluded with a radical division of social and psychological interpretations (see Gadd & Jefferson, 2007) so that questions of masculinity became dismissed as unrelated to 'repressed or subconscious factors' (Bartlett, 2007: 592) or understanding perpetrator 'lives with little direction and histories of violence, suggesting hostility and anger' (593).

THE MASCULINITY AND HOMICIDE STUDY

In Australia there were protests over the death of a homosexual law lecturer killed in Adelaide in 1972 in circumstances suggesting the likely involvement of police officers as assailants (Willet, 2000). A more critical turning point in the local community activism against anti-homosexual killings was the reaction to the death of Michael Stevens, a 23-year-old gay man who was assaulted and left dying by a gang of youths on a Sydney street in 1985. This attack coincided with an expansion in the gay and lesbian media which began to report on issues of violence and discrimination, and the first tentative moves towards a new form of homosexual–police consultation. One of the city's first openly homosexual councillors added his voice to public concerns about this killing and the assailants who walked free or were not charged ('Acquittal inquiry called for', *Sydney Morning Herald*, 28 May 1987).

It also attracted wider media coverage that included tabloid press sensation about a killing on 'notorious Oxford Street', the mystery 'transvestite witness' said to have comforted the dying victim and even the victim's friendship with a local transsexual who was killed at home in an unsolved shotgun attack ('Police seek unidentified transvestite', *Mirror*, 2 July 1985). As this street attack did not involve any behaviour which could be reasonably construed as provocative or blameworthy, much of this coverage was sympathetic ('Youths jailed for cowardly attack', *Sydney Morning Herald*, 2 May 1987). The appearance of one of the survivors of the attack on a national television talk show also marked a significant moment in the creation of a wider community consciousness about this form of crime ('Fear on the streets as gay bashings turn into murder', *Sydney Morning Herald*, 25 June 1985). As well as its key impact on gay and lesbian consciousness of the dangers of violence, this crime appeared to reflect a growing perpetrator awareness of the availability of victims in urban areas with a high concentration of gay men, lesbians and transsexuals. Stevens and two gay male friends were attacked near Oxford Street by assailants who later admitted they went to the area because they were likely to find a homosexual victim among the people they encountered.

In the 1970s, Oxford Street was an unfashionable part of inner Sydney. Its rapid transformation into an area of bars, nightclubs, restaurants and new shops was spearheaded by the influx of gay men in the subcultural boom of the late 1970s and early 1980s. Yet the history of the area was underwritten with the complexities and contradictions of the relations between homosexuals and the local legal system. Early expansion as a gay district was only possible because of the deep level of corruption of the area's notoriously homophobic police (Wotherspoon, 1991). Links between underworld figures and local officers had often allowed venues to flourish despite obvious breaches of liquor licensing laws. By the 1980s there was a lauding of the tourist value of 'pink precincts' around the globe, and local gay and lesbian tour operators referred to this strip as the 'golden mile' and site of the annual Mardi Gras parade (Faro & Wotherspoon, 2000). There has been a growth of publicity marked by fascination and even celebration of the new position of this 'pink precinct' as a tourist attraction. More recently, the large numbers of heterosexuals drawn to the nightlife of the area has sharpened debates about safety, sexuality and urban space.

The new indignation over fatal and non-fatal bashings signalled the importance of a shared sense of spatial identity related to the growth of commercial gay and lesbian precincts in Western cities including Amsterdam, Berlin, London, New York, San Francisco and Sydney in the last 30 years. This public visibility and sense of 'gay space', and mixed feelings of safety, ownership and siege, often inflected the politics against violence and wider debates about the extent and nature of the gay and lesbian community (Tomsen, 1993). Such 'gay' areas have proven attractive to those seeking a place of refuge and a sense of local community within a wider heterosexist society. Reasons for 'sexual migration' (Rubin, 1993) from suburban and rural locations include issues of discrimination and personal safety. Paradoxically, this can also make some forms of victimisation more possible as new opportunities exist for perpetrators in the increased visibility of homosexuals within such districts and the growing publicity about them. Such districts have been perceived as safe although they may be targeted by people intending to harass and assault locals and in reality they only offer a 'freedom to be openly gay, to challenge the norming of public space as straight, rather than freedom from violence' (Rushbrook, 2002: 195).

At various points in time, such as the victories of openly gay male candidates in city elections in San Francisco and Sydney in the 1970s and 1980s, they have been a focus of political strength as well as an alternative sexual culture. These locations have been eroded and sometimes shifted due to such impacts as the AIDS crisis and exclusive levels of gentrification with burgeoning accommodation and retail costs. The very existence of such urban areas has also been sometimes criticised for a separation from the social mainstream, and the way in which a grounding of sexual identity in specific urban spaces can result in a marginalisation of those homosexuals who for reasons of social class, age, gender, race or even elements of choice, have not been part of this process.

In the early 1990s, concerns grew about a jump in the annual number of reported killings of homosexual men in inner Sydney. As could be expected from the heirs to a movement that strategically focused on issues of law and legal equality, this interest particularly surrounded the direction and outcome of the criminal trials of arrested suspects. Many of these accused men alleged that their use of fatal violence was caused and justified by homosexual advances or assaults from their victims. This development necessitated a coherent and informed response by gay and lesbian organisations in their dealings with police, legal officials and political figures. Against this backdrop, the author's research filled gaps in knowledge about victimisation by studying homicides in which victims were selected out for attack by their killers on the basis of their perceived homosexuality. This was achieved by a use of information from overlapping sources, and detailed analyses of perpetrator motive and evidence about the unfolding of different fatal incidents as interactive encounters between victims and perpetrators. To counter the uncertainty of police monitoring, a wide search of press records was conducted.

This research set out to critically assess the notion that these killings can always be completely understood as 'hate' crimes with an in-depth analysis of motive. This search was directed at finding probable 'anti-homosexual killings' with these being broadly understood as homicides in which the sexuality of the victim was reasonably judged as having a likely important relation to the fatal incident. This excluded cases of fatal domestic violence within homosexual couples, conflicts where the homosexuality of the deceased appeared to be coincidental to the victimisation and killings that resulted from conflicts between men in which terms such as 'poofter' or 'faggot' were traded as simple insults in a preceding argument. Seventy-four anti-homosexual killings that occurred over two decades in the state of New South Wales were uncovered. Of these, 55 were classified by police as solved and the other 19 as unsolved.

The study analysed trial records and transcripts concerning 40 matters, as well as court exhibits, witness statements, dock statements and final judgments on sentencing. Whereas some of these trials had resulted in murder convictions, in other cases pleas of provocation and self-defence regarding alleged sexual assaults or advances by the deceased had resulted in manslaughter convictions and full acquittals. This suggested a parallel with the allegations being raised in American courts ('Developments: sexual orientation and the law', 1989; Comstock, 1992; Mison, 1992). This study explored the form and presentation of claims about sexual advances in different killing scenarios. Further information was obtained from coroners records regarding 12 unsolved matters. An archival search of records that included post-mortem reports, forensic reports, incident narratives, police exhibits and interviews with key suspects in these matters was conducted.

All killings were summarised and analysed for basic information regarding the location and pattern of the offences, relevant situational factors and the characteristics of the parties involved. Records were examined for details regarding victims and perpetrators, aspects of victimisation, and the relative importance of levels of anti-homosexual sentiment and notions of sexual and male identity in the motives of perpetrators. Police records of interviews with freshly arrested suspects were a useful source of insights regarding motives for offending. These were often conducted close in time to the actual killing and gave a more immediate record of the perpetrators' explanations and rationalisations of their own violence.

Lastly, the author's study also considered the depiction of the sexual identities of both perpetrators and victims in courtroom settings and how these could have critical outcomes in sentencing and the determination of guilt. These depictions were subjected to a content analysis concerning the themes of honour, masculinity and sexual deviance. This was done to unearth commonsense categories of understanding male violence and sexual identity that could impact on judicial findings.

VICTIMS AND PERPETRATORS

These 74 killings represented approximately 14 per cent of all homicides with male victims occurring in the state over a 20-year period (Tomsen, 2002). They peaked in 1989–1993, with six victims killed in 1987 and 1990, and seven in 1992. The research analysis produced striking findings regarding the age and social class of victims. These were notably older than other male victims of homicide. Age is often given a negative correlation to victimisation with younger men regarded as most at risk of fatal involvements with violence, but this did not hold true with these attacks. Most victims were middle-aged or older males, with a peak in the thirties and forties age brackets. Thirty-six were in their thirties or forties, 21 were in their fifties or sixties, and 15 were in their twenties. Only one case with a teenage victim was found. This raised the possibility that the real and perceived physical vulnerability or social isolation of older homosexual men may be factors in opportunistic killings, especially in cases where the victim and perpetrator were friends or acquaintances.

The general risk of homicide in men is heavily concentrated among those with low socio-economic status (Polk, 1994). This finding must be qualified for anti-homosexual killings. The victim's occupation was known in 59 cases. Seventeen were unemployed or pensioners, partly reflecting the older age profile of the group. Five worked in blue-collar activities, 23 in small business, clerical or hospitality positions, and a further 14 in management or professions. A high proportion of men who are middle-class professionals and semi-professionals are at risk of victimisation in such attacks. Unusually, the victims included a diplomat, an ex-city mayor, a physician, a dentist, an accountant, a journalist, three wealthy businessmen and five schoolteachers. The insulation from violent crime those with higher social status generally experience is counteracted by factors related to sexuality.

The designation of these homicides as 'gay-hate' killings was avoided as a prior classification of the sexuality of each victim. From a constructionist point of view 'gayness' is a historically specific label for a similar culture and outlook among certain sexual groups, rather than the actual sexual practices of individuals (Connell & Dowsett, 1992). For decades, the homosexual male and lesbian population of inner Sydney has comprised one of the largest in the southern hemisphere (Wotherspoon, 1991). However, victims comprised a mix of men from city, suburban and other locations. Many of the victims had only marginal or no apparent links to any homosexual or 'gay male' subculture. Fifty-two victims could be termed as homosexual, bisexual or transsexual. Others may have been more secretive about their sexuality or engaged in same-sex activity without identifying as non-heterosexual. Activist concerns about anti-homosexual violence have principally focused on the threat to inner-city gay men and lesbians, yet victims lived in a variety of areas that included urban and non-metropolitan settings.

Twenty per cent of killings occurred at sites of public same-sex cruising. Locally, these are known colloquially as 'beats'. In other English-speaking nations they are referred to as 'tearooms' (US) and 'cottages' (UK), though contemporary sexual globalisation has resulted in a more frequent interchangeability of these terms (Humphreys, 1970; Moran, 1996; Dalton, 2007). These sites also still attract many men who are circumspect about overt displays of their sexuality, but regard themselves as homosexual or gay (Hodge, 1995). Such locations are an alternative to commercial gay venues which may be too public, expensive, inaccessible or alienating for rural, suburban or various other homosexual men. Valuable ethnographic research conducted on such locations suggests that many 'beat-users' do not identify as homosexual and it is not accurate to caricature this entire group as 'closets' in need of liberation from the moral strictures of society. There is a mixed pattern of sexual identification by men with divergent sexual identities. As attacks occur frequently at public locations where men seek out casual sex partners, this raised the likelihood that many victims of anti-homosexual violence at such locations have minimal or no homosexual self-identification. For this reason, they have presented similar difficulties as targets for anti-violence campaigns as they have for HIV workers and educators.

Paradoxically, the dissemination of research knowledge about such locations has run in tandem with an increased official scrutiny. Anonymous same-sex public cruising has been a long-standing concern for public authorities and incites much police animosity towards gay/homosexual men (Dalton, 2007). Swivel (1991) demonstrated how these became the subject of an increased degree of localised regulation, and a 'war of position' between users and police and authority figures, which generally went unnoticed among official gay and lesbian organisations. Features of this were derived from situational crime prevention with the immediate environment altered by measures (space, lighting and surveillance) aimed to prevent and contain same-sex activities. More directly, revived and strengthened contemporary offensive behaviour provisions resulted in police crackdowns and arrests at such locations (Tomsen, 1993). The limits of liberal public tolerance and the divisions between respectable and disrespectable patterns of homosexuality that arise from conflicts over these locations are obvious. Victims bashed or killed at such places are attacked in circumstances that have rendered them subject to moral disputes about risk-taking and blameworthiness.

The identity of victims is relevant to the issue of sexual motives for prejudice and violence. Violence is directed against victims who are viewed by their assailants as homosexual or 'gay' in a simplistic way. Regardless of the appropriate label for the sexuality of each victim, a fatal assault can still be reasonably termed as an anti-homosexual killing if the perpetrator(s) perceived a victim to be homosexual or their hostility to same-sex desire had a significant relation to the motive for the attack. Three victims were best described as transsexual or transgender. Furthermore, some others appeared to be conventionally 'heterosexual'.

For example, in one incident a young soldier who had been drinking heavily with friends fell asleep next to a public toilet in a park known for homosexual cruising and violence. He was killed by youths who offered no plausible reason for the vicious assault but repeatedly referred to the crime scene as the 'poofter park' (*R v. Turner & Nash*, NSWSC Finlay J, 14 September 1990). In another incident, the killing of a middle-aged man in a non-gay bar was preceded by repeated and personal anti-homosexual abuse. When the escalating dispute moved onto a city street the perpetrator tried to involve young onlookers in his conflict with the alleged 'poofter'. The accused had no rational basis for believing his victim was homosexual (*R v. Gellatly*, NSWDC Wall J, 22 December 1995).

In other cases the homosexuality of the victim was real but not publicly divulged and this was resented by some friends and close relatives of the deceased. One mother only learnt of her son's sexuality after he had been killed in an alley at the end of a night of heavy drinking in gay bars (Tomsen, 2002). In another matter a well-respected and married professional was killed by a younger man he had been drinking with and the victim set off a fatal dispute by attacking the perpetrator 'without reason' while in the 'vulnerable' position of urinating. The sexuality of the deceased, the sexualised aspects of this interaction and suggestions that the victim and perpetrator were longstanding acquaintances were not openly discussed in the courtroom (Tomsen, 2002).

This study reaffirmed that the great bulk of assailants in violent anti-homosexual attacks are young males. In the solved homicides, 88 of the 92 perpetrators or co-perpetrators were males. This is similar to the general pattern of homicides between men (Polk, 1994). Yet this was most pronounced in these data. Whereas many victims were middle-aged or older, the killers were significantly younger. Eleven perpetrators were more than 30 years old, 38 were in their twenties and 43 were teenagers. A total of 65 perpetrators and co-perpetrators were aged 25 years or less at the time of the offence. Young perpetrators tended more to attack in groups. Forty-five were involved in the 23 solved killings carried out by two or more perpetrators. Twenty young perpetrators were involved in the six attacks which had three or more assailants. Key suspects in unsolved matters also comprised groups of teenage boys who had come under police surveillance for ongoing involvement in bashings of homosexual men. This factor of youthfulness and the greater age of victims created very substantial gaps. Victims were at least 10 years older than perpetrators in 17 killings. In a further 25, victims were 20 years or more in age than their killers.

Only four females were involved in these killings. These were two teenage girls and two women in their twenties. None acted without a male lead and all four were the partners of male key perpetrators. One directly participated in a murder by stabbing and another had a peripheral involvement in a fatal public gang attack. The other two assisted partners in attempts to conceal killings. Overall, six male perpetrators carried out double-killings. Two had both a heterosexual and a homosexual victim. A pair of killers and two other perpetrators acting solo all killed two homosexual victims. Of these six killers, one was a heroin addict, one an alcoholic, three were heavily involved in male prostitution and two were classified as having dangerous 'psychopathic' personalities (see Chapter 7).

A fact that is not stressed in activism and public campaigning around 'homophobic' violence and other forms of violent 'hate crime' is the majority of perpetrators have low socio-economic status. This was a very pronounced feature of these killings. Some perpetrators were schoolboys at the time of their offence. Nevertheless, most had a very limited education and were unemployed or in unskilled manual jobs (such as a labourer, driver or storeman), or in sex work with a homosexual clientele. The highest levels of occupational status were a few cases of skilled trade qualifications (a boilermaker, a plumber, a gardener) and a killer employed in a minor clerical role.

Although official records concerning the social backgrounds of these perpetrators are fragmentary, examples with full detail suggest a common pattern of family breakdown, poverty, petty delinquency escalating into more serious police matters, substance abuse and marginality in the job market and housing. This evidence of social disadvantage suggests the distinction that some commentators have drawn between traditional working-class and more impoverished 'underclass' social positions that may be characterised by extensive and violent offending and victimisation (Murray, 2003).

Full details for 65 perpetrators were found in trial records. Eleven had a history of violence, 23 had a criminal record and three had served a prison term. Twenty-four had experienced family breakdown, and 25 had a history of illicit drug and alcohol abuse that sometimes dated from childhood with a likely link to episodes of personal violence. The substance use ranged from binge drinking mixed with marihuana smoking and the taking of amphetamines, to serious addiction to heroin. Only five (including two double-killers) were discussed in court records as having a serious mental disturbance linked to acts of killing. The profile of the great majority reflected social deprivation and marginality rather than psychological pathology.

FATAL SCENARIOS

These fatal attacks took place in a mix of areas, with the bulk happening in inner-city or suburban locations. Nineteen killings took place in a rural, small-town or regional location. Five victims were killed near Oxford Street or by someone they evidently met in a bar there. Another eight were killed at three public cruising locations around the city. However, the number of fatal attacks at beats and public locations (30) was exceeded by the number of killings occurring in the victims' or perpetrators' own residence (33).

Most assailants relied on kicking and punching with great force to kill and often as a group activity. The common means of death was bashing (33). All victims who drowned (five) were bashed before dying. Four more died of strangulation or suffocation. Twenty-two were stabbed with knives. Other weapons included scissors, forks, a rock, stick, claw hammer, saw, bottle, bowling pin, fire-extinguisher, metal tape dispenser, spade, auto wheel brace, ceramic money-holder, plaster garden statue and a hunting bow and arrows. Only six victims were attacked with a firearm and this may be because young killers have less access to such weapons. In the five solved instances of firearm killing, 7 of 10 perpetrators were 25 years old or more. Possibly this non-use of firearms also reflected a preference for a more hands-on approach providing a greater level of gratification for killers.

In one case a victim was stabbed 65 times and most blows were delivered after he had already died (*Sydney Morning Herald*, 17 October 1981). Another victim was stabbed 47 times in the face with a screwdriver by an enraged young man who approached him at a beat. Other examples of heightened violence included the castration of one victim before his death and the blinding, binding and torture of another. This finding corresponded with the overall level of violence uncovered by Mott (1996). Likewise, in a Florida-based analysis of the injury patterns of deceased victims, many offences were notable for their exceptional brutality and the frenzied form of attacks with victims tormented and wounded repeatedly (Bell & Vila, 1996).

Assailants attacked in a spontaneous outburst or planned group assault which soon reached a fatal crescendo and most killings were characterised by the perpetrators' reckless indifference to the lethal results of their actions. Sixteen of these crimes appeared to be the result of a conscious prior decision to kill. The great bulk had the quality of 'poofter bashings', retaliatory assaults intended to punish a homosexual advance, or robberies in which the victim perished. A fatal outcome often surprised killers who unleashed violence with little appreciation of the full danger of such attacks for victims.[1]

In recent decades researchers have grown increasingly critical of any simple categorising of homicides as either domestic or stranger killings (Decker, 1993). Records of these homicides reflected the dual significance of attacks at beats/public locations and those occurring in private homes. Twenty-seven killings were public bashings or gang attacks, 20 comprised situations of socialising between friends and acquaintances and 19 were sexual 'pick-ups'. This suggests a mixed pattern of danger from locations and relations to perpetrators.

The victim's relation to his killer(s) was known in 69 cases. Twenty-eight cases involved complete strangers and 24 cases involved friends or acquaintances. Half of the homicides that occurred in a private dwelling involved killers who were barely known to their victims. Assailants were typically met in bars or the street, or they were male prostitutes and other men contacted via telephone sex services. Given that in 45 of these 69 cases victims either barely knew or did not know their killer or killers, these homicides suggest a much stronger aspect of danger from strangers (even in private dwellings) than is the case with fatal attacks on women or even more general cases of homicide with male victims.

Two general scenarios of killings were found in this evidence. The first was a fatal attack carried out in public space on a victim who was homosexual or presumed to be. He was usually a complete stranger to the assailant or assailants—they often attacked in groups. Some victims were killed at locations that were near to areas with bars, nightclubs and restaurants favoured by a gay clientele. Victims seemed to have been most vulnerable when attacked at beats. The statements of a number of arrested suspects were marked by a tone of outrage concerning same-sex activities at these places. But such locations were selected as places to seek homosexual victims because of their expected ready availability. Some perpetrators were attracted by the relative seclusion of locations (beachfronts, parks, trails and nature reserves) which are dark and deserted at night, and the compromised situation of victims who had been seeking out casual sexual activity. Around one-third of the fatal attacks fitted this scenario of a public attack by strangers operating in a group.

In the second scenario for these crimes a personal dispute leading to violence typically occurred between two men in private space. Commonly, assailants in this second scenario alleged a sexual advance came from the deceased. These amounted to 33 homicides. A significant internal variation exists between two forms of these. These comprise situations of friendly socialising and drinking (12), or the more continuously sexualised situations of men linking up for the purpose of a casual sexual encounter (15). This distinction was significant to assessment of the plausibility of perpetrator claims about being subjected to an unexpected and provocative sexual advance. Such claims are generally less believable in the more openly sexualised type of setting.

Thirty-three killings were marked by robbery or the intention to rob as a motive. This has an uneven relation to the motives of perpetrators. In many instances the theft of property had an incidental relation to the anti-homosexual assault. Property of little value was stolen as an after-thought or a further means of victim degradation. In a minority of kill-ings it appeared to be a principal motive. This operated in the context of awareness of the homosexuality of victims who could be soft targets with an expected vulnerability to attack and robbery and reluctance to report crimes. In a few such cases, unexpected victim resistance served to escalate violence to a fatal level. The large number of attacks in which violence well exceeded the level needed to overpower a person and steal property sug-gested anti-homosexual sentiment had an important role. Like many gang bashings, or sudden violent responses to homosexual suggestiveness, these robberies were mostly not planned killings but the perpetrators' fury or contempt for the victim outweighed restraint with a lethal result.

ADVANCE ALLEGATIONS AND THE LEGAL RESPONSE

Forty trials were analysed in full detail. In 31 of the trials, perpetrators made allegations of a homosexual advance or advances by the deceased. The nine trials in which this was not raised included seven fatal attacks in public space as well as one case of a targeted group attack on a victim's house in which the claim about a sexual advance was later alluded to outside of trial evidence. Trials in which courtroom advance allegations were made comprised 26 instances of private-scenario disputes between men who were friends or acquaintances and 19 instances of killing by a solo assailant. Half of the cases which involved multiple perpetrators and where allegations about a sexual advance were made referred to a previous occasion of a sexual advance between the deceased and the per-petrator or a third party. To the extent that these claims were taken as plausible evidence, crimes involving multiple perpetrators were recast as being about matters concerning past occasions of the more private sce-nario of sexual advance.

The evidence suggests that both real and alleged homosexual advances are more typical of cases in the second general scenario of violence, that is, due to a dispute between two men socialising privately. Even if allega-tions are not true, the only surviving direct witness is the accused killer or a co-perpetrator. And such claims about the predatory behaviour of the deceased will be interpreted as being far more plausible in this par-ticular social context rather than the circumstances of public violence or a group attack on a stranger. The 16 successful uses of homosexual advance claims (resulting in findings of manslaughter or acquittals) reflected these characteristics. Most occurred in private space, and half of the public-space killings with successful allegations took the form of the private-dispute scenario between acquaintances.[2] Ten of these killings had solo perpetrators. Half of those with multiple perpetrators referred to an occasion of previous one-on-one sexual abuse. Additionally, half of these 16 killings involved teenage perpetrators, and another killer was a teenager at the time of the alleged sexual abuse by his eventual victim. Courtroom themes regarding the enhanced credibility of a thoroughly heterosexual image and the legal duty to safeguard teenage boys from homosexual desire are discussed at greater length in subsequent chapters of this book.

Homosexual advance claims should be deconstructed to critically analyse the killers' rationalisations of their violence against the weight of evidence. In different cases that are more or less plausible these allegations have been made to explain away killings motivated by prejudice, opportunistic robberies, recreational violence and group attacks that enhance male identity or even an inflated response to the undermining of a sense of social honour implied by homosexual objectification. Despite the success of advance allegations in many trials, this work critically rejects the prevailing legal view that violence is a partially excusable response to a nonviolent homosexual pass. This is a perspective that reflects the masculinity of legal doctrine and rulings and that can ultimately serve to downplay and condone anti-homosexual violence.

5 Killings as 'Hate Crimes'?

CRIME, VIOLENCE AND MASCULINITY

A fresh understanding of 'homophobic' violence as it is acted out by perpetrators can be found in the expanding research and activism around masculinity and crime. An appreciation of the complex interrelation of anti-homosexual attacks and masculinity is fundamental to understanding the motivation of assailants. Explanations of anti-homosexual assaults as exclusive examples of hate crime derived from prejudiced sentiments among perpetrators will not suffice for a complete understanding of these offences as they relate to issues of male identity and masculine culture.

In particular, any analysis of assaults and killings requires some explanation of the very heavy rate of offending by young men and their compelling attraction to this form of criminal violence. The involvement of male perpetrators in incidents of violence directed against sexual minorities has been noted by most researchers studying attacks on gay men, transsexuals, lesbians and bisexuals (Comstock, 1991; Ehrlich, 1992; Harry, 1992; Plummer, 1999). In the author's own previous study of killings the great majority of assailants were males and to a marked degree they were young men and teenage boys. Only four females were involved in these, either as co-perpetrators or accomplices. In two of these cases they had a direct involvement with the violence, which raises thoughts about female offending that contradict essentialist views about the links between gender and violence. Although anti-homosexual attitudes have been linked by researchers to a mainstream masculinity (Herek, 1984), this is by no means an exclusively male outlook. Female participation in the persecution of sexual minorities more characteristically takes the form of vilification and other non-violent abuse and, at worst, the condoning and active encouragement of violence by male partners and peers. The deployment of serious and even fatal violence to act out hatred and prejudice and to physically intimidate sexual minorities is virtually a male-monopolised activity.

At first glance this phenomenon may seem to simply fit the general correlation between criminal activities, particularly acts of violence, and the high proportion of male perpetrators which is found in more general studies of crime. However, in the case of attacks directed against sexual minorities, and most obviously in instances of the killings of homosexual men, this has a deeper significance for the identity of perpetrators which accentuates the 'maleness' of such acts. Even more broadly, analyses of masculinity can illuminate the historical pattern of institutional responses to this violence and its cultural and public condoning. Such violence has been and often still is legitimated by the criminal justice system through legal rules, discourse and courtroom findings, and even directly perpetrated by members of the more masculinised sectors of state bureaucracies such as the military and police.

Until recently, the wide level of male violence against other men has not been well researched or examined as a form of gendered violence. Similarly, there has been little analysis of masculine attitudes towards subjection to violence beyond the general finding that men as a group tend to be less fearful in relation to crime. Research in the 1990s and after studied the experience of confrontational violence by tracing the role of victimisation in establishing power relations between men, and the mixed effects of attacks on victims that both undermine and reinforce conventional ideas of manhood (Stanko & Hobdell, 1993; Goodey, 1997; Tomsen, 2005). This gestures towards the need for ongoing research on the major differences in social power (e.g., on the grounds of race, social class, age and sexuality) that exist between groups of men and how these are reproduced and reflected in the definition, production and punishment of criminality and an unequal access to legitimate victimhood.

In particular, the widespread pattern of male victimisation (especially from criminal violence) around the globe appears to defy commonsense notions of the male privilege that characterises most aspects of civil and public life in contemporary societies. A full understanding of the cultural generation of violent masculine identities ultimately cannot be divorced from an analysis of these patterns of male victimisation and the response of criminal justice systems to them. The respected status given to men who have both stoic involvements with violence and a general indifference to it have often served to reproduce toughened masculine identities which can cause alarm at moments of civil and political unrest. Equally, the daily confrontation between criminal justice authorities and many working, poor and minority men only affirms a commitment to delinquent and criminal identities that are strongly inflected with elements of masculine protest (Tomsen, 2008). But the production of violent, and even dangerously destructive, forms of masculinity has also been usefully harnessed by nation-states for their own purposes; both in the recruitment of masses of such men for the purpose of fighting wars and in the physically repressive form of social control that is often exerted by traditional police systems.

Male offenders carry out the great majority of crimes. Aspects of the general tie between masculinity and crimes of violence have been discussed repeatedly by researchers with a broad range of evidence. International and cross-cultural studies of official records for detected crime, including police notice, arrest, conviction rates and imprisonment, all reflect the masculinity of offending (Messerschmidt, 1993, 1997). This is reflected also in victim studies and surveys of victimisation. Men commit the majority of homicides, rapes and sexual attacks, assaults in both domestic and public situations, and armed robberies. Although criminal justice agencies focus heavily on detecting, prosecuting and punishing the offending of working-class, poor and minority males, it is apparent that high levels of recorded and reported offending reflect a real and pervasive social phenomenon of disproportionate male criminality.

The reasons for this have been a puzzle for researchers, officials and commentators. Since its origins at the end of the 1800s, criminology had ongoing difficulty with explaining the link between masculinity and crime, and research often disregarded the link between offending and maleness. Feminist writers have argued that although the link between masculinity and criminality has always been evident in crime research, this has been disregarded as a result of the masculinity of criminology itself wherein the bulk of research has been done by men from a unitary male perspective. Much traditional criminological discourse had a close concern with the study and control of 'dangerous' forms of masculinity, particularly working-class male delinquency, but did not tackle the relation between criminality and the socially varied attainment of male status and power.[1] It studied crime by a male norm and never developed a sufficiently critical view of the link to gender, especially to non-pathological and widespread forms of masculine identity that are tied to offending. The result of this has been a tendency to naturalise male offending and reversion to gender essentialism by explaining male wrongdoing as an inherent and presocial phenomenon that men are drawn to.

The positivist stress on biology often viewed crime as a reflection of defective male and female identities (Gould, 1981). A range of subsequent accounts also disregarded the social link between crime and masculinity, including sociological accounts that focused on class differences to explain crime and then either relied on biological sex differences to explain the gendered pattern of most criminal offending or else said nothing about it.[2]

This broad legacy that mostly disregarded or skewed understanding of gendered offending has been challenged by contemporary research on the social construction of masculinities and the everyday qualities of their aggressive and destructive forms (Stanko, 1990). This shift since the 1980s has been a response to the wider reflection on gender and identity from social movements including feminism, gay and lesbian activism and sections of the men's movement. In particular, research on violence against women stressed the relationship between offending and everyday and often legitimated constructions of manhood. In the academy, there has been a growth in research on male violence and a general expansion of research on masculinity or 'men's studies' (see Kimmel, 1987; Segal, 1990; Connell et al., 2005).

This new field also owes much of its inspiration to the theoretical contribution from a sociologist developing a key explanatory model of different forms of masculinity. 'Hegemonic masculinity' has been defined not as a particular character type, but a whole complex of historically evolving and varied social practices in societies which either legitimate, or attempt to guarantee, the shoring up of patriarchy and male domination of women (Connell, 1995b). This model of 'hegemonic' and other masculinities has been very influential but also much contested in social sciences, including criminology.[3]

For some liberal critics, this model could seem too closely tied to Marxist ideas about an overarching dominant ideology as a ruling set of oppressive masculine beliefs. Yet much of the critique has come from the Left and postmodern camps. Critics have suggested this model downplays social class and reflects a degrading view of working-class men as inherently violent and destructive (Hall, 2002). Jefferson suggests that this model results in a narrow view of true masculinity as a wholly negative set of personal attributes (2002). Another argues that the model offers an imprecise notion that 'masculinity' comprises whatever men are or do, though from his own adoption of a corporeal binary that overstates gender difference and does not explain the diversity or contradictions of different masculinities (Collier, 1998).

Additionally, it is noteworthy that a stress on the dual threat of the dangerous and unregulated peacetime masculinity of men from racial minorities and the impoverished underclass and the socially feminising influence of welfare systems in liberal democratic states has become a recurrent feature of conservative political discourse about crime and crime rates in many industrialised nations. This discourse finds reinforcement in the pronouncements of some key figures in contemporary criminology and echoes the concerns and claims of the revisionist wings of the men's movement (Clatterbaugh, 1990) in a way that signals not all accounts of the crime–masculinity link are progressive intellectual moments.

Nevertheless, the notion of hegemonic and marginalised masculinities has been deployed in a rich and widening range of criminological studies that examine the spectrum of masculine offending. The strong correlation between maleness and rates of criminal offending, especially with regard to crimes of violence, is now more openly acknowledged among researchers. The complexity of the cultural construction and reproduction of masculinities that are interwoven with much criminal activity is a likely reason why prevention, deterrence and rehabilitation have universally taken the form of such elusive and intractable problems, and why single-factor explanations of crime (as an outcome of poverty, unemployment, drinking or even age and social class) so often fail to hold up to the further scrutiny of researchers seeking causal explanations.

In the 'new masculinities' approach there has been an emphasis on the relations between different masculinities, the causes and patterns of most criminal offending and victimisation, and the broader workings of the wider criminal justice system of public and private policing, criminal courts, corrections and prisons (Newburn & Stanko, 1994). These scholars share the view that masculinities are plural, socially constructed, reproduced in the collective social practices of different men and embedded in institutional and occupational settings. Furthermore, masculinities are intricately linked with struggles for social power that occur between men and women and among different men. They vary and importantly intersect with other dimensions of inequality, and the major pitfall of any gender-centric analysis of criminality is overlooking a skewed criminalisation process that frequently targets, criminalises and punishes men and boys from disadvantaged and marginal social settings. Messerschmidt's influential accounts of crimes as 'doing masculinity' are understood within a structured action framework incorporating differences of class, race/ethnicity, age, sexuality and the common concern with power. As there are different forms of masculinity that are differently linked to the attainment of social power, crime itself is a means or social resource to achieve masculinity and analyses must balance consideration of structural forces and human agency (Messerschmidt, 1993, 1997).

Moreover, these new studies draw out the importance of insider perspectives and detailed case analyses to understanding the links between masculinity and violent offending via knowledge of both the masculine unconscious and the male body. Notably, Jefferson argues that researchers in this field should not ignore the psychic aspects of any criminal masculine identity (Jefferson, 1997; see also Gadd & Farrall, 2004). In one of Messerschmidt's studies of male juvenile offenders a dynamic interplay of hegemonic and other masculinities occurs against the backdrop of different relations to the body and achievable masculinities that shape offending in different criminal pathways (Messerschmidt, 1999).

This approach has also impacted on the study of particular offences and most notably on the recent study of killings. Key analyses of homicides from the 1990s that exemplified this new exploration of masculine offending concluded that the typical 'masculine scenarios' of most killings are disputes between men regarding insults and slights to personal honour or assaults directed at controlling female spouses and domestic partners (Polk, 1994). Detailed examination of many incidents reflects the masculine and everyday forms of most fatal interpersonal violence. Furthermore, the criminal defences (particularly provocation) that are invoked by many accused and defence counsel have been generally less available to women who kill, and the status of these suggests a link with notions of masculine violence that have respect in the criminal justice system and wider culture (Howe, 2001).

MASCULINITIES, MALE PRIVILEGE AND
ANTI-HOMOSEXUAL VIOLENCE

Although a radical disavowal of all of the trappings of male status was advocated in early 'effeminist' political writing and strategies (Carrigan et al., 1985), gay men's analyses of masculine privilege and power have been far less pressing than those evolved in the women's movement. Nor have these gay reflections on power been typically characterised by the widespread guilt of heterosexual men in their own responses to feminism, or the earnest self-examination evident in some wings of the men's movement (Clatterbaugh, 1990; Edwards, 1994). Nevertheless, as the more recent gay research in this field (Nardi, 2000) suggests, masculinity must be regarded as far more than just a target of satire, cultural parody and objectification for gay men. The toll of this violence, and the overwhelming involvement of men as perpetrators in its more serious instances, has signalled a further need to explore fully the relationships between these acts and different forms of masculinity. Regardless of whether or not masculinity and men, as some contemporary social commentators insist, really are entering a stage of full 'crisis', both homosexual and unconventional heterosexual men and boys are often direct targets of anger and anxiety related to the gendered social practices of men (Connell, 1995b; Plummer, 1999).

Connell (1995b) defines hegemonic masculinity such that any attainment or approximation of this hegemonic form by individual men is highly contingent on the levels of real social power reached in different men's lives:

> hegemony is likely to be established only if there is some correspondence between cultural ideal and institutional power, collective if not individual. So the top levels of business, the military and government provide a fairly convincing *corporate* display of masculinity, still very little shaken by feminist women or dissenting men. It is the successful claim to authority, more than direct violence, that is the mark of hegemony (though violence often underpins or supports authority). (77)

A dynamic series of relationships and tensions exist between the hegemonic and other 'subordinated' and 'marginalised' forms, and a recognition of diversity leads to the questions of power relations between different masculinities:

> To recognize diversity in masculinities is not enough. We must also recognize the *relations* between the different kinds of masculinities: relations of alliance, dominance and subordination. These relationships are constructed through practices that exclude and include,

that intimidate, exploit, and so on. There is a gender politics within masculinity. (37)

The major example of a subordinated masculinity offered is male homosexuality. This contravenes dominant ideals of manhood and meets with legal bans, extensive stigma and violent hostility as 'no relationship among men in the contemporary Western world carries more symbolic freight than the one between straight and gay' (143). Male homosexuality has a fraught relationship with hegemonic masculinity which is epitomised in anti-homosexual violence:

> violence becomes important in gender politics among men. Most episodes of violence (counting military combat, homicide and armed assault) are transactions among men. Terror is used as a means of drawing boundaries and making exclusions, for example, in heterosexual violence against gay men. (83)

This view has the strength of allowing for an explanation of anti-homosexual violence as it may be perpetrated by groups of men with very different levels of social power (as soldiers or police, in street gangs, etc.). But the actual practice of direct intimidation and violence is mostly explained in Connell's account by the contradictions that underlie one of the forms that are described as marginalised: The life histories of a group of young working-class men who have little formal education and minor criminal histories and subsist on the edge of the market for unskilled labouring jobs are the key examples of 'protest masculinity'. This term (which has been used before by criminologists and sociologists and appropriates some of Adler's psychoanalytic description of 'masculine protest') here describes a form of masculinity that is a characteristic of men in a marginal location of social class, with the masculine claim on power contradicted by economic and social weakness:

> by virtue of class situation and practice (e.g., in school), these men have lost most of the patriarchal dividend. For instance, they have missed out on the economic gain over women that accrues to men in employment, the better chances of promotion, the better job classifications. If they accept this loss they are accepting the justice of their own deprivation. If they try to make it good by direct action, state power stands in their way. (116)

The protest masculinity of this group of young men is reflected in the frequency of hypermasculine aggressive display (often at a collective level), antisocial, violent and minor criminal behaviour. It exhibits a juxtaposition of overt misogyny, compulsory heterosexuality (a vital element of hegemonic masculinity) and homophobia (some freely admit to gay-bashing and most are disgusted by the idea of male homosexuality). Sex and violence figure very highly in this configuration of manhood. Connell is struck by the extent to which the social circumstances of these men appear to have led to an indifference towards the supposed psychological and emotional contrasts between men and women, in favour of a heightened awareness of violence and sexual activity as the most important markers of true gender boundaries established in natural body differences (109). This raises the possibility that an exaggerated (though highly conformist and culturally reproduced) homophobia may reflect the extent to which male same-sex activity is understood as a major symbolic threat to the gender differences which are not clearly marked by much else than anatomical sex in the circumstances of social marginalisation.

'THERE'S NO POINT BEING A POOF'

The statements of perpetrators in police interviews and criminal trials reflect the importance of male group status, the contextual and ad hoc nature of the course of these killings, confusion and fear of same-sex desire and a measure of rage about the categorical uncertainty of some victims and their identity. But most importantly, killers assume the role of policing the public sexual identity of different victims and potential victims. This signals the wider social importance of the enforcement or inscription of essentialist categories through acts of harassment and violence.

In January 1990 Richard Johnson, a 33-year-old gay man, was bashed and killed at a Sydney beat by a group of young men. This occurred in an inner-city working-class district with a high concentration of poverty. The partial gentrification of the area with the influx of gay men and professional heterosexuals in the 1980s and 1990s created a new mix of local residents and the social tensions that went with it. The death of Johnson raised issues about contested social space and the class sentiments which inflect some of the motivation behind anti-homosexual attacks. Homophobic sentiments among local residents in this and similar areas around the globe may be reinforced by a common belief that all gay men live on high incomes and their presence inflates housing and rental costs for everybody. In the early 1990s this stereotype sat oddly with a further factor in the expanded numbers of gay men arriving in this location and similar locations. Gay/homosexual men with HIV who were impoverished by illness had little free choice about their place of residence. A significant number moved into clusters of public housing which dotted low income areas in inner Sydney. In so doing they risked a regular pattern of harassment and violence in their daily lives that included danger from hostile neighbours as well as street attacks.

In this killing, the perpetrators were eight youths. Six were aged between 15 and 17 years, and the other two were 18 and 19 years old. All of them became friends through attendance at a local school or football clubs. After learning through media reports about the death of their victim the perpetrators planned a clumsy effort to cover the crime. They concocted a story in which they claimed that they had all been in the location just prior to the killing, but met up with a group of large Polynesian or black men who had chased them from the park and presumably then murdered Johnson (police interviews with JL, 23 January 1990: 4–5; MJ, 26 January 1990: 1–3; RM, 27 January 1990: 2; AF, 31 January 1990: 1).

The considerable difficulties of maintaining narrative consistency when so many perpetrators were involved was soon apparent. This account was soon altered to a story in which the deceased was described as an aggressive drunk who almost ran them over as he drove by the park, stopped his car, approached them and by himself challenged all of them to a fight after an exchange of abuse (police interview with AM, 1 February 1990: 2–7). The next, and even less plausible version of events which clearly betrays a homophobic motive, was that the victim was an unusually aggressive and brazen beat-user they chanced upon in the park. He then attacked all of the perpetrators by swinging his fists and calling them 'faggot bashing bastards', after being referred to as a 'faggot' by one of them (police interview with AM, 2 January 1990: 1).

Despite the contradictions in statements by the perpetrators and other evidence, there was a central consistency around certain facts and events which the police and trial court finally accepted as accurate. On the evening of the killing, the youths played basketball together in the grounds of a local high school which many had or still attended. Afterwards they crossed through a park where there was a men's toilet they already knew served as a location for homosexual cruising. They selected one of several telephone numbers which, along with an invitation to have sex, had been scribbled on the door of a cubicle. M called Johnson from a nearby public phone. He covered the mouthpiece to hide the comments and sniggering of the others, and invited him for a meeting, a promise of sex and the alleged remark that 'I like giving headjobs' (police interview with RM, 3 February 1990: 5). In the later words of one perpetrator:

> The guy wanted him to wear a long sleeved shirt and tie, so he could tie him down and piss on him, and he also said, that he wanted his hot cum in his throat. (Police interview with AF, 3 February 1990: 4)

The victim welcomed the offer of sex and arrived close to the arranged time wearing a tie for recognition. He walked into the park and toilet block but perhaps sensing a hoax or some danger he commenced walking back to his car. Details of the actual attack which followed were summarised by the presiding trial judge as follows:

> The eight young men, who had been waiting in the school grounds at a point where they could observe the toilets without themselves

being seen, ran towards the toilets whilst their intended victim was inside the building, and when he emerged seven of them (but not Y) set upon him without mercy. One punched him heavily and without warning to the jaw and he fell to the ground. He was still conscious as most of the group assaulted him in various ways. At least two of them stomped with one heel on the right side of the victim's head above and behind the ear, causing a subarachnoid haemorrhage and almost certainly unconsciousness. Many of them kicked him in the head and trunk. One at least jumped on the victim's right chest as he lay on his back, landing with his full weight on both knees. One or more such impacts caused multiple rib fractures and the liver injury which was the actual cause of death. (*R v. M, H, M & Y*, NSWSC 15 April 1991, Badgery-Parker J, pp. 2–3)

The brevity of this account fails to convey the full brutality of a killing which at trial the crown prosecutor referred to as 'one of the most vicious, severe bashings that one could possibly imagine without the use of weapons, just with fists and feet'. The attack on Johnson was totally one-sided; in the words of one assailant, 'he didn't have a chance' (police interview with MC, 3 February 1990: 14). At its commencement, some of them yelled 'get the poof' (police interview with RM, 3 January 1990: 2). In a comment that suggested a genuine anger and puzzlement about homosexual identity he was told 'there's no point being a poof' (RM interview: 3). He was subjected to a round of blows and taunted with anti-gay comments and laughter as he pleaded 'leave me alone, I'm sorry, I'm gay' (RM interview: 3).

In the estimation of one participant the attack lasted 'for about three minutes', well beyond what was required to merely frighten, rob or even seriously bash the victim and a dangerously long time to sustain a barrage of blows from so many assailants. Johnson drifted in and out of consciousness at different points during the assault. One perpetrator admitted that the victim was still kicked and battered while in an unconscious state that was apparent 'because he was snoring'. After the group had robbed personal items from the victim, he was left lying on a patch of grass and making 'weird noises' and saying 'someone help me'. Two of the youths returned later in the evening to check on the victim who still lay motionless and battered. Nobody called for medical help. The assailants' stomping left imprints of sandshoes on Johnson's scalp and caused his brain to bleed. His jeans were split and torn by repeated kicks to his groin, and he was covered in lacerations, cuts and bruises, with seven smashed ribs, likely brain damage and a ruptured liver. Although the victim was found in an unconscious state next morning by a passer-by who called an ambulance, he died soon after.

The reasons why these youths were in a toilet they knew to be a homosexual beat, or read the obscene messages that were written inside, were not explored in the courtroom. But the presiding judge did suggest that a hatred of homosexual men and their sexual cruising at this location were the over-whelming reasons, noting that:

> the motivation for the original plan to lure Mr. Johnson to the scene and assault him was not a desire for violence for its own sake, but re-lated to anger at the conduct of homosexuals in the toilet. (*R v. M, H, M & Y*, 15 April 1991, Badgery-Parker J, p. 21)

Four of the accused youths were convicted of manslaughter, with maxi-mum jail terms of ten, nine, eight, and six and a half years. During the trial of the four other participants, the new pressures on the criminal justice system that derived from a heightened gay and lesbian scrutiny of these sorts of crimes became evident. The judge and defence counsel expressed considerable irritation with an article about the killing that was written by a leading local gay journalist (M. Goddard, 'In the gay killing fields', *Syd-ney Morning Herald*, 6 April 1991). In their view this wrongly implied that the perpetrators were probably involved in other bashings, or even killings, of homosexual men (*R v. M, H, M & Y*, 15 April 1991, Badgery-Parker J, p. 14). Nevertheless, activist pressure for weighty sanctions was maintained. At the conclusion of this trial, three accused were convicted of murder with maximum sentences of 18, 18 and 13 years. Another perpetrator was con-victed of manslaughter with an eight-year maximum term (*R v. M, H, M & Y*, 15 April 1991, Badgery-Parker J). These sentences may seem inconsistent or even lenient to some observers. But it is possible that even more lenient sentences could have been expected by a similar group of offenders in an earlier time or different context well away from the critical gaze of activist groups and a new gay and lesbian media.

This killing had a historical importance in mobilising an activism against the murders of homosexual men which had fewer reservations about the possible lack of legitimacy of victims killed at beats. The courtroom out-comes and heavy sentences imposed on some key offenders appeared to reassure gay men and lesbians that the law had become more responsive to their concerns. Yet this was complicated and thrown into doubt by other cases which featured controversial allegations of a sexual advance by vic-tims (see Chapter 6).

HATRED OR MASCULINITY?

This planned and fatal group attack on a stranger appeared to illustrate the relevance of aspects of the activist and social-movement understanding of the typical 'hate crime'. Yet it also called for reflection on the relevance of issues of male identity as a cause of violence, especially among young male peer groups. The offenders' contempt for their target was evident in the reckless and sadistic nature of an ongoing attack on a helpless and apparently unconscious victim. This hostility extended to gay/homosexual men as a class of people encroaching onto a traditional working-class neighbourhood. Group disgust about beat activity appeared as a mere further rationalisation of this violence. Other victims were quite probably attacked on other occasions with impunity. In police interviews, some freely admitted the intention to 'bait a poofter'. One said in planning the attack 'if he's a fag bash the shit out of him'. Another perpetrator claimed that previous attacks had been carried out by 'everyone' involved in the killing. A suggestive remark hinted that the perpetrators may have meted out such a severe bashing to Johnson because their previous assaults did not result in any deaths:

> like it's said sometimes, the boys tell you, that they can't believe how much of a belting that they [homosexuals] get and then get up and walk away like nothing happened. (Police interview with RM, 3 February 1990: 10)

Another statement explained the victim was 'a fag' and was therefore 'like an enemy' (police interview with MC, 3 February 1990: 14). The interviews suggested that all were aware of sexual activity in the park and the way that it attracted men to the location. Territorial feelings about the area they lived in appeared to translate into anger about this. The viewing of homosexual men as social outsiders, both sexually and spatially, raises the element of class identity in this hostility to homosexuals. One explanation noting 'it's our place', seemed like a weak justification for murder, but this view appeared to have had a real force in the consciousness of these youths.

Moreover, this level of anti-homosexual hostility may appear to be highly irrational, but the evidence of any serious psychological disturbance or full criminality in any of the youths was wanting. One had a criminal record, though as the amateurish quality of their shifting alibis reflected, these young men were inexperienced in dealing with investigating police and courts. With a fair degree of exaggeration a few were even described in court as school 'high achievers'. In reality, these were ordinary examples of youth drawn from their own inner-city community characterised by life in public housing clusters or low income rental accommodation. This was a social location that placed a high value on patterns of hard working-class masculinity attained by body strength in manual labour, trades and contact sports such as Rugby League. The specific social positioning or 'habitus' (Bourdieu, 1997) of these teenage boys included the absence of most fathers and a submission to maternal authority in cramped accommodation; mostly female school instruction with uneven academic success; limited work prospects in a city increasingly founded on finance, services and hospitality; and restricted or no contact with girls who were presumably not attracted by their immaturity and lack of disposable income.

Among similar groups of perpetrators in public gang killings this marginal social location also appears to have produced a disproportionate sense of male honour. This outlook could accommodate extreme and one-sided violence against homosexual victims, alongside an unlikely sense of guardianship about local families and communities. Suspects in one unsolved matter sought to explain their violence at beats by reference to the need to protect local children playing nearby. In the Johnson case, a further reminder of this lack of proportion arose in police interviews. In the presence of his mother, one youth gave a graphic account of his role in the killing to police officers. When he was asked which particular sexual activities the victim requested over the phone, male chivalry prevailed. He became embarrassed and protective of his mother and asked if she could leave the interview room (MC interview: 6). Afterwards she returned to the room to learn more violent details of her son's involvement in the killing.

In police interviews and reports of psychiatrists there was clear evidence of anti-homosexual hatred and some admissions to previous involvements in bashings. These attacks should not be taken as a universal behaviour pattern among disadvantaged young men, but they do reflect ideas similar to those held by many other people in their own communities. One piece of evidence from a police interview provided a startling reminder of the wider community attitudes that form part of the backdrop to anti-homosexual assaults. This revealed that two local middle-aged men were walking with a dog in the park when Johnson arrived. Apparently, these men witnessed the entire assault without any reaction to it. They never intervened, called for medical assistance or reported the matter to police. They were standing an estimated 25 metres from the scene and the young men even walked past them on leaving the park. This revelation puzzled an officer who asked why the presence of these men as witnesses did not distract or bother the perpetrators. Knowingly, the youth simply responded that 'we didn't think it would matter' (MC interview: 11–12).

Overall, there is a remarkable likeness between the social histories, characteristics and attitudes of Connell's sample of semi-criminal young men engaged in 'protest masculinity' and many of the perpetrators who featured in this crime. The majority of the assailants involved in these group killings were younger, working-class and poor men with a marginal existence in the labour market and low social status. Much of this violence, especially the planned gang attacks on homosexual men, suggests an underlying compensatory search for masculine status among perpetrators and an important cultural paradox which appears to shape many of these attacks. Assaults on these victims take the outward form of a type of rebellion or protest against dominant social values and partly attract young marginalised men for this reason. In reality, continuous backdrops to the motives of perpetrators are mainstream constructions of male identity and the deviant positioning of male homosexuality in the codes, practices and discourses that reproduce social understandings of masculinity. The attraction of these assailants to anti-homosexual violence is continuously linked to a widespread social understanding of a desired 'hegemonic masculinity' as thoroughly hetero-sexual, and engagements with violence as a possible means of establishing a respected male identity. The hegemonic form remains beyond reach for those with little or no material wealth or institutional power, and violence and harassment directed against sexual minorities serve as ready means of establishing a respected male identity within the less empowered pattern of 'protest' masculinity.[4]

With the value of violence to these marginal groups of young men, it is unsurprising that several involved in group killings and others questioned in regard to unsolved deaths had a strong interest in fighting and some formal training in boxing and martial arts. In the worst cases, the group status of some assailants was built on a reputation for unrestrained street violence. The key perpetrator in one gang killing could not resist describing his violence to numerous friends and apparently expected to make a positive impression about his manhood on a girlfriend by writing to her of his intention to bash homosexuals (*R v. D*, NSWSC, 7 August 1992, Wood J). With his subse-quent arrest and conviction for murder, these public boasts appeared to be idiotic. They also reflected the very limited material and cultural resources available for the achievement of a masculine status among the groups of young men who carry out many of the attacks on homosexuals. A further reminder of the powerful influence of these young male concerns and how they can lead to fatal violence was evidence about the entire involvement of one offender in the Johnson killing to counter a reputation for being soft and a 'wimp' (*R v. RM*, NSWSC, 6 February–30 April 1991, Badgery-Parker J).

HATRED AND THE POLICING OF GENDER IDENTITY

As well as punishing presumed sexual deviance, 'hate' violence also disci-plines gender identity. Anti-homosexual violence and harassment result in the direct and indirect control of homosexual men and others who are out-side conventional gender boundaries. Different activists and commentators have perceived prejudice against transsexual/transgender people as a similar or separate phenomenon from anti-homosexual outlooks (Moran & Sharpe, 2004). Nevertheless, the gendered features of this are evident in perpetra-tor concerns about corporeal threat and a perceived desecration of the male body by feminine adornment. In specific social circumstances such as the Sydney Gay and Lesbian Mardi Gras and other celebratory events frequented by heterosexuals, there is a suspension of prejudice, and transsexualism is viewed as playful and sexually exciting—at other times it may be perceived as a serious threat to gender norms that must be strictly enforced.

A killing which suggested hatred, a shared male pleasure in violence and the imposition of strict gender codes by marginal young men was another public gang attack. Gordon Tuckey, aged 22, was killed on a public cycleway on the south coast of New South Wales. The circumstances of his death as summarised by the trial judge were:

> At about ten minutes to twelve midnight . . . the figure of a person was observed lying beside the eastern side of the concrete cycleway which follows the coast line near East Woonona in the Wollongong area. This figure was facing in an easterly direction towards the ocean lying on its left side, with the head towards the north and feet towards the south. Later that night following a telephone call, police and ambulance officers attended the scene and the body of the victim, Gordon Tuckey, was found lying face down, the head in a pool of blood, partly on the cycleway and partly off its eastern edge. The body was naked from the waist down, except for a strip of nylon fabric wound around the penis. Items of women's clothing, including underwear and a short black skirt, were found nearby. The body of the deceased showed evidence of multiple injuries including lacerations, abrasions and bruising to various parts including, in particular, the head, consistent with multiple blows which brought about death. The evidence of the forensic pathologist established that the cause of death was a massive cerebral haemorrhage associated with a fracture of the floor of the skull resulting from multiple heavy blows to the head and temporal area. (*R v. Dunn*, NSWSC, 21 September 1995, Ireland J, pp. 1–2)

Confused and contradictory stories from witnesses and the parties involved appear to have been intended to deny blame for the attack. The judge substantially accepted the final version of events offered by the accused 19-year-old, Dunn. He was charged with murder and two friends who were at different times present at the crime scene were charged with concealing a crime. According to Dunn, after a night of drinking with a 19-year-old friend named Rees, both were riding their bicycles on the public cycleway. In the darkness, the victim leapt from the bushes, sexually assaulted Dunn and wholly provoked the retaliatory violence which led to his death:

> as I was coming around the corner someone jumped out behind me and I've turned around he . . . grabbed me by the leg, and he sort of pushed me and I've gone down and he's got down the bottom of me leg, he's holding on to it and that's when I've twisted me ankle I think it was and then he's kicked me in the knee and he's on top of me, sort of, just rubbing—he did not have no pants on him and he was rubbing his dick up and down me leg and then as I've come up I've just started throwing punches at him. . . .

> . . . he was going on about something, just looked really weird to me . . . he's just started saying his stuff and just going on and on about 'I'm gonna give it to you good' or something like 'young man' or something,

and then I just started throwing me hands, hitting him in the head. . . . I've tried to get up . . . and he jumped back out and he was laughing and spat on me. . . . I think I threw a few more punches and I sort of kicked him away. . . . I was just throwing me hands and they were, they were, just hitting him.

He had something on his face. I think, I think he had make-up on. I'm not sure because he just looked—ah it just made me feel sick . . . and then he's grabbed me and it just went on from there. (Police interview with Dunn, 3 July 1993: 12–16)

Dunn played down the extent of his own violence and represented himself as the real victim of a macabre and traumatic sexual attack. He told police the entire incident took 10 to 15 minutes, though it seems unlikely that all of this time was needed by him to get away. Dunn insisted the victim was injured but still alive when he left him:

he was breathing and he was mumbling something and then he's just laid down on the concrete. . . .

. . . then I've gone up to the railway station and washed me hands and me shoes and rung an ambulance. (Dunn interview: 12–13)

If Dunn can be believed, it took a great level of violence to repel the sexual interest of the deceased. Tuckey's head was repeatedly bashed into the concrete pathway so that his face was not recognisable. He was assaulted with a tree branch that was found later with blood on it, subjected to repeated and ongoing punching and kicking and had been crushed in the ribs by someone jumping from a wooden cycle rail.

Dunn eventually admitted that after the attack he and Rees visited the home of a friend who lived in a nearby public housing estate. He told the people there about the encounter, began to wash blood off himself and then returned to the scene. He later claimed that this was done to check on the victim's welfare, but while there he carried out another attack. He returned again to his friend's house, allegedly with more blood on himself which he also set about cleaning away. A friend then went with Rees to also check on the victim. Dunn later walked to a public phone. After one o'clock in the morning an emergency call was received from a male voice seeking an ambulance and suggesting that a person had been attacked on the cycleway and was looking 'pretty crook'. Investigating police later found bloodstains on the phone handset.

Dunn returned to his mother's home and set about washing the remainder of the victim's blood from his clothing and shoes. Tuckey was dead when the ambulance arrived. At the crime scene, police found earrings and a pair of black high-heeled shoes, a skirt and pair of black stockings nearby, giving rise to tabloid reports of a 'bizarre sex murder' in the area ('Sex link in brutal death on cycleway', *Sun-Herald*, 4 July 1993; 'Date with death for man in drag', *Tele-Mirror*, 22 September 1995). At his trial Dunn was found to have been provoked by Tuckey's advance and the public cross-dressing of the deceased. His violence comprised a 'gross over-reaction' but did not amount to murder, and the accused was sentenced to a maximum term of 11 years imprisonment (*R v. Dunn*, 21 September 1995, Ireland J, p. 8).

This conviction left open many issues about the killing. Any simple notion of 'hate' crime may discount both the masculine motives and the gendered interaction between offenders and victims in such cases. One witness insisted that Rees took an active role in the attack. It is also uncertain if Rees and the other friend only went to the scene to merely check on the body. Tuckey's parents later insisted that their son was heterosexual. The victim may not have been gay or homosexual, but it does not seem that this distinction was understood by his assailant(s). His perceived deviance in the sexual and gender order sparked the violence against him. The theft of some property suggests robbery as a partial motive. However, there is a remaining uncertainty about how the accused first met his eventual victim. According to Rees, he and Dunn both cycled past the victim and then Dunn put down his bike and walked back and asked for a cigarette. This may have been a sexual overture. In the darkness, with make-up, skirt, high heels and a hooded top, the victim could have had the convincing allure of an attractive woman who was alone and vulnerable.

Rees later claimed that a fight broke out when Dunn realised he was speaking to a male. If this was so, his anger at being fooled in this way may have overlapped with a sense of sexual frustration and a contempt for any male dressed publicly as a woman. The location of the killing was not known as a homosexual beat. It is therefore unlikely that the perpetrators were seeking to carry out anti-gay violence in any preplanned way and may have only been spontaneously taking up an unexpected opportunity to sexually harass someone they thought was a lone woman. Nevertheless, a consciousness of Tuckey's sexual difference played a pivotal role in triggering the attack and the extreme level of savagery.

A witness whom police interviewed saw the body after the first assault. At that time, it was not semi-naked and the victim was mistaken for a drunk who had passed out near the path. The black dress was apparently removed and a stocking tied around his penis as a form of victim humiliation during the second attack. Dunn also abused his victim by calling him a 'poofter' and a 'rockspider', eliding different categories of sexual deviance, but still clearly viewing the victim as contemptible (police interview with JR, 4 July 1993). In another statement, a witness suggested that the accused had bragged that he 'had just bashed a rockspider' as he washed the victim's blood from himself (police interview with CD, 27 July 1993).

Despite confused and contradictory statements, this killing left an over-all impression of the complexity of perpetrator motives though with a con-tinuous undercurrent of rigid male views of sexual expression and gender identity. It is apparent from attacks such as these that anti-homosexual violence may or may not be preplanned; it is often spontaneous and situ-ationally structured. It might also not distinguish clearly between homo-sexuality, transsexualism, paedophilia and other stigmatised sexualities as its target.

The killing of Tuckey also reflected the urgency with which men in groups can assume the role of policing the public sexual and gender behaviours of other men. Perhaps most importantly of all, the effects of this form of violence reverberate among all men. Anti-homosexual violence and harass-ment do not just result in the public control of homosexual men who are regarded as a sexually deviant minority. This crude and immediate means of policing male identity was reproduced in the local culture of specific groups of youths who trained themselves in, practised and initiated others into such violence. Again, as in the Johnson case, evidence regarding these perpetrators suggested a high value was attached to this activity among men who were young and socially marginal, and themselves had a limited status in a patriarchal social order which prized masculinities built on a direct share in the male control of institutional and material resources including regular sexual access to women. They were among those most likely to ini-tiate and carry out this form of violence which is both denounced but also condoned in masculinist and heterosexist cultures.

Even when most closely linked to issues of masculinity, this violence has motives which can appear to be contradictory and inconsistent. Some kill-ings reflect an outright disgust and rage about the breach of gender norms implied by public displays of effeminacy, especially through clothing and grooming. Dunn was shocked and revolted by his victim's female cloth-ing, grooming and facial make-up which made him 'feel sick'. This disgust does not fit with the much-vaunted new tolerance for cross-dressing or even a revelling in its transgressive pleasure that might accompany aspects of urban cultural queering. Obviously, such tolerance is highly constrained by social context. In the majority of circumstances, public cross-dressing evokes anger by a disturbance of the binary opposition between male and female anatomies (Garber, 1992).

It is apparent that anger at such public effeminacy and defence of conven-tional masculine self-presentation shapes the motives for anti-homosexual violence in a culture which often erroneously conflates male homosexual identity with an overt feminine appearance. However, attacks which are sudden and carried out in darkness with little interaction between per-petrators and victims, and attacks perpetrated on men who appear to be conventionally masculine, do not reflect this. Homophobic sentiments and actions can be carried through or modified in varied situations. The jury in Dunn's trial never learnt that he had previously shared a house with a male friend whose homosexual activity did not trouble him (*R v. Dunn*, NSWSC, 21 September 1995, Ireland J).

Research evidence about the widespread harassment of and violence against homosexual men may also appear to be difficult to reconcile with evidence regarding the widespread pattern of actual same-sex activity and desire among men in the general community. Same-sex engagements are common in situations which are defined as being without personal choice such as those that arise during periods of detention in male juvenile institutions and prisons. However, what these violent incidents often share is hostility to any open and public assumption of a homosexual identity by victims. This appears to confront and undermine the perpetrator's own determination to achieve manhood in a socially honoured though often difficult heterosexual pathway. An evident resentment towards men who have appeared to abandon the social struggle to sexually dominate women in favour of easy pleasures lies behind this policing of publicly acceptable male sexualities. Confusion about the diverse possibilities of male sexuality, and a troubled and simplistic view about the element of choice in sexual identity, were apparent also in the peculiar question put to Richard Johnson by his killers as he was first attacked. This victim was asked 'why be a fucking poofter?' (police interview with RM, 3 January 1990: 2–3). In response, Johnson apologised for being gay. This did not satisfy their urgent curiosity or need for some reassurance about their own sexual choices, and he was killed soon after.

COMMUNITY HOMOPHOBIA, MASCULINITY AND LAW

It is apparent from the details of these incidents that the violence of the young offenders in these types of homicides is notably vicious. This savagery is often juxtaposed with evidence about the everyday qualities of the young men who perpetrate it. The obvious inexperience with criminal charges and confusion about the serious repercussions of their violence shown by many offenders reflect this. Furthermore, the social and psychological ordinariness of the majority of these killers strongly points to the mainstream origins of their views on sexuality and violence. These views are moulded by matters of social class, youth and especially by male identity. Details about the assailants in the Tuckey killing suggest histories of violence, petty crime and contact with police and juvenile courts more typical of 'disrespectable' working-class households and lives. But offenders in these public group killings were young men similar to the many others who have an occasional and eventually diminishing involvement in petty disorder and street violence.

These facts highlight one of the pitfalls of the ideal 'hate crime' model suggesting an abnormal level of perpetrator hatred while there is a considerable level of public support for the actions of such offenders and a sharing of their view of homosexuals among members of the wider public.

Evidence about a wider level of public support for these and similar attacks in the 1990s can be found in the community complacency which complicated police inquiries into unsolved killings. Some of these appear to have been the result of similar attacks by gangs of young men. Investigations gave much reconstructed detail of these incidents and the involvements of suspected offenders in such attacks.

A prime location for unsolved killings and assaults in the 1990s was an area of steep and dangerous cliffs at South Bondi in Sydney where gay/homosexual men had gone missing or been found bashed to death. The frequency of attacks in this location and the regular involvement of different and unconnected groups of assailants appear to have slowed and complicated police inquiries. The evidence taken from men who were beat-users indicated a low level of reporting of very serious violence, and information from local residents suggested a degree of public support for the bashings, which drew an expression of outrage from the coroner sitting on the inquest into one unsolved death (K. Waller, 'Ugly stain of homophobia continues to pollute Sydney', *Sydney Morning Herald*, 24 September 1992).

A similar role for community norms as a backdrop to anti-homosexual violence was reflected in an unsolved killing at another suburban park. Investigation revealed that the location was the site of regular violence, and that at least two different gangs of suspects had ongoing and unrelated involvement in attacks at the scene. On the night of the killing nearby residents heard the shouts of someone being attacked but they ignored these as they came from the homosexual beat and such cries were a common occurrence. On hearing of the crime, one local also appeared to quickly offer an unlikely alibi to cover for the major suspect who happened to live in the same block of flats (Tomsen, 2002). Other victims who were killed as a result of such attacks by strangers at well-known sites of sexual cruising died without seeking the assistance that may have saved them. For example, one victim who was severely bashed in public later died in his own home from the resulting wounds, and another ignored questions from onlookers who found him bleeding and dazed in a city park and then minutes later drowned unnoticed in Sydney Harbour (Tomsen, 2002). Such actions may seem foolhardy but these victims were aware of their tenuous claim to a status as legitimate victims seeking public or official help.

An awareness of the contradictory public response to anti-homosexual violence may also have been behind the naïve boasting or frankness about involvements in killings and the initial sense of puzzlement at the serious investigation of attacks among arrested perpetrators. A general lack of monitoring of such offences reflected a long history of police and legal indifference to violence against homosexuals. This was in part due to the long-term criminal status of male homosexuality in the legal system. It also reflected elements of the 'official masculinity' of police and legal bureaucracies and the daily reproduction of valued male identities within these workplaces and occupational cultures. There is an underlying relation of this violence to the masculinity of both perpetrators and gatekeepers to the legal system. This signals the general relation of the criminal justice system to different masculinities and culturally constructed views of victimhood among subordinated social groups.

In cultures that promote strong links between violence and masculinity, 'gay-bashing' serves a dual purpose of constructing a masculine and heterosexual identity for perpetrators. This is achieved through a simultaneous involvement with violence and clearly establishing homosexuals as an opposed group of social outsiders. These attacks have been part of a compelling and difficult struggle to achieve the features and status of adult masculinity, though this struggle is often doomed to fail or left unresolved in the situation of many of these assailants. Past evidence regarding anti-homosexual killings reminds researchers that many of these are also experienced by perpetrators as a form of group recreational violence that both signals and affirms a masculine heterosexual status to others. In this way, these gang attacks can also be read as masculine crimes and are importantly characterised by the group production of masculine identities among assailants (Messerschmidt, 1993).

More broadly, this pattern of anti-homosexual violence and killing exemplifies the mostly unstudied way in which the trivialisation of male victimisation is linked to the social construction of violent and aggressive masculinities, and also how this is intimately linked to the construction of male identities among criminal justice personnel. Contemporary comment about the masculinity of the judiciary and police agencies has also taken the form of concern about what heavily sexist occupational cultures mean to women who are seeking entry to these workplaces. Research on lax police responses to domestic violence and the negative experience of the law courts for many female victims reiterate this focus. There is a need to anchor accounts of such practices with a perspective on the gender politics of the highly masculinised sectors of public bureaucracies (Connell, 1990, 1995b).

The masculinity of these state agencies also produces and orders power relations among groups of men by selectively criminalising male behaviour and trivialising victimisation. Culturally valued and empowered masculinity is sanctioned and defined by these practices. Male sexualities are 'policed' in both the violence of perpetrators and the masculinist responses of the law. With no intended irony, defence counsel representing perpetrators in the Johnson trial suggested that the fighting skills and a strong interest in casual violence among his clients were actually the hallmarks of 'good character' because they were acquired through years of training at boxing and martial arts classes in Police Boys' Clubs. It is significant that these organisations were originally founded to channel working-class youth delinquency and aggression into socially respectable modes of masculinity. The official ignoring and the partial condoning of such harassment and attacks are tied to the general production of a 'respectable' gendered hostility against homosexuality and these assaults can even be seen as a form of 'dirty work' (see Hughes, 1962) that is performed by younger, lower status males and is both disavowed and appreciated for its wider social consequences. For this reason, challenges to the criminalised status of homosexuality and to allegations of sexual advances raised as excuses for masculine violence have not been merely symbolic struggles in the efforts to counter such violence.

6   Male Honour and the 'Homosexual Advance'

INTRODUCTION

The further limits of discounting the role of perpetrator masculinity in 'hate' attacks have been evident in the controversy regarding the 'homosexual advance' defence. In the 1990s and afterwards, activists and commentators in a range of nations voiced concern about the status and impact of this defence in criminal trials of assailants. The pattern and outcomes of these trials suggested that accused perpetrator claims about unwanted homosexual advances from victims, which both caused and necessitated retaliatory violence, had been used with significant effect.

Locating the cause of anti-gay violence in the sexual desire of victims has an established basis in popular stories and jokes about homosexuality in which attacks are reconstructed as a form of invited punishment for a deviant sexuality. In the Australian legal arena, cases involving homosexual advance allegations date back at least to the 1950s.[1] It seems probable that a contemporary increase in the level of police arrests of suspected killers in a range of jurisdictions had brought these claims into courtroom accounts of fatal attacks with increasing regularity and controversial results. Thus, these claims have been seen as an important contemporary obstacle to having these crimes taken more seriously and to the attainment of legitimate victim status and equality in criminal justice systems.

Sexual advance allegations of this sort have been difficult for gay and lesbian lobbyists to evolve a confident response to. Confusion about the apparently successful appropriation of victim status by some assailants has shaped divisions over the appropriate reaction to such claims. There have been misgivings about the inability of a deceased victim to respond to these allegations and the possibility that many claims are a convenient explanation for attacks with anti-homosexual motives or the selection of homosexual victims as soft targets for assault and robbery (Lesbian and Gay Anti-Violence Project, 1995).

Yet an outright dismissal of such allegations by anti-violence groups has a curious ring to lesbians with backgrounds in feminist politics and a care not to readily dismiss claims of sexual assault heard in legal settings as fictitious.

Furthermore, a public taboo concerning intergenerational sex overshadows any response to cases that involve violence and advance allegations from young perpetrators, with a wariness about matters which involve a very wide age gap between an offender and victim.

The plausibility of these allegations is best judged from detailed evidence regarding different attacks and killings. The author's homicide study suggests such claims are made in a variety of circumstances with a considerable diversity in fatal scenarios. Claims are made in circumstances involving preplanned 'hate' attacks, and on arrest assailants seek out an excuse for their violent actions. In the cases of killing that conform to the scenario of a public gang attack, claims about sexual advances are less credible. The light sentences meted out to the killers involved in the brutal killing of Gordon Tuckey (see Chapter 5) seemed more related to the advantage won from trading information about other criminal offences (*R v. Dunn*, NSWSC, 21 September 1995, Ireland J), rather than lame claims about sexual victimisation from a marauding transsexual.

As outlined in Chapter 4, the second major scenario for anti-homosexual homicides are cases of a dispute resulting in violence during an episode of shared drinking and socialising by male friends or recent acquaintances—typically in private space. Sexual advance allegations can be more difficult to counter as implausible when they arise from these circumstances. Many such claims are transparently false and are made in relation to incidents involving preplanned attacks or robberies. Others are superficially credible. Among these are killings that suggest an offender awareness of the sexualised context of the interaction with their victim. This can include a conscious inducement of an advance and an opportunistic response that includes an exaggerated surprise and retaliatory violence. Despite the brutality and callousness of their actions, these offenders act in a rational and methodical manner to carry out a criminal action they had already intended.

An example of a killing which went to trial, and where there is a lingering suspicion that the statement of the accused about being subjected to an unwanted homosexual advance or assault could be a convenient rationalisation for violence, was an attack by a killer who met his victim in a gay sex-cinema and accompanied him home to purchase drugs, and then later claimed that he could only ward off persistent sexual advances with extreme violence (Tomsen, 2002: 59–63). This case resulted in controversy due to the level of bloodshed, the theft of property from the victim and the full acquittal of the accused perpetrator after his delivery of an ingenious dock statement to explain his actions as unplanned and sexually innocent.

Here, perpetrators appeared to understand cultural codes of masculinity with crimes structured around a prior creation of a respectable explanation for any necessary use of force. In so doing, they demonstrated more guile and social perception than the arrested perpetrators who carry out straightforward 'hate' bashings. They established themselves in a crime scenario to take possible advantage of the widespread notion that heterosexual men can often be expected to respond with force to a homosexual pass. In addition to filling a need to rationalise violence in the legal context if the crime was solved, acting out this code of anger and violence may have assisted an actual robbery as a way of making the victim more fearful. In these circumstances where a homosexual pass was consciously induced, it may also give such attacks the feeling of 'righteousness' that characterises much predatory violent crime (Katz, 1988).

Most importantly and against the expectations of many activists, the research evidence also suggests incidents where claims about a homosexual advance are plausible. This is even though a clear distinction must be drawn between a forceful sexual assault and a mere sexual pass that could be rebuffed. Cases of this sort form the subject matter of this chapter and the next. Although the masculinity of perpetrators is fundamentally involved in all the various major forms of anti-homosexual killing, the differences in type and apparent motive have significant implications for an understanding of anti-homosexual violence and the relationship between homophobia and male identity. In particular, a narrow view that incidents involving sexual advance claims are just further examples of 'hate crimes' derived from homophobic sentiments among 'gay-bashers' downplays an understanding of these offences as they relate to issues of social honour.

HONOUR AND MALE VIOLENCE

A key aspect of the criminological discourse which seeks to explain why violence is a predominantly male activity suggests the importance of issues of personal honour and self-respect among male participants in many disputes, assaults and fatal attacks. Some studies refer to the relation this has to violence against women, but this type of analysis has been mostly credited with explanatory power in regard to incidents of violence between men. A considerable literature now exists on the importance of male honour among men, and the connections it has with the occurrence and escalation of violent incidents between them (Campbell, 1986; Archer, 1994). This research suggests that many disputes between males that result in serious injuries and death are prompted by overreactions to minor affronts or reputational slights which challenge male honour and necessitate revenge (Archer, 1994; Polk, 1994; Mullins, 2006). These sorts of conflicts arise regularly in everyday activities like drinking in bars, driving in traffic, travelling and socialising in public space (Felson & Steadman, 1983). They may seem minor in cause but are often highly meaningful among certain groups of males and particularly to low status youth:

Young men at the margins of society are particularly prone to violent fights, and these mostly occur on the streets around where the protagonists live, and also in and around bars and other places selling alcohol. Violent acts usually develop from an escalating exchange of verbal aggression and minor physical acts. The exchange begins with an event which one of the protagonists perceives as an identity threat. Although this often appears trivial to outsiders, or even to the protagonists in retrospect, it initiates a series of threats, insults and commands which transform the nature of the dispute into one which arouses anger through perceived threats to personal self-esteem or becomes a matter of face-saving and reputation. (Archer, 1994: 137–8)

Cognitive explanations have missed the links between this quarrelsome sensitivity to slights in public social interaction, widespread homosexual desire and the Freudian insight concerning how fear and confusion about unconsciously indistinct sexual rivals and love objects can feed masculine paranoia (see Lewes, 1995). Nevertheless, there is strong empirical value for crime researchers in this interpretation of much violence between men, especially public violence among young male strangers and casual acquaintances.[2] Although a wide range of research literature suggests a regular connection between drinking, violence and social disorder, much doubt remains as to the actual nature and significance of this link. Strong insights into this come from consideration of the tie between heavy group drinking and the importance of issues of male honour in the social interaction that leads to violent behaviour. Social psychologists explain great variation in reactions to intoxication in different social contexts by noting that collective drinking is often marked by 'power displays' in which an assertion of social power, and a heightened sensitivity to challenges to it, is maintained, and this will make for a very volatile social setting (Boyatzis, 1974; Archer, 1994).

This contextual model of group drinking can be merged with criminologists' accounts of many assaults as incidents characterised by an escalating confrontation over social honour where the generation and protection of a masculine identity is most valued. This approach has also been partly confirmed by the author's own observational research on public violence and male drinking (Tomsen, 1997a). The importance of this guarding of a tough male identity by surviving public slights, challenges and actual assaults in drinking venues was often observed in the field and many violent incidents could be readily understood in terms of male honour. This was also confirmed in semi-structured interviews focused on the topics of public violence and the personal male experience of assaults as assailants and victims (Tomsen, 2005).

This analysis of male honour in the social context of violent incidents has been demonstrated by other researchers, and has particularly extended understanding of many street attacks and homicides (Katz, 1988; Polk,

1994). This may appear to be a trivial or meaningless factor in the motivation for violence, yet the protection and creation of self-esteem and keeping 'face' among men is of fundamental importance in shaping the interactive process of violence. These analyses highlight the sequence of violent events to indicate what varying features of social interaction distinguish scuffles and minor assaults from the scenarios of attacks resulting in severe injuries and death. In so doing, the most lucid of these studies (e.g., Polk, 1994) have also dynamically illustrated the relation of violence to masculine identity as this is negotiated, challenged and rebuilt in ongoing social conflicts.

It is important to note that this interactive form of analysis alone cannot offer a full explanation of the social, legal and cultural circumstances of this violence. It may also overstress the social role of victims and their own active self-destruction. A frequent trivialisation of victimisation still pervades official, researcher and popular thinking about much violence, including attacks against homosexual men. Furthermore, these accounts may ignore the important role of authority figures in condoning such violence and the relationship of male violence with the general culture that has been stressed in the new literature on masculinity and crime. Also, its links to the everyday struggle to attain an identity which approximates hegemonic masculinity, and the limited social and material means by which many perpetrators can attain culturally reified forms of manhood, remain unexplored if a paradigm of brittle working-class honour prevails in general explanations of the phenomenon of male-on-male violence.

Nevertheless, the interactive analysis offers a useful starting point to an understanding of cases of killing characterised by a homosexual advance and shared socialising and heavy male drinking. In these, an offender can react with a great level of violence that reflects real shock and outrage. These attacks are explicable in terms of the affront that a homosexual advance can comprise to a sense of male honour and orthodox notions of the sanctity of the male body. Killings in which the claims of arrested perpetrators about a homosexual advance from the deceased appear to be true, but where the violence seems to have been a very exaggerated and irrational response to a sexual pass as a verbal invitation to sexual activity and/or physical touching, illustrate the usefulness of the analysis of male honour.

'HE DID WORSE TO ME'

Questions about how male honour can set off and partly excuse violence were raised by a well-publicised killing in which sudden and extreme violence was used in response to a probable homosexual advance. In 1993 Don Gillies, aged 36, was killed in the house where he lived in a rural town. He was a small-businessman who was well respected in the local community and was not open about his homosexuality. His killer was Malcolm Green, an unemployed 22-year-old friend.

The victim invited his friend to his house to eat, drink and socialise. They drank heavily, talked and watched television. At about midnight Gillies invited Green to stay for the night as it was late and cold outside, and both were too intoxicated to drive a vehicle legally. Allegedly, Gillies entered a darkened bedroom in a totally naked state and made sexual overtures, placing his hand on the younger man's buttocks and fondling his groin. Green responded with a frenzied round of violence with a pair of scissors that he found lying on the floor. In addition to the stabbing wounds, the victim had received an estimated 20 blows to the head. These injuries also suggested that his face had been slammed against a wall. Green phoned his brother-in-law and later told police that he had killed Gillies and 'he did worse to me. I killed him and I will tell you about it. He put it on me and I just snapped' (*R v. Green*, NSWSC, 7 June 1994, Abadee J, p. 9). His statement related how he became subjected to persistent homosexual advances that so shocked him that he lost all self-control:

> After a while when I was fully unclothed, Don entered the room I was in, slid in beside me in the bed and started talking to me how great a person I was. Then he started touching me. I pushed him away. He asked what was wrong. I said, 'what do you think is wrong? I'm not like this'. He started grabbing me with both hands around my lower back. I pushed him away. He started grabbing me harder. I tried and forced him to the lower side of me. He still tried to grab me. I hit him again and again on top of the bed until he didn't look like Don to me. He still tried to grope and talk to me. That's when I hit him again and saw the scissors on the floor on the right hand side of the bed. When I saw the scissors he touched me around the waist, shoulder area and said, 'why?' I said to him, 'I didn't ask for this'. I grabbed the scissors and hit him again. By the time I stopped I realised what had happened. I just stood at the foot of the bed with Don on the floor laying face down in blood. . . . I didn't know what to do, didn't know where to go. (*R v. Green*, NSWSC, 7 June 1994, pp. 10–11)

This killing resembles other cases in which a killer's sense of identity and self-worth, was so threatened by a homosexual pass that the circumstances triggered a frenzy of retaliatory violence. Green was intoxicated at the time of the killing and his friend was a larger and older male, but he did not appear to have been placed in a situation with the real possibility of homosexual rape or even an injurious assault. The violent struggle did not begin until Green punched Gillies and no violence was done to him. Whereas Gillies was completely naked, Green was mostly clothed. The deceased may have already been completely disabled as a sexual or physical threat before he was repeatedly stabbed and killed. During the multiple stabbing it seems that Gillies also tried to speak with his killer. Green later admitted that Gillies had 'gurgled' something at him. The perpetrator also agreed in police interviews that he could have left the room or house at any time when the advances were made. He insisted that he was instead 'trapped' and scared by confusion and feelings of betrayal.

This perpetrator was an unskilled worker and not regularly employed at the time of the offence. He was a poor student and early school-leaver with a criminal history that comprised only convictions for minor drug matters. The violence was characterised by the trial judge as an 'explosion' (*R v. Green*, NSWSC, 7 June 1994, p. 18). The critical moment in this episode was the sexual touching:

> He grabbed me by both arms and pulled me towards him till there was no room in between us. Then he moved his hands down my backside, arse. I pushed it away. Then he slowly touched my groin area. That's when I got aggressive and hit him. (*R v. Green*, NSWCCA, 14 December 1994, p. 5)

Green clarified, 'I suppose it was gently but I didn't respond' (5), but the key feature setting off the outburst was the sexualised nature of the fondling and the particular sacrosanct body parts that were being fondled.

After the event, there was strong evidence of deep remorse. The victim and perpetrator were close friends. Green insisted he derived no pleasure from the killing and told police that he could not understand how some people 'get off' on such an act. Important evidence in court related to Green's father and episodes of violence and abuse within his family. This suggested that his sisters had been sexually abused by their father. He had also referred to this in police interviews by stating that during the killing he could see his father 'over two of my sisters . . . and they were crying and I just lost it . . . lost control' (*R v. Green*, NSWSC, 7 June 1994, p. 25).

Other evidence suggested that the perpetrator had never actually witnessed such attacks on his sisters but had instead formed his own mental images of what they may have been like. Despite the courtroom discussion about such images, the suggested unbroken causal link to the violent response to a homosexual advance appeared to be quite distant and it strained belief. A psychiatrist characterised the killing simply as 'a period of extreme discontrol due to sexual touching', and did not suggest that Green had a disturbed personality which rendered him distinct from the general population.

As will be demonstrated in the following, allegations of childhood abuse are usually treated more seriously in cases of homosexual desire with a significant age gap between parties. But this concern about sexual advances has also reflected judicial and legal imagining of male homosexual activity as being a form of violence in itself. In this case the suggestion of ongoing (hetero)sexual abuse in a family setting was projected onto a homosexual victim, with male homosexual desire as the general signifier of corruption and sexual violence.

This trope appears to have critically shaped the reasoning behind a major legal precedent that favourably viewed the killer's efforts to be retried and paved the way for his eventual success in securing a much lesser sentence. A first appeal against a murder conviction failed but a majority of the Australian High Court later granted Green the right to appeal. In the late 1990s he was convicted of manslaughter on the grounds of provocation with a 10-year sentence (Tomsen, 2002: 78). This legal case attracted much local and international publicity as it appeared to entrench the use of the homosexual advance defence in law. At the same time, this outcome signposted the links between the masculinist views of the socially marginal young men who comprise the bulk of perpetrators and those of eminent and institutionally powerful members of the judiciary.

HOMOSEXUAL ADVANCE AND THE 'UNDER-AGED' PERPETRATOR

The Green case demonstrates how claims about an unwanted homosexual advance—even in the form of a non-violent pass—shape the results of trials because of the legitimacy given to notions of the defence of male honour and the heterosexual male body. This effect is greatly reinforced where a perpetrator is below the legal age of consent for homosexual activity and notions of male honour overlap with concerns about vulnerable male sexualities and magnified fears of intergenerational homosexual desire. These factors then inform legal and expert pronouncements about the motives behind the actions of both perpetrators and victims.

A key focal point for late twentieth-century homosexual politics was the struggle to remove a whole category of adult sexual activity from the 'non-consenting' legal barrier. And much of the stigma which still attaches to homosexuality in more open and pluralist societies is linked to the recent nature of this shift away from total legal prohibition (see Moran, 1996). This sort of sexual ban can apply to a range of other activities, including freely entered relations of prostitution and sadomasochism. This was evident in the notorious arrests of the men involved in consenting group sadomasochism that followed on from 'Operation Spanner' by British police surveillance in the 1990s. In the resulting trial, male judicial pronouncements made a contorted distinction between the sort of consent to mutual assault that enhances heterosexual masculinity (e.g., in boxing and football or various forms of military bastardisation described as mere "horseplay") and circumstances that signal the horror of homosexual degradation of male bodies (Moran, 1995; Stychin, 1995).

The legal age of sexual consent for both males and females is historically and culturally varied and also substantially differs between national and regional jurisdictions. Gay and lesbian activists and their adversaries in most contemporary liberal democracies are well aware that associated criminal laws have been subjected to heated public debate, legal challenge and regular revision. Nevertheless, in the criminal courtroom these legal barriers are treated as beyond contention and sacrosanct.

This sexual ban also applies with state prohibitions of all sexual contact involving young people, who are regarded as being unable to arrive at autonomous decisions to enter or refuse sexual activity—especially with the possibility of coercion and manipulation from an older partner. Such views form the backdrop to the official response to anti-homosexual killings in which there is evidence of real or alleged sexual activity between the deceased and young perpetrators. These claims suggest that the deceased either had committed, or had intended to commit, an act which is criminal in all circumstances.

The distinction between a sexual attack and a mere sexual advance dissolves in these cases because of the legal fiction that all such behaviour comprises a non-consensual assault. Whenever a perpetrator is an under-aged male, an allegation of a homosexual advance will amount to a claim about a serious criminal offence by the deceased. A further consequence is that in cases involving a young perpetrator's violent response to an alleged advance, provocation will be found to have occurred in a much wider range of circumstances. This will have a continuous and often controversial impact on the outcome of trials related to killings given the wide age gaps between many perpetrators and their victims, and the attractions of anti-homosexual violence to immature youths drawn to the ease of establishing a masculine status through an involvement in this activity.

In Green's trial and those of several other killers, acts of sexual abuse were said to have been perpetrated on someone other than the actual killer by persons other than the deceased and years before the actual killing that occurred in response to an alleged homosexual advance. Whether or not such claims are directly related to the experiences of the perpetrator and victim, it is evident from these cases that the alleged sexual abuse linked to a killing either was real or was artificially constructed as a rationalisation for a serious crime. Sometimes these claims seem to veil a simple robbery. In these trials, childhood sexual experiences are referred to as episodes of abuse which created a special hypersensitivity to sexual advances from an older person. Arguably, among male victims of real sexual abuse this victimisation could be associated with feelings of emasculation that create insecurity and fear about homosexual relations which culturally imply feminisation. In these latter circumstances, a violent reaction reflecting the psychological effects of significant abuse will be very hard to distinguish from cases of the commonplace defence of male honour by forcefully repelling a homosexual pass.

However, the courtroom impact of provocation pleas linked to evidence about sexual abuse of young perpetrators has been considerable, especially when this abuse was alleged to have come from the deceased himself. This outcome is unsurprising as by law all of the sexual experiences of the under-aged are deemed to be assaults. This legal situation also cannot be divorced from a widespread point of view in which all intergenerational homosexual relations or advances are regarded with the suspicion of being abusive.

Homosexual desire is commonly understood as a type of sexual contagion (Moran, 1996) which younger men with their heightened sexual drives need protection from through unequal age of consent laws. A history of legal inequality built on a supposed urgent need to regulate and channel youthful male sexuality can create strong suspicions about intergenerational friendships and relations which characterise the circumstances of many killings. It may also reinforce a view that either all killers below the age of lawful consent who meet with a homosexual advance, or those who demonstrate past victimisation from sexual abuse, are without agency or any motives in their violent interaction with victims.

'A GROSS OVERREACTION'

The privileging of notions of honour in relation to anti-homosexual violence and a denial of any sexual agency for a youthful killer was demonstrated in a further killing and related trial. In 1993 Kevin Marsh, a 60-year-old invalid pensioner who lived alone in a flat in a regional city, was bashed and killed by T, a local 17-year-old. The pair were drinking and talking together for a short time, when an alleged sexual pass by Marsh resulted in a physical confrontation and his violent death. This fatal episode was summarised by the judge at the perpetrator's trial:

> On 30 June 1993 the prisoner visited a friend L at his home. . . . While amusing themselves with a computer they consumed some drinks . . . the prisoner had separated from L and another companion by about 8:40 p.m. Shortly thereafter the prisoner . . . encountered Kevin William Marsh who was passing the time smoking whilst standing on the verandah of the block of flatettes in which he resided. Mr. Marsh—who was to become the victim—invited the prisoner to come in for a couple of beers. . . . There is no evidence that they were previously acquainted. Subsequent to conviction the prisoner has told a probation officer that although he was aware of the victim's reputation he succumbed to the victim's offer of a few free drinks. After consuming some liquor the prisoner sought to leave . . . at some stage the prisoner became concerned that his exit from the flat may have been going to be impeded. This concern was magnified into a loss of self-control that followed the victim coming behind the prisoner and grasping him on the buttocks . . . the prisoner's reaction to molestation was to grasp a concrete object which was used as a door stopper

and which was referred to as a garden gnome. It was not constituted of light plaster. . . . The prisoner struck the victim on the head with the gnome, thereby crushing his skull and causing death. Immediately thereafter—although death had already been caused—the prisoner acquired a kitchen knife and stabbed the deceased many times. (*R v. T*, NSWSC, 14 July 1994, Grove J, pp. 1–2)

After this attack a neighbour saw 'a baby-faced teenager' leaving the building with a knife in his hand. T threw this weapon under a tree and returned to his parents' house where he lived. He drove about the local area in a confused state, and when meeting up with friends he said that he had assaulted a man who had made a sexual pass at him and that he had just 'freaked out' in response to this (*R v. T*, 6 April 1994, Grove J, p. 39).

T cleaned his bloodstained shoes while at home the next day. His jeans and a coloured sweatshirt were sent over to his grandparents' house for washing and later recovered by investigating police. Officers were called to the crime scene after neighbours noticed a pool of congealed blood coming from under the front door of his flat. The injuries to the deceased were very extensive. A post-mortem report indicated that he had been punched repeatedly and then died of severe head injuries before being stabbed. T was interviewed a few days after the killing and immediately claimed that it was a homosexual advance from Marsh which entirely provoked this violence as 'I done it, but I done it in self-defence. . . . He tried to crack on to me' (police interview with T, 2 July 1993: 4).

The perpetrator cooperated with police investigations and helped locate the knife he attacked the victim with. In further interviews, he admitted that the victim was lying facedown when he was struck on the back of the head and killed with a plaster 'garden gnome'. Marsh was prostrate on the floor, and possibly unconscious, when he then turned him over and stabbed him with a knife so many times and with such force that the blade bent out of shape.

In court, T addressed the jury with a dock statement which described himself as a well-mannered young man who became the unsuspecting victim of sexual molestation, and whose actions were directed by feelings of being trapped in the flat and a fear of homosexual rape:

I had a fair bit of drink that night but I wasn't really drunk so I can remember what happened. . . . He entered the unit and I followed. I felt uncomfortable when I was in there but I sat down and stayed for twenty minutes or more. I stood up, I said goodnight to him and I think I said, 'ciao'. I think I said, 'no more beers thanks'. . . . I got near the doorway and he grabbed my bottom hard, both hands and he said something. I pushed him away from me as he swung the punch back at me. I punched him a couple of times and he fell to the floor and was still coming back at me. I was really frightened and I picked up the door stopper. He was still coming at me. I have never been molested in this way before ever. I hit him with the door stopper. I don't know how many times. I did not mean to kill him. That thought never crossed my mind. I only wanted to stop him. He was still coming at me.

After I hit him with the door stopper I saw a knife on the coffee table. I stabbed him with it, I don't know how many times. I went to the door, security door. It wouldn't open. It was one of those—Marsh had locked me in. I was really frightened although I was trying to get the keys from his pocket. I got the keys, I let myself out. I threw the keys on the ground. I ran home, I took Mum's car. I did some really crazy things . . . but they won't matter now. I think I was trying to tell people what happened. I wasn't proud of myself. I think I was still frightened . . . I never deliberately hurt anyone in my life. I'm terribly sorry. (R v. T, 11 April 1994, Grove J, pp. 99–101)

T stresses that Marsh had locked the door but it seems that he may not have known this until after the alleged sexual assault. He did not adequately explain why he did not leave the flat after punching Marsh to the ground, or why he had to use the statue and knife to repeatedly wound and overcome the older man. Contradictions in statements by the perpetrator also created doubts about how the first violent blow was struck and by whom. It is uncertain whether or not Marsh really did punch T or just fend off a first punch.

The very ambiguous statement that 'I pushed him away from me as he swung the punch back at me' suggests that he really struck the first hard blow. Similarly, the second use of the phrase 'he was still coming at me' breaks up the sequence of events so that it appears very different to what was apparent from forensic investigations at the crime scene. This phrase appears to refer to the interaction before the fatal blow with the gnome, but it is placed in the statement in a way that could suggest in the minds of jurors that Marsh was virtually unstoppable until finished off with the knife.

The principal motive for this killing was not the theft of property, although T obtained free smokes and drinks and after the attack took the victim's cigarettes. T gave an account in court of a more even-handed fight than that which really appears to have taken place since it is unlikely he was in any real danger of a sexual assault that he could not ward off. He also knew of Marsh's reputation for homosexual interests, having already admitted in a police interview that he had heard 'just rumours and that like . . . he had to be a poofter or something' (T interview: 17). There was no evidence of any comments of a suggestive nature coming from the victim prior to the conflict. Nevertheless, T would probably have known that his sexual attractiveness was the basis of the hospitality.

According to the evidence of a neighbour, he stayed in the flat much longer than he later claimed. It is likely that T may have consciously played on

Marsh's sexual interest in his youth and good looks. It must have seemed likely that a sexual proposition was forthcoming. But the fine line between gratified male narcissism and sudden hostility to homosexual objectification could have been crossed when Marsh affronted the perpetrator's masculinity by touching him on the buttocks. T then carried out a killing characterised by its frenzied nature, and the multiple stabbing of a victim who was probably killed by the first blow.

The pattern and level of the killer's violence indicates that he was thrown into an instant and total rage by this sexual touching. T told police the victim had grabbed his buttocks with 'a good grip' and this was the critical moment in the lead-up to the slaying:

> I was gonna walk out and he come up behind me and grabbed me on the backside . . . he was just moaning and groaning a bit . . . you know like he was getting turned on or something . . . and then I turned around and pushed him and he punched me and I started. (T interview: 15)

Read together, interview records and trial transcripts indicate a shifting account of the events surrounding the death. This is not unusual in such cases and by itself does not suggest a very devious character. According to the trial judge, T had an 'immature personality' reflected in the act of going near the victim despite his being 'an older man about whom the prisoner had some knowledge of adverse reputation' (*R v. T*, Remarks on Sentence, 14 July 1994, Grove J, p. 4). T had no previous criminal history and he was not known among his friends for acts of violence. Equally, he appeared to have had genuine feelings of remorse and immediately after the killing he felt compelled by a need to confess the matter to friends.

When talking to friends he did not brag of his attack on a homosexual and thereby claim the male status that this sort of violence could give him. Elements of fear and shock are important in understanding the effect of the affront to T that came from the sexual touching of his body and his own frenzied response to that threat. In reality, T seems to have been frightened more by his own actions, and the self-discovery of a capacity to kill, than by the actual sexual pass. In his statements, he seems only half-conscious of the power of the heterosexual imperative to respond with rapid force to these bodily affronts, and how widespread the capacity for this violence is among ordinary men who are not viewed by others as having violent personalities.

The final outcome of this trial was a further reminder that this male response to a homosexual advance is partially excused at the highest levels. As in the trial of Gordon Tuckey's killer, a presiding judge described this killing as a 'gross overreaction' to the 'sexual overture' from the deceased (*R v. T*, 14 July 1994, Grove J, p. 5). But despite the offender's extreme reaction to homosexual touching and the brutal and gratuitous quality of his violence directed against an unarmed old man, the court accepted a plea of provocation. At the end of his trial, the killer was convicted of manslaughter with a maximum six-year term imposed. At the time of this killing the perpetrator had not reached the (then unequal) local lawful age of consent for homosexual activity. Nevertheless, he could have been reasonably expected to make his own sexual choices. It seems likely that the sentence had a deeper relation to his relative youth, the much greater age of his victim and more legal unease about the dangerous possibilities of mixing homosexual objectification and interest with youthful sexual longings.

HOMOPHOBIA OR BODILY HONOUR?

Much of the activist confusion about these cases and the difficulties involved in labelling such homicides as 'hate-killings' is the failure to appreciate the masculine qualities of this violence and the added legitimacy that these give to it. This has been a critical aspect of the cultural backdrop to these cases and the expanding use of sexual advance allegations by young men charged with killing other men. Existing rules regarding pleas of provocation and self-defence are coupled with allegations of a homosexual advance to powerful effect in a range of jurisdictions. In this way, the official response to anti-homosexual killings reflects the potency of claims about the affront to heterosexual manhood that derives from a homosexual pass.

The sudden and frenzied violence of both Green and T, which in both cases far exceeded the level needed to rebuff a sexual pass, was 'out of character' for both young men. More deeply, it reflected widespread notions of the integrity of the male body and its sexual parts on which a sense of male status is itself founded. Evidence in both trials suggested that male honour was temporarily undermined by the emasculation of homosexual touching, and then quickly restored by the immediate and exaggerated violence which is a common and sometimes respected masculine behaviour in situations of personal anxiety or threat. The matter of bodily touching featured as the critical aspect of this provocation to violence. The accused in these and other recent cases strongly stressed the threat to their masculinity involved in this sexual fondling. Masculine heterosexual identity is built around ensuring the sanctity and integrity of the body, with rigid limits imposed on the circumstances and socially admitted forms of male physical contact (Connell, 1995b). Theoretically, this phenomenon also suggests a link with corporeal feminist interpretations of the major significance of bounded understandings of male bodies (Grosz, 1994; Walby, 1995). Walby has exposed the significance of what she called 'hegemonic bodily imagos of sexual difference' (1995: 268) to explain the dual somatic grounding of misogyny and homophobia:

> The culture's privileging of masculinity means that the hegemonic bodily imago of masculinity conforms with his status as sovereign ego.

The destroyer, and that of women with the correlative status of the one who is made to conform to this ego, the destroyed. The male body is understood as phallic and impenetrable, as a war-body simultaneously armed and armoured, equipped for victory. The female body is its opposite, permeable and receptive, able to absorb all this violence. In other words, boundary difference is displaced outwards from (imaginary) genital difference. The fantasy of the always hard and ready penis/phallus characterizes the entire surface of the male body . . . any kind of penetration, or even the threat of penetration, is up against a clearly defined and absolute boundary, crosses a property line . . . even the momentary possibility of penetration, the very fantasy of penetration, counts as absolute violation. (268–9)

The martial metaphor might not attract all readers here. Nevertheless, what remains insightful and of vital importance is that the real-world penetrability of men is a feared matter that they become most aware of in their considerations about homosexual practice. Any enactment of this threat has major destructive consequences for the corporeal anchoring of male identity.

To reiterate, many allegations about a homosexual advance appear to be fictitious rationalisations for violence and in a large number of cases prejudiced views and the motive to rob or attack homosexual men as soft targets structure the real interests of perpetrators. Yet there is as well a considerable diversity in fatal scenarios and instances of sexual assault in which the accused had reasonably founded fears about his physical safety. A small number of the incidents analysed in the author's study gave rise to the possibility that the accused killer was, in reality, subjected to a substantial sexual assault which physically endangered him. By contrast, extreme responses to real though very minor sexual advances also had a real role that underlay a substantial number of killings. Many other cases of the male honour and minor sexual pass scenarios were found in this study of killings. For example, in the extraordinary 1987 'bottom pinch murder' a man shot a workmate dead for pinching his buttocks and then held police at bay with an exchange of gunfire in a subsequent siege ('Man killed for sex harassment: court told', *Sydney Morning Herald*, 10 February 1988).

Just as gang attacks on homosexual targets reflect evident concerns with questions of masculinity these incidents suggest a further relation between matters of male identity and anti-homosexual killings. More broadly, this violence is also more complexly linked to the historically shifting and dynamic relations between differently empowered and subordinated forms of masculinity. It may not be the case that masculinity and men really are entering a stage of 'crisis' as some commentators and sociologists have suggested (Simpson, 1994; Jefferson, 2002). Yet the increasing media objectification of male bodies, the very homoerotic quality of much popular culture and more mainstream representations of gay and lesbian lifestyles as fascinating and pleasurable, induces contradictions in the public representation of dominant and desirable forms of masculine identity (Dowsett, 1996a). It is against this social backdrop that we may best appreciate T's flirtation with his victim, his sudden violent rage and his endless confusion about his own actions.

Many discussions of this violence rely on an excessively pathologised view about the roots of anti-homosexual prejudice and overlook the importance of this fear of sexual objectification and bodily affronts to honour as aspects of heterosexual masculinity. Warding off the dishonour from a homosexual pass is a distinct concern from either genuinely fearing or fighting off a sexual assault, but aggression and violence are viewed by perpetrators and others as the most appropriate response to a sexual advance. Questions of the male honour of accused perpetrators have been critical to the recent controversy surrounding the use of the 'homosexual advance defence' in homicide trials in the United States, Australia and other nations. These notions have an even wider level of community respect than obvious homophobia, and due to the masculinist understandings of violent behaviour inscribed in the law they also have had a substantial courtroom impact.

Far from reflecting the individually experienced pathology of 'homosexual panic' discussed in the next chapter, evidence about the commonplace occurrence of anti-homosexual violence suggests considerable male unease with ruptures in the simple linked dichotomies of unmasculine/masculine and homo/hetero. These many acts of harassment and assault are not just the symptoms of episodic difficult changes in individual male identities. They are an intricate and defining part of these social forms. Heterosexual and homosexual masculinities are created, reproduced and then to some extent destabilised in the urgency of such instances of violence and the official and wider social responses to them.

Fanning this confusion are the mixed signals about violence and homosexual desire that are now offered by the law. The more serious investigation and prosecution of such attacks sits uneasily with the success of claims about homosexual advances and the often linked and prominent role of law courts in expounding a sense of dread and panic about same-sex desire. An interesting paradox concerning contemporary forms of masculinity and male sexuality arises here. The success of offender claims about the horror of being subjected to a homosexual advance is premised on the certainty of the homo/hetero divide. The law appears to wholly affirm the reality of this symbolic border. But such legal cases also rely on and reflect wide social and political concerns about the sexual sensitivity of youth to contagion and corruption. Evidence of and anxiety about the ambiguity and fluidity of male sexuality always threaten the shaky underpinnings of the homosexual advance defence.

7   Violence, Identity and Panic

THE ORIGINS AND USES OF 'HOMOSEXUAL PANIC'

'Homosexual panic' suggests that episodes of acute anxiety and fear characterised by guilt about some past homosexual experience or aspects of homosexual desire may result from a lack of heterosexual integration in an unstable individual. It can be traced back to the conservative reworking of Freud's insights into undifferentiated sexual desire and the ambiguous legacy of his views about homosexuality in the human unconscious. In *Psychopathology* (1920), Edward Kempf first developed this new term. This major tome was a patchwork compilation of the diverse insights and anecdotes about mental illness intending to offer 'an unprejudiced insight into human behaviour' (Preface) collected by a psychiatrist who spent years in practice at a mental hospital in the United States.

Although moralistic in tone, this work reflected a view that was even more focused than Freud on the significance of sexuality and sexual desire in the achievement of a rounded balance in individual and collective psychological health and 'the universal struggle for virility, goodness and happiness' (Kempf, 1920: 118). His readers were offered a curious mix of psychoanalytic insights including a wide range of case studies of different neuroses and psychoses and their psychological and physical (including postural and facial) manifestations, the depiction of sex in myths, sculpture and art, and the animal origins of human sexuality. Kempf also documented the influence of 'autonomic affective cravings' and the fear of sexual inferiority in humans. This offered warnings about the dangers of sexual perversions along with a social Darwinist insistence on the vital role of the 'sexual selection' of the human 'herd'.

Kempf emerged here as one of the champions of new heterosexual identities as society must recognize that '. . . instead of despising and discouraging heterosexuality it should encourage and promote the development of heterosexual potency' (719).

In particular, he declared great admiration for cultural items and works of art such as erotic Rodin sculptures that served to express 'the eternal vigor and constructive power of uncensored heterosexual love' (143). Prudery must be rejected and opposite-sex desire actively and universally promoted and protected. There is some parallel between these views and the better-known psychoanalytic accounts that also celebrated heterosexuality and the new role of collective sex education and excoriated homosexuals as a threat to the sexual health of the entire society (Reich, 1975). Nevertheless, Kempf viewed licentiousness and promiscuity as reflecting a lack of sexual balance. As a result he offered a seemingly even more sanitised vision of sexual normality and the attainment of social happiness with a correct balance of intellectual and physical training promoted by educators, professionals and state agencies. This meant the development of youth in an education that corrected the 'evil' (Kempf, 1920: 150) of non-heterosexual desire. Furthermore, in addition to the fundamental and constant threat of homosexuality, the collective attainment of a balanced species reproduction was threatened by the particular cultural, religious and racial mix, and discouragement of reproduction that prevailed in contemporary America:

> Prostitution, masturbation, homosexual and heterosexual perversions as a tendency to biological abortion and waste, and social deterioration, are always to remain among the great problems of the human race and incessantly require society's counter-efforts to train the individual to enjoy living a socially constructive sexual life. Society can not possibly escape the laws of nature (because of the fatal tendency to autoerotic and homosexual reversion) by erecting barriers against normal sexuality. There is but one solution and that must lie in a profound revolution of social and religious conventions and the ideals of education in order to bring about a more healthful and happy career of sublimation of the sex cravings with virility as the goal. (158)

In this perspective, sexuality was a mixed blessing that constituted the very foundation of society and its potential ruin. He accepted the original bisexual disposition and widespread levels of same-sex desire among humans. Homosexuality was a universal possibility and universal threat.[1] For this reason, Kempf exhibited a visceral hostility to it as a key marker of psychological disturbance and social pathology. A 'reversion tendency' (139) meant the likelihood of a shift back to homosexuality whenever a confident heterosexuality was not encouraged in young men and women. Like the unconscious desire for incest, sexual and gender confusion were lurking everywhere (123).

Unsurprisingly, Kempf's account closely associated a range of major psychological illnesses, mental breakdown and homosexuality. 'Homosexual panic' reflected the general danger of same-sex desire, especially among men. Sufferers typically experienced a physical collapse and acute dissociation of the personality with perverse hallucinations and paranoia running with 'a protracted course from several weeks to many years' (514). The majority of case studies were of males who experienced an episode of panic in such same-sex environments as the army, navy, prisons and certain asylums. Despite the dangerous ubiquity of same-sex desire, Kempf's asocial essentialism meant this was only ever conceived as a psychological reversion. The various ways that social groups and cultures can incorporate homosexual practice into models of manhood were not considered. Thus, any reader could wonder who the 'erotic companions' (477) in these hypermasculine environments setting off desire and panic in Kempf's patients really were.

For the purposes of analysing the legal response to cases of anti-homosexual violence, it is important to note that these case studies purported to detail a very serious mental illness and associated implosion of personality. This occurred in the medium to long term and entailed an overall inability to function socially among sufferers. Psychosis and a range of disturbing behaviours typically resulted from paranoia about homosexuality that had been projected as social anxiety, avoidance and the fear of gossip from friends and colleagues, along with passive fantasies about becoming a sexual object. In fact, there was no suggestion or description here of a link between acts of violence directed at those with homosexual identities and 'homosexual panic'. *Psychopathology* described the psychotic imagining of sexual advances or interest from other males, rather than the real circumstances of any sexual assault and a resulting violent reply from a sufferer. Furthermore, a fear of heterosexuality and avoiding the possibility of sexual advances from women were other elements of this panic.

It is evident that any determined advocacy of 'homosexual panic' in the context of police investigations and criminal courtroom discussions about assaults and fatal violence would do well not to refer too closely to the full original account of this condition. If this did occur, it seems that few judges or jurors could take seriously the claim that a perpetrator of violence was certainly suffering from this condition. Kempf's detailed account of actual traumatic incidents of 'homosexual panic' is well removed from the familiar circumstances of quick annoyance and violent rage from otherwise socially functioning men that characterise an overwhelming majority of cases of anti-homosexual killing with sexual advance allegations.

Kempf's own anti-homosexual bias was fed by an awareness of the fluidity of human sexual desire. Yet over nine decades the notion of 'homosexual panic' has come more and more to suggest the essentialist idea of one fundamental (though often 'repressed') heterosexual or homosexual identity for each individual and that this is the very basis of hostility to homosexuality. The term was used by psychological research with links to early work on homophobia (Glick, 1959). And despite his best intentions, Weinberg's (1972) own key description of homophobia as repressed homosexuality drew close to this model. Although the 'homosexual panic defence' has no formal existence in law, it seems it has strongly influenced medical/forensic and legal experts involved in criminal investigations. It entered courtroom argument soon after the 1920s (Green, 1992). The controversial circumstances of trials in the United States in which 'homosexual panic' has been referred to by defence counsel and expert witnesses have led to arguments that this term creates the misleading impression that many offenders have acted violently because of an advanced pathological condition, and that by reducing levels of responsibility it seems to exonerate this violence ('Developments: sexual orientation and the law', 1989; Mison, 1992; Comstock, 1992; Sedgwick, 1994; Suffredini, 2001).

The controversy about 'homosexual panic' arguments has been mirrored in contemporary debates about the legal status of 'homosexual advance' allegations in homicide trials and the significance of the final legal rulings in relation to the violence of Malcolm Green discussed in the previous chapter (see Coss, 1998; Howe, 2001). Against many activist expectations, it is apparent that defence allegations about a homosexual advance from the deceased victim have more success when linked to common notions of masculine heterosexual identity. Dressler (1995) pointed out the masculine qualities of the use of the provocation plea in sexual advance cases that partly excused sudden anger and unrestrained violence from perpetrators. This observation was extended in the present author's research regarding the apparent emergence of the 'homosexual advance defence'. The latter confirmed that allegations of a sexual advance are most powerfully raised by perpetrators in regular courtroom claims of provocation as a threat to male identity and bodily integrity.

A cogent discussion of the notion of 'reasonableness' in murder cases focused on a range of American killings in which advance claims were raised (Lee, 2003). This drew out the anti-homosexual and deeply gendered aspects of the resulting trial outcomes. Particular forms of male aggression and protection of heterosexuality have been so naturalised that unjust distinctions between hypothetical advance scenarios that could have male/female or hetero/homo aggressors, appear trite or go unnoticed:

> A man who responds to a (homo)sexual advance with violence resulting in death claims he acted as any ordinary (i.e. heterosexual) man would have acted. . . . A woman who responds with deadly force to a man who whistles at her, tries to kiss her, grabs her buttocks, or fondles her breasts is quite unusual, not at all typical. Ordinary women are supposed to accept a certain amount of unwanted male attention, and while they might frown, struggle or protest, they are not supposed to use lethal violence to dissuade or thwart men who suggest sexual interest. . . . Men in this society are supposed to be happy if a woman shows she is sexually attracted to him by taking off her clothes, kissing him on the mouth, or grabbing his crotch. If a man, however, shows his sexual interest in another man by acting in a similar manner, he is asking for a violent response. (Lee, 2003: 84–5)

Unsurprisingly, it has been less psychologically complex allegations of a 'homosexual advance' and everyday hostile male response to it that are more usually and effectively raised by perpetrators and defence counsel. These do not use the specific defence of 'homosexual panic' and rely instead on the conventional notions of the protection of masculine honour discussed in the previous chapter. Yet much of the recent interest regarding the 'homosexual panic defence' has been in regard to the possible social and political consequences of the imagery about violence that follows deployment of this explanation of retaliatory force as a courtroom tactic. In stressing that a perpetrator himself had uncontrollable feelings of homosexual desire or guilt, it seemingly re-pathologises homosexuality and disavows and denies mainstream homophobia.

This merges with conservative and fundamentalist views of sexual morality that have characterised American and other political landscapes in recent decades (Vance, 1994). Its attraction to these forces is that it depoliticises the issue of anti-homosexual violence by implying that no heterosexuals are themselves responsible for this form of crime. It seems instead that it is 'practising homosexuals' who criminally prey on each other, with offending and victimisation remaining internal to this unfortunate social group. This appears to justify the traditional trivialisation of this form of crime.

A view that hostility and violence towards homosexuals may be linked to repressed sexual desire is also regularly implied in gay and lesbian politics, writing and culture. In its most simple and essentialist expression this can come awkwardly close to the notion that 'gay-bashers' are most often closet homosexuals. This means of explaining anti-homosexual violence and same-sex activity among men shares with sexual conservatives and the dominant culture of the contemporary West a commitment to the centrality of the hetero/homo dyad as the key means of understanding human sexuality. An often related notion is that although many people may be confused and mistaken about their positioning in this simple sexual hierarchy, each individual has an essential sexuality to which they will be inclined as the master term of their personal and social identity.

'I WAS ASHAMED OF IT'

In anti-homosexual homicides, both killers and their victims include homosexually active men who are not homosexually or gay-identified. It is evident from the analysis of official records that a notable heightened anxiety about sexuality marks the consciousness of perpetrators who have engaged in publicly known same-sex activities, when this has serious implications for their masculine social identity. Trial evidence has provided an illustration of how these anti-homosexual attacks have reflected the fluidity of male sexual desire, and in the extreme circumstances of fatal assault, involved perpetrators with ordinary masculine motives such as the protection of a heterosexual public reputation. The social fears of perpetrators and legal confusion in dealing with the meanings of same-sex activity were both evident in cases that involved killers who—like many other men—did not identify as homosexual but found pleasure in covert homosexual encounters.

The criminal justice system has evident difficulty classifying and interpreting situations that suggest the involvement of killers in same-sex activities with their victims. In incidents involving under-aged offenders this activity can be readily classified by courts as abuse. But even in matters that involve adult offenders, a willing engagement in homosexual activity is generally viewed as signalling a psychological disturbance that was also the predominant cause fatal violence. Such sexual activity is deemed to be the marker of a past history of abuse or repressed homosexual urges which produce guilt and self-loathing. The psychological stresses resulting from this have been expressed in acts of anti-homosexual violence in which perpetrators have attempted to distance themselves from the homosexual identity implied by their own sexual activity and desires. The shared anxiety of both perpetrators and legal officialdom about the implications of same-sex activity is evident in another case studied in detail. This involved a killer who found ongoing physical pleasure in homosexual encounters. The consequences of this sexual activity eventually threatened his sense of masculinity and honour in a way that resulted in explosive fatal violence directed towards a friend.

In 1990 Gary Webster, a 43-year-old openly homosexual man who had just been released from jail, visited a suburban charity in outer Sydney. He met up with a long-term friend, 26-year-old Graham Hort, and his girlfriend, Tricia. All three went to a local hotel and drank heavily. In a shared hotel room, a dispute developed over an alleged remark in which Webster told Tricia that he and Hort had an ongoing sexual liaison and that her boyfriend would one day leave her. In a further alleged argument Webster ridiculed and taunted Hort by saying, 'I am going to fuck you like the kid that you are' (*R v. Hort*, NSWSC, 13–18 May 1992, Judgment, Finlay J, p. 25). Webster was soon after stabbed repeatedly and killed by the couple. They shared a drink and smashed the glasses against a wall. A foil cross and a page from a book on psychic and occult experiences was placed on the body, and the word 'poof' was carved into the side of the bed with the knife used to kill the victim. They then had sex next to the dead body. A few days later Hort confessed fully to police (police interview with GH, 27 August 1990). He was charged with murder and his girlfriend gave evidence against him. After a long trial, a maximum term of 14 years in prison was imposed on him (*R v. Hort*, 13–18 May 1992, Sentence, Finlay J).

The official examination of the perpetrator's motive referred to his substance abuse and family upbringing. Though he had no previous criminal record for violence and only one conviction for marihuana possession, reports suggested that he was a frequent user of alcohol and amphetamines.

A key feature of the trial was the issue of whether or not he was a 'true' homosexual. One psychiatrist diagnosed a 'borderline personality disorder'. Hort's homosexual contacts were due to self-destructive impulses and a push to demean himself. He was described as a homosexual who denies being homosexual 'in his head', and then also as a sexual 'enigma'. Notions of unconscious repression were used to explain his ambivalent attitude to homosexual activity and to suggest that the killing was an instance of 'homosexual panic'. His fears about homosexuality were seen as reflected in a request to be put on protection in jail and fear of rape by other inmates. This was said to reflect a 'rape mentality' (which the court was also told is not unusual in women who are raped) rather than a reasonable fear (*R v. Hort*, 13–18 May 1992, Finlay J, p. 44).

A second expert regarded the perpetrator's behaviour (rather than his personality) as pathological and respected him as fundamentally heterosexual, but noted the troubles that came from sexual relations with a variety of other men. The killing was a result of the trauma experienced due to an alleged sexual assault by a football coach when he was a teenager, and 'probably to a series of other homosexual encounters which appear to have been very alien to this man and have led to a build up of a tremendous set of conflicts within this man which his unconscious mind could not accommodate' (*R v. Hort*, 13–18 May 1992, Judgment, Finlay J, p. 42).

A last psychiatrist also disagreed with the diagnosis of a full personality disorder and noted that the causes of the killing were largely circumstantial: The perpetrator had no money, was drunk, tired and fearful of losing a girlfriend. When intoxicated he was very vulnerable to the tensions produced by homosexual advances. If he was released and continued to drink and lead a 'disorganized lifestyle', he was 'likely to encounter further situations with other men and where doubts about his sexuality will again arise, and this would put the other person at risk. This situation is well known in legal history' (*R v. Hort*, 13–18 May 1992, Judgment, Finlay J, p. 20). The perpetrator was diagnosed as a confused heterosexual without the social skills to cope with homosexual advances. He had previous relations with women that 'were not too bad' and with 'no sexual difficulties', including a failed marriage, numerous girlfriends and a passionate affair with the manageress of a KFC store (*R v. Hort*, 13–18 May 1992, Judgment, Finlay J, pp. 14, 38). Even in this explanation of the killing as a consequence of drunkenness and the stresses of social marginality, homosexual contact was still viewed as suggesting significant psychological problems and sexual 'doubts' (*R v. Hort*, 13–18 May 1992, Judgment, Finlay J, p. 18). At one point this expert conveyed disbelief about the limit of four sexual contacts which the perpetrator claimed to have had with the deceased. In response to blunt questions from the prosecutor, he agreed that the relation was a 'financial transaction' (*R v. Hort*, 13–18 May 1992, Judgment, Finlay J, p. 93). He then also added that 'there may have been some abnormal sexual side to it too' and noted that for a while Hort seemed to have adjusted to his relations with the victim (*R v. Hort*, 13–18 May 1992, Judgment, Finlay J, pp. 86, 93).

Overall, none of these physicians or counsel participating in the trial seemed to have directly considered the possibility that the accused was a homosexually active male who derived real physical pleasure from his same-sex encounters. Although Hort voiced later disgust about his homosexual activities or hinted at a financial need, his most revealing comments refer to a substantial fear about these activities becoming publicly known and the threat to masculine identity that this entailed. In police interviews, he also interprets and downplays his participation in these activities ('a couple of headjobs') through a commonplace discourse of male sexuality as hedonistic, unrestrained and unemotional. Male same-sex activity for pleasure might result in amusement or ridicule according to circumstances but it does not suggest a deeper homosexual nature in participants. The victim's possible attempt to invest their sexual relations with a sensitive or romantic content in the mischievous remark to Tricia undermined this protective way in which the perpetrator interpreted his own sexuality and also further outraged him. As he told one psychiatrist, 'he made it seem like we were full-blown lovers' (*R v. Hort*, 13–18 May 1992, Judgment, Finlay J, p. 17).

Although definitely linked to the perpetrator's experience of a profound threat to his masculine social status, the courtroom discussions of his underlying motives were preoccupied with matters of identity. These reflected an urge to classify and search for essential sexual identities with heterosexuality assumed to be a natural and psychically healthy pattern and homosexuality a signifier of abuse, illness or potential for violence. The difficulties that medical authorities and legal counsel experienced with this process of labelling Hort suggest that his sexual history and actions were resistant to any easy classification.

'GAY' KILLERS AND EROTICISED VIOLENCE

Reworked notions of 'homosexual panic' suggest that episodes of violence directed against homosexuals result from a lack of full sexual integration in an individual and are often characterised by guilt about some past homosexual experience or aspects of homosexual desire. It is evident from an analysis of the extent and forms of anti-homosexual violence that this model is too narrow and simplistic in failing to account for the widespread levels of both homophobic sentiments and homosexual desire in the general population of men who do not manifest any psychological abnormality. As the discussion of killings in Chapter 6 suggests, anti-homosexual views are not held exclusively by perpetrators, but are shared with respectable figures, are inscribed within social institutions and also reflect elements of the representation of prized and devalued sexualities and masculinities in the general culture.

Yet some perpetrators who have bashed and killed homosexual men have appeared to fit this disturbed pattern of a pathological response to homosexual inclinations and behaviour. There has been a sensationalised media focus on those anti-homosexual killings perpetrated by men who themselves appeared to be homosexual. In being both killers and homosexuals, these perpetrators became folk devils with a doubly bad repute. And there has been an even greater level of lurid interest in the triple deviance of the dangerous but small number of apparently homosexual perpetrators who become serial killers. The detailed international reporting on a series of killings which occurred in the United States in 1997 and culminated in the deaths of the fashion designer Gianni Versace and his alleged killer, Andrew Cunanan, clearly reflected the heightened popular fascination with this very particular type of crime (Douglas et al., 2006: 448–52). This matched the previous high and ongoing interest in the crimes of such homosexually active serial killers as Gacy and Dahmer in the United States, or Nilsen, Ireland and Moore in Britain (Carr, 1997). In particular, the notorious crimes of Jeffrey Dahmer sparked a wave of anti-homosexual sentiment and revulsion in American culture. As with much public representation of the HIV epidemic, this conflated same-sex activity with death as it implied a direct link between this serial killer's homosexual 'lifestyle' and his violence, sickness and evil (Schmidt, 1994).

The image of psychopathic perpetrators has had an ongoing influence on media speculation and official inquiries regarding killings studied by the author. For example, in 1981, GB, a 27-year-old gay man who was holidaying in Sydney, was found dead in a friend's inner-city flat where he had been staying. He was killed by someone who cut his throat and in a frenzy of violence stabbed him 64 times. The flat was not disturbed and no property had been taken. Police believed the victim met his killer in a local gay bar and they found evidence of sexual activity. As this incident was close in time to the similar brutal killings of other homosexual men, press speculation arose that a 'gay blade' killer was frequenting local gay venues in search of victims whose homosexuality placed them in grave danger. Along with police commentators, these press reports hypothesised the perpetrator was probably a homosexual so disgusted by his own sexual activity that he reacted to sexual contact with extreme and murderous violence ('Sydney's unsolved murders', *Mirror*, 7 December 1981).

As noted earlier, the notion that whoever has sexual relations with a person of their own gender is necessarily a 'homosexual' (conflating identity with sexual practice) is contradicted by research evidence about casual same-sex activity engaged in by many men with no identification as homosexual. But in these killings, evidence of sexual activity usually gave rise to speculation about each crime as the handiwork of a psychologically disturbed homosexual. In 1995 Kenneth Brennan, a 53-year-old gay schoolteacher, was stabbed to death in his inner-city residence in Kings Cross and his body was discovered by his lover a day later. Police found no signs of a break-in, though a violent struggle had accompanied the stabbing. Evidence that the victim had sexual intercourse with someone who called by or had been picked up and asked home was also found. Detailed investigations did not result in any arrests, and this case remains unsolved. Remarkably, the killer's apparent act in wiping down the victim after the attack was reported as a gesture of tenderness that reflected sudden feelings of remorse and guilt from a psychologically confused homosexual perpetrator. This was not considered as a likely rational strategy to elude identification by wiping fingerprints, blood or semen from the body. A 'homosexual panic' understanding of the killing also led to the curious final police belief that:

> the frenzied attack, the positioning of the body with the pillow under the torso, the sponging down of the body and the signs of sexual intercourse, may indicate that the perpetrator or perpetrators may be homosexual or homophobic. (Police statement, 18 January 1996: 54)

At the end of the later coronial inquest into the death, this passage was quoted for its supposed particularly helpful insights into possible motive and the perpetrator's identity, and the suggestion that homosexuality and homophobia were 'the two ends of the spectrum if you will' (*Death of KB*, Coroner's Report, 11 September 1996, Abernethy J, p. 55). In the popular and legal imagination, these uncommon cases become iconic instances of the self-destructiveness of homosexuality and its relationship to violence (Dalton, 2001).[2] This is projected with the imagery of a homosexual violence that reflects a lack of stable masculinity in both perpetrators and victims.

There is a deep symbolic value for such real or irrational and assumed instances of killing by 'homosexuals' and the social avenging role of those who might kill them. This stems from a basic equation of homosexuality and violence itself as twin evils in the collective unconscious. Three decades ago, the importance of this set of conflations was recognised in a perceptive analysis of a sensational instance of a son carrying out a killing of a homosexual to revenge the murder of his father and his subsequent lenient treatment by legal officials and public opinion:

> The paranoiac association of homosexuality with crime is not only a defence against the homosexual libido, it also decorates it with blood. . . . Homosexual murder is paranoiacally experienced as murder for pleasure, the main danger to civilised society. The avenging murder [of a homosexual] deserves respect because it affirms the rights of the family. (Hocquenghem, 1978: 55)

Issues of the identity, culture and political situations of gay men are linked to their own contradictory position in societies which, in one major system

of social stratification, ascribe the fullest status and power to heterosexualised masculinity. This has been manifested in arguments over such issues
as the ironic eroticising of masculine power in gay male culture, the gender
parody of drag and involvements with apparently masculinist sexual tastes
and practices. These divisions have particularly concerned the 'macho'
personal style and imagery of the denim-and-leather fad in the burgeoning
gay men's urban subcultures of the 1970s, a prominence of pornography
and erotica and the mixed responses to such practices as sadomasochism,
sex work and casual, group and intergenerational sex (Edwards, 1994;
Levine, 1998). It has also shaped the possibilities and limits of coalitionism with lesbians, and gay men's relation to now widely varied, pro-gay
or puritanical and even viscerally anti-gay brands of polemical feminism
(Jeffreys, 2004).

None of these attacks on gay male physical fitness and masculine dress-
ing acknowledge the enhanced sense of personal safety and the repelling of
likely perpetrators of violence that may result from these practices. The fire
in these various debates, and the moral execration of gay men that can con-
clude them, is linked to a commonplace puzzlement about eroticised representations of masculinity which are a frequent element of gay male culture.
Gay literature, art and culture (including the output of Genet, Mappletho-
rpe, Davila or the even more salacious and popular drawings by Tom of
Finland), and most obviously different genres of gay pornography, often
focus on and objectify the masculinity of aggressive heterosexual men. This
transgressively renders the links between power and desire more explicit.
In leather and sadomasochistic subcultures, this is built around a symbolic appropriation of the power and markings of status that derive from
the often violent masculinity of those same groups of men (street toughs,
police, the military and so on) who have been most directly involved in the
physical oppression of homosexuals.

This frequent gay male eroticising of the actual or potential perpetrators
of violence has a far more difficult outcome than the mischievous offence
it gives many prudes. At worst, the very ambiguous pattern of this subcultural representation of sexualised destructive masculinity can meet with
a confused and literal interpretation. This obfuscates the understanding
of motive and the circumstances in anti-homosexual assaults and killings.
It can also assume the form of a superficial view which suggests that such
crimes are the general result of the unbridled desire of victims. Furthermore, as objects of desire, some perpetrators have at least symbolically lost
an unblemished masculine identity. They can therefore also be thought of
as homosexual.

Possibly the most widespread example of this elision of the homoerotic
and the homosexual can be found in stage, literary and film representations of German Nazism. In these, the homosexual activities of some of
the early Nazi leadership are given a far greater significance than the continuous vilification of homosexuals in Fascist ideology and the systematic

persecution, imprisonment and murder of thousands (Plant, 1986; Haeberle, 1989). The simple equation of male homosexual desire and class exploitation or 'bourgeois decadence' has persisted in Leftist thought.[3] Even more offensively, an equation with Nazism has been familiar across the political Left and was most notably and crudely expressed in key Freudo-Marxist writings (e.g., Reich, 1975). This interpretation of Fascism as 'repressed homosexuality' can only offer a muddled understanding of the renewed involvement of neo-Nazis in attacks on gay men and lesbians in Central Europe and North America, and it dovetails with the popularised 'homosexual panic' model to explain such violence. It is obvious that some victims had been sexually attracted to their eventual killers and it is necessary to interrogate elements of the 'heterosexuality' of many perpetrators. But the murky yet culturally powerful notions of the always desiring victim and the 'closeted' killer with his repressed urges form a major part of the backdrop of the legal response to homosexual advance allegations.

SEX WORKERS AS PERPETRATORS

Fatal attacks have been carried out by youths and men who are mostly heterosexually identified but whose own culturally shaped relationships to dominant notions of masculinity are especially and continuously rendered unstable. Prostitutes featured as both suspects and confirmed perpetrators in the author's research. In other studies, they formed a larger proportion of the perpetrator group (Miller & Humphries, 1980; Mott, 1996). Considerable variation exists across location and time in such factors as the extent, form and regulation of such commercial sex work and the ready availability of casual outlets for homosexual activity. Despite this difference, the role of male sex workers as perpetrators in the local context was found to be significant. For example, unsolved killings of the regular clients of sex workers regularly led to police investigations focused on what were in one case called 'the male homosexual heroin-addict type offenders in the prostitution area of Kings Cross' (*Death of WD*, Coroner's Report, 12 December 1994, Abernethy J, p. 14).

Evidence about these killings suggested robbery was a major motive. This finding was expected given the underlying commercial basis of sexual contacts with homosexual men. More insights into motive in such cases were found in the old records of the trials of the perpetrators who jointly killed two men in separate incidents in the early 1980s. The victims had been tied up and stabbed to death in a similar fashion. These were Peter Parkes, a 41-year-old gay schoolteacher found dead in his flat and the Greek Consul, Constantine Giannaris, killed in his harbour-side home a month later. The social status of Giannaris and the circumstances of his death led to an immediate high level of lurid media interest and speculation about the crime. This included a theory that the killing was carried out by the same terrorist group who were thought to have assassinated a Turkish diplomat in the previous year ('Police hunt mad louts', *Mirror*, 17 November 1981).

Michael Caldwell, aged 19 years, and AT, a 16-year-old youth, were charged with the killings. AT lived with Caldwell and Caldwell's girlfriend. He had befriended Parkes and had sex with him twice before his killing. On the night of the first killing Caldwell had suggested that they visit, rob and murder someone. The pair called at the home of another man who had paid them for sex. Because he was not there, they contacted Parkes at four o'clock in the morning. The Consul was also visited at home and killed in the next month. The obvious motive was robbery and property was taken from both victims.

In this and other similar killings, it appears that the typical perpetrators are young heterosexual men who are not extremely homophobic or acting out a major psychopathic crisis of personal identity in their violence. They do seem more like calculating killers who view the men using their services as ready targets for extortion and robbery. Evidence suggests that many are participating in sex work to meet the cost of their own illicit drug use. Fatal incidents arise out of disputes over payment for sexual services or where amounts are insufficient for the perpetrators' own drug needs. In these two killings, both of the accused were admitted prostitutes but during legal proceedings strongly denied that they were homosexual. They insisted they had sexual contacts for profit only. Their subsequent statements suggested a mix of resentments about their male clients and ambiguous views about gay men and their newly expanding subculture.

AT insisted that he disliked Giannaris but would ring him when he could not get any other clients, and that this second victim paid him whether they had sex or not (*R v. MC & AT*, NSWSC, 26 November 1982, Lee J, p. 6). In a later statement AT told a psychiatrist that this victim treated him with disdain and had once also tried to cheat him out of a fee (p. 19). He said that Parkes was also derogatory towards him in their sexual encounters. AT repeatedly stated that he did not like being a prostitute and one psychiatrist noted he had a 'hatred of homosexuals who he felt degraded him' (p. 23). The occasional expression of such animosity could be expected as the relations between all prostitutes and their clients are underwritten by the logic and tensions of sexual transactions for cash. However, this sat incongruously with the intimate sexual and positive social contact with homosexuals arising from their form of employment.

AT also told a psychiatrist that the 'gays' were always very kind to him (p. 14). He and Caldwell frequented mainstream gay as well as hustler bars. The judge at AT's trial noted very disapprovingly that there was 'no evidence to suggest that the prisoner ever made any worthwhile effort to keep away from homosexuals or to find another job' (p. 24) and imposed a substantial prison sentence. It is uncertain whether the court believed they were or were not heterosexual, but it is apparent that the perpetrators lost any possibility of judicial sympathy regarding their youth and drug addiction given the hostility evoked by the ongoing debasement of masculinity that this form of sex work comprises.

This contradiction captures the precarious state of the masculinity of such perpetrators due to the cultural responses to male sex work and homosexuality. Same-sex relations can be sheltered from notions of being unmanly for some or all participants. But a lowered male status is especially likely when these are not entered into freely and have become a principal source of livelihood. Commodification of the male body and sexual parts in these transactions seriously violates culturally dominant views of physical inviolability. The resulting stigma that heterosexually identified male sex workers experience will lead to the heightened contempt and mixed hostility and dependence towards clients that these youths clearly demonstrated in their actions and statements.

THE GAY PSYCHOPATH?

The evolved discourse of 'homosexual panic' appears to be even more suggestive in relation to a small number of killings that involved perpetrators with a dangerous disturbance concerning matters of sexual identity and evidence of violent psychoses and schizophrenia. Professional definitions of criminal psychopaths are variable but descriptors include being manipulative, callous, unemotional and impulsive and denying responsibility for personal actions. In homicide studies this is associated with persistent aggression, sadism and deceitfulness (Williamson et al., 1997; Porter & Woodworth, 2007).

In 1994 Richard Leonard and his girlfriend, both of whom had just taken LSD, stabbed a taxi-driver to death in order to evade paying their fare. The press subsequently featured accounts of the special tragedy of the senseless murder of a good family man ('Cab driver killed in drug frenzy, jury told', *Sydney Morning Herald*, 5 November 1997). At the time, Leonard was already charged with carrying out a previous killing. Earlier in the year he had killed Stephen Dempsey, a 34-year-old gay man, at a bush area that was well known for homosexual cruising.

Police found no trace of the victim until late in the year when his body (without its head and limbs) was found wrapped in chicken wire and floating in water north of Sydney. Dempsey was killed by a single arrow wound to the heart. Dismembered parts of the body were stored in a refrigerator before they were dumped months later. Some of the victim's property was taken, including his car, though the decision to steal this may well have been an afterthought. When arrested and questioned by police about this offence, the perpetrator alleged that he killed in order to ward off persistent sexual advances that could only be rebuffed with serious violence.

The perpetrator was well aware that he was at a homosexual beat and felt hostility towards the men who went there. Other men had reported to police that they were threatened by a man armed with a bow and arrows at this location. The perpetrator also derived a considerable degree of pleasure from the killing in itself as a premeditated and sadistic experimentation with violence including the acting out of a hunting fantasy and the dismemberment and storing of a corpse. These features of this murder were the ritualistic elements of the behaviour pattern of a dangerous psychopathic killer suffering violent psychoses and hatred of openly homosexual men. The perpetrator enjoyed his violent action and was later taped engaged in sadistic boasting about the death.

It was evident that he had also been involved in homosexual activities for either pleasure or profit. Police surveillance revealed that he had contacted male escort agencies with a homosexual clientele, in search of work to meet the costs of his regular illicit drug use. Remarkably, his claim that provocative and upsetting sexual advances by the deceased prompted his violence meant a jury took over four days to reach a verdict of murder. By contrast, the presiding judge quickly convicted the perpetrator to a life term and spoke of him as a disturbed sadistic criminal, who beyond his homophobic violence comprised a major threat to the wider community (*R v. Leonard*, NSWSC, 10 November 1997, Badgery-Parker J).

The crimes committed by such pathological perpetrators with homosexual contacts and homosexual interests may appear at first to be best explained by psychiatric analysis removed from the social and cultural sphere. Yet it has to be maintained that even in these cases, the perpetrators' efforts to shore up their own personal and public masculinity remain significant. Leonard obviously felt that his manhood was under threat from his homosexual activities and he took real actions to compensate for this in his daily life. A history of same-sex involvements that included sex work sat alongside his keen interest in acts of violence, dangerous weapons, hunting and powerful motorbikes. He pursued body-building with meticulous note-taking about the planned and resulting masculine bodily changes recorded in confiscated diaries. Part-time work in the security industry and a planned career as a private police officer also suggested the strong attractions of uniformed male authority.

This everyday concern with the protection of masculine identity was also evident in the consciousness of another equally disturbed and sadistic double-killer who at different times had sex with two homosexual men and then killed both of them; in one case with ritualistic elements of torture and interference with the corpse. This teenage perpetrator was very fearful of the discovery of his homosexuality in a conservative migrant family and an industrial working-class neighbourhood characterised by a culture of aggressive machismo and anti-homosexual hostility. Like Leonard, this youth was readily classified as a violent and sadistic psychopath without empathetic feeling for others, or any guilt and remorse about his actions. He also made a claim about an unwanted homosexual advance from his tortured victim that fell flat alongside evidence of desired and ongoing homosexual contacts, and was subsequently sentenced to a life term of imprisonment (*R v. Valera [Van Krevel]*, NSWSC, 21 December 2000, Studdert J).

The considerable social and psychological difficulties of those sex workers who are driven to enacting extreme violence and the sadistic perpetrators in these fatal incidents cannot be denied. However, as with other killings, it remains likely that these crimes were strongly linked to tensions in heterosexual male identity akin to those of many other men in contemporary societies. Therefore, it is also still the case that these crimes could be viewed against the cultural backdrop of male heterosexual anxiety about the homoerotic gaze and the attractive possibilities of widespread homosexual desire.

HOMOSEXUALITY AS MALE RISK

These tropes of masculinity and same-sex desire are not fixed in time but are shifting with some contradictory new ways of understanding male sexuality evident in cultural representations and explanations for both sexual activity and violence. In general, criminal courts have leaned towards classification of same-sex activity as a marker of pathology. It is unsurprising that this reflects the traditional overt essentialism of legal and medical discourse that has direct links back to nineteenth-century sexology and the intensified regulation of modern sexuality (Weeks, 1985). More interestingly, shifts in understanding and interpreting sexual desire now reflect some modification of crude essentialism though with some unintended and negative secondary effects.

Analysis of another trial suggests an apparent progression in expert and legal thinking by having no outward search for a final sexual label to categorise another perpetrator who either did, or intended to, engage in sexual activity with his eventual victim. In March 1999, BM, a 29-year-old gay man, replied to a message left by another male on the 'Hot Gossip Chat Line' that requested casual female sexual contacts. G, a 20-year-old man, later contacted BM and said that he was inexperienced but interested in trying sexual activity with other men. That night they met, talked for a while and then went to a secluded park to have sex. According to G, BM insisted on receptive oral sex and pulled him to the ground and a serious fight began. BM wrestled with G and allegedly chased him. Ultimately G strangled BM to protect himself from what he described as a violent sexual advance and because of his fears of anal rape. As he was 'freaking out' G then stole the victim's wallet, mobile phone and motor vehicle. G was later found guilty of manslaughter, with a maximum term of five years imprisonment imposed by a judge who suggested that G was 'having doubts or uncertainties about his sexuality' that motivated his behaviour (*R v. Graham*, NSWSC, 10 November 2000, Whealy J, p. 8).

During this trial there was ongoing argument between prosecution and defence counsel about whether or not G's actions were due to a pressing need for self-defence or merely provoked by the sexual advance from BM. It was also suggested by the prosecution (contesting self-defence) that this violence could have been due to his sudden repulsion at his own homosexual desire and activities, with this reflecting a lack of mental balance due to uncertain sexual identity. Throughout proceedings the forceful and actual nature of the alleged sexual advance was not challenged. The likelihood that the real origin of the dispute between G and BM was due to the manner in which oral sex could be engaged in was unexplored. Giving (and not receiving) oral sexual pleasure is the frequent fate of gay/homosexual men engaged in casual encounters with heterosexual or non-gay-identifying men. BM may have either refused to give oral sex at all or having done so he expected a form of reciprocation in a way that could have culminated in an escalating argument.

A much lesser role was given here for expert witnesses than in the trials discussed earlier, but final sentencing was influenced by a report from a psychologist finding a potential for reckless, dangerous and antisocial behaviour. Seeking excitement and stimulation by G were responses 'consistent with his reported history of chat line involvement and willingness to meet people through this medium' (p. 43). It is significant that in this more recent proceeding there was no outward inquiry about the perpetrator's 'true' sexuality, but an expert search for mental disturbance still occurred. The inquiry did not drive a process of sexual classification on the basis of evidence about actual sexual practice and desire. And this classification was left open at the end of the trial when G had been dumped by his regular girlfriend, either because of the fatal encounter with his victim or because he had been seeking casual sex with women and men via a telephone sexline. Impulsively seeking out same-sex pleasure was deemed as reflecting a serious character flaw that required professional treatment. Same-sex activity for pleasure here signalled disturbance rather than a muddled homosexual identity: A decade of HIV activism and popular media comment about the levels of mutual casual sexual activity engaged in by men had recast this behaviour as a troublesome form of masculine thrill-seeking. This typified the new problems that mark life in societies characterised by a heightened awareness and attraction to 'risk' particularly as a gendered phenomenon (Whitehead, 2005). In the sexual arena, this can even be equated with a hedonistic and unregulated male search for excitement or stimulation from either female or male partners.

This novel pattern of understanding the identity and motivations of some perpetrators appears to acknowledge evidence against essentialism and to acknowledge fluidity and widespread same-sex activity. This is distinct from the view of those killers and assailants (including sex workers and violent psychopaths) whose 'true' or pathological immersion into homo-sexual activity undermines the credibility of sexual advance claims. Yet an essentialist thread runs through all of these depictions and understandings of perpetrators and their violence. Perpetrators such as G are deemed to be essentially non-gay but irresponsible male 'risk-takers'. Thus, their own advance claims may be given more credence with a greater likelihood of a lenient sentence.

WHAT'S IN A NAME?

The analysis of these killings and related trials gives a different and more blurred view of male sexuality than this dominant sexual discourse would lead an observer to expect. Variations in practice, desire and iden-tity produce a complex and uneven relationship with dominant and mar-ginal forms of masculinity that inflect the interactions between offenders and victims and the self-understanding of individuals in either category. Involvements in same-sex practices have mixed implications for their mas-culinity. Although there is a real level of fluidity and frequent diversity of practice in men's sex lives, this desire and activity does not occur in a social vacuum. The force of the culturally dominant distinction between heterosexual and homosexual identities gives this hierarchy a reified and seemingly natural status; it has become the most important reference point for individuals who assign a key identity to themselves based on their sexual experiences.

Within this hierarchy heterosexual acts and desires have become the fundamental embodiment of a dominant ideal of empowered masculin-ity, while others may disallow a claim on this. Consequently, men have constructed and lost masculine identities around their same-sex activ-ity. In closed male institutions such as prisons, these have been elabo-rated around relations of domination, force and sexual submission which both alarm and puzzle outsiders (Heilpern, 1998; Sabo et al., 2001). The recent historical backdrop to this tension between fluid male desire and the social imperatives of heterosexual identity has been the wide and public rejection of patriarchal sex-dominance as a model of life by communities of gay men in liberal nations. A simple view of all 'gay-bashers' who engage in homosexual activities as being sexually repressed homosexuals is a popularised model of causality which itself reflects the pervasiveness of essentialist notions of sexuality. It is evident from an analysis of official records that a notably heightened anxiety about sexu-ality marks the consciousness of offenders who have engaged in publicly known same-sex activities, when this has serious implications for their masculine social identity.

Ultimately there is no clear answer as to what extent these various sex workers, sadistic 'psychopaths' and sexual adventurers can be referred to as homosexuals. It is evident that serious mental pathology can be manifested in fantasies and behaviours that feature homosexual desire and practice (Lewes, 1995). Framing these crimes through the simple homosexual panic discourse would lead to an insistence that this is always the case. Yet the panic discourse necessitates a denial of the fluidity of sexuality and perpetrator actions are only reduced to understanding through a presumed inherent homosexuality. This psychic and social proximity (Dollimore, 1991) of homosexual and heterosexual identities is a universal male conundrum which is much sharpened in the circumstances of young working-class men and marginal men who typify the patterns of 'protest masculinity' in a way that can foster aggression and violence. These various perpetrators are not closet homosexuals but are better understood as failing heterosexuals in a culture that generally collapses heterosexuality and masculinity together.

The expert drive to classify according to essentialist categories and the difficulties explaining same-sex activity are evident in the courtroom confusion about the killers' core identity. These discussions do not consider the ubiquity of same-sex desire among gay/homosexual and non-homosexually identified men and their homoerotic interaction. Same-sex activity is mostly interpreted as reflecting a serious mental disturbance, and perpetrator anxiety about the implications of this desire and sexual practice are further fed by the spread of sexually fixed views in contemporary Western culture and their privileged status in medical, psychiatric and legal discourses. This anxiety is closely tied to contradictory and shifting representations and discourses about what is entailed in being 'a man' as regards sexual practice and identity. The most disturbed of these killers are at the extreme end of the widespread male tension about gender and sexual identity, yet with their pathology and violence linked to social and cultural pressures towards male gender conformity and outward loyalty to the homosexual/heterosexual dyad.

8 Demons and Victims

ANTI-HOMOSEXUAL DEPICTIONS

Critics of criminal courts, the judiciary and various judicial findings in regard to the treatment of women and racial and ethnic minorities as victims, have become more vociferous in recent decades. Whether or not outcomes in the trials related to anti-homosexual violence measure up to liberal notions of equal justice is difficult to quickly gauge. Public opinion about the relative social worth of different victims and the personal merits of different perpetrators and their culpability for their actions is varied. In addition to this, there are important albeit fine differences between crimes which are at first glance identical.

The criminal justice system has recently appeared more ready to punish those planned and public homophobic attacks which come to light. This reflects growing community sensitivity about violence against gay men and lesbians, and the political mobilisation around this issue. Although the hearts and minds of police and legal authorities may be reluctant or even resentful about this shift, the actual authority of the courts and the judiciary would be potentially undermined by a wavering public response to obvious cases of hate attacks. In fact, it is likely that a type of micro 'legitimation crisis' (see Habermas, 1976) in this sphere will ensue once a matter of unequal access or treatment in an ostensibly liberal system of law is convincingly publicised. The law's role in firmly punishing and discouraging hate-related violence among divided social groups appears to be essential for social order and to ensure the smooth functioning of a pluralist democratic culture. The modern form of the political state was founded in a fundamental monopoly of legitimate violence (Weber, 1970). It is the state that will choose who is executed and by what hand. This vital feature of public political authority still persists in liberal democracies even though it may only occasionally display itself in a commitment to war and such controversial circumstances as the regular exercise of the death penalty (Sarat, 2005).

This official determination to punish killers is not so evident in cases where perpetrators allege that fatal violence was needed to repel, or was provoked by, a sexual advance from their victim. This different pattern begs explanation. As demonstrated earlier, the 'homosexual advance defence' has had an extended impact on the outcome of trials which some observers might view as straightforward cases of opportunistic homicide or the protection of masculinity with lethal violence. Perhaps because of the increased number of matters which are being prosecuted seriously or the lessons learnt among defence counsel from previous legal scores and victories, these are growing in frequency. A further variation on this pattern of partly exonerating male violence is the impact of evidence concerning previous occasions of alleged sexual assaults, often from years ago. Claims are made that a perpetrator has previously been subjected to sexual abuse by the deceased. Or the killing of a homosexual victim can even be rationalised by reference to previous paedophilic abuse by another person.

In practice, the tactical use of such claims has become interwoven with critical patterns of depiction of victims and perpetrators. The evolution of the essentialist sexual classification of individuals and groups and its durability are evident in the courtroom and media portrayals of victims and perpetrators in violent incidents. Criminal law has filtered its understanding of homosexuality through the motifs and language of 'addiction, seduction and contagion' (Stychin, 1995: 126), and even by a 'vampiric' model of homosexual desire (Dalton, 2006b).

Key media and trial portrayals still rely on negative stereotypes of gay/homosexual men as morally corrupt, unregulated and illegitimate victims who assumed a key role in setting off the crimes directed against them. A major part of the gay and lesbian activist discomfort about trials involving the homosexual advance defence is due to the difficulty of judging the truthfulness of allegations about sexual behaviour of the deceased. These are made about a person who is not alive to speak on their own behalf, yet such allegations often have a critical impact on the final result of a case. The airing of such claims may be more easily characterised by disparaging images of the deceased.

An emphasis on the sexual normality and male honour of the accused killer frequently runs alongside the negative pattern of representation of the characters and 'lifestyles' of victims in court. As social and legal attitudes towards homosexuality, even in the recent decades, are still contradictory and in a state of flux, this pattern can take the obvious form of stereotyping homosexual victims as sexually predatory and therefore in some way deserving of their fate.[1] Trials such as these provide striking instances of the importance of the reproduction of conventional sexual taxonomies in criminal justice system responses to anti-homosexual violence. They especially favour a minoritising discourse about homosexuality in depictions of victims and heterosexualised representations of perpetrators. The cultural privilege attached to this divide and the importance of legal discourse to regimes concerning sexual boundaries are evidenced in these responses to allegations of a sexual advance through what Sedgwick has called a 'doubly minoritizing taxonomy' of the hetero/homo divide (1994: 19). This both denigrates victims and locates the explanation for their killing in their own sexual desire. In a generally homophobic culture, this also falsely creates a sole responsibility for homophobic murders in the temperament of individual perpetrators. The final result is a simultaneous disavowal and part toleration of this form of violence.

A key example of this was found in one courtroom depiction of a victim killed by a male friend in a drinking bout. His killer was fully acquitted after he successfully claimed that a homosexual advance from the deceased could only be repelled by a fatal knife wound to the throat. News of this outcome added further fuel to gay and lesbian misgivings about the criminal justice system. Very different depictions of the perpetrator and victim were drawn throughout the hearing. It was evident that the most successful use of the homosexual advance defence relied on simple 'boy next door' depictions of the wholesome heterosexual masculinity of killers that might become violent in specific circumstances. A pattern of representation that seemed quite distinct from the literal use of the 'panic defence' was the frequent stressing of the heterosexual identity of the accused. In his unsworn statement delivered to the jury, the perpetrator emphasised:

> I want to make it clear, I am not a homosexual, I never have been homosexual and never had any homosexual experience of any kind. I have always had girlfriends. I hold no prejudices against homosexuals, I have friends who are gay, I treat them the same as anybody else because they are the same as anybody else. (*R v. Bonner*, NSWSC, 17 May 1995, Dowd J, p. 90)

This implied that normal and fundamentally heterosexual men carry a sympathetic or even chivalrous attitude to homosexuals. This contrasts with the irrational and violent response of a homophobic minority that will itself reflect repressed homosexual urges. An overlapping view was also raised by defence counsel who reminded the jury that the accused was a thorough heterosexual with no involvements in anti-homosexual violence at beats or near gay venues:

> you have seen this man, you have seen his father, you have heard the family friend from long ago who has known him. If one thing is crystal clear in this case it is Steven is not homosexual and you may think it is equally clear he is not a person who is a gay basher or a poofter basher. (*R v. Bonner*, 17 May 1995, Dowd J, p. 129)

> He does not have convictions for assaulting people, carrying concealed weapons, bashing up homosexuals at Green Park, or causing trouble in Oxford Street. (*R v. Bonner*, 18 May 1995, Dowd J, p. 145)

The defence further argued that the homosexual assault which triggered the fatal stabbing was an expression of the unsatisfied and uncontrollable sexual lusting of the deceased. This underlay his attitude to a physically handsome male friend. Accordingly, the defence further argued:

> let us accept that Tom was indeed homosexual with the propensity with which that sexual orientation entails. What are the propensities?. . . . Clearly [these are] to feel towards male persons, because they are homosexuals I am talking about, feelings of love and sexual desire which non-homosexual men and women feel towards each other; which men and women together desire, touching, holding hands, kissing, by sleeping together and indeed by having sexual intercourse. (*R v. Bonner*, 18 May 1995, Dowd J, p. 140)

This passage gives the outward appearance of making a fair and equal comparison of heterosexual and homosexual passion. But the rest of the address hints that a lack of self-restraint and sexual excess is an inherent element and distinctive marker of this 'propensity':

> Years ago when the subject of homosexual behaviour was still—to use the vernacular—in the closet, many people in the community may have been uncertain about male sexuality and may have been totally ignorant of what it meant to be a homosexual person. But we now live in a time when people are more educated about these matters and for many years you may have seen in Sydney each year . . . [the] gay Mardi Gras that is seen by thousands of people, the pilots of which you see on the television, and as jurors you bring into the jury box your knowledge of these matters and indeed you are aware of that phenomenon, and anyone who has ever seen the gay Mardi Gras would be in no doubt what the conduct of the participants says in terms of the attitude of gay men towards homosexuality. (*R v. Bonner*, 18 May 1995, Dowd J, p. 140)

The pretended expertise and superficial tolerance of this passage was a cogent example of the 'interpellation' of its intended audience. This term refers to a process whereby individuals come to recognise themselves in specific ways that may be unknowingly distorted when they are addressed by authoritative figures or sources (Althusser, 1971). Jurors were constructed as people familiar with urban sexual diversity, notably the Sydney Gay and Lesbian Mardi Gras. The sting in this was the focus on public sexual 'conduct' (a word with legal associations of public order crime) that in all likelihood fitted with ignorant understandings of gay and homosexual men as hedonistic and corrupted by overriding sexual desires. This would have served to devalue the perceived social worth of the deceased in the eyes of the jurors. This depiction of the victim and the group of men he belonged to by virtue of a shared desire was then also coupled with an account of the killer's physical appearance. This was deemed to be irresistible to any gay or homosexual man:

> At the time of the incident Steven was sporting a beard. You can see in some of those photographs he looks—from the perspective of a young lady or a homosexual man—he is fetching, an attractive young fellow. And I submit to you, you would find it entirely credible that the scenario of Tom's behaviour, which I have outlined to you, could be explained in simple and basic terms of a person with homosexual inclinations. (*R v. Bonner*, 18 May 1995, Dowd J, p. 142)

THE DANGEROUS 'NON-GAY'

This and similar cases have reflected how obvious stereotyping of perpetrators and victims may permeate the legal proceedings that deal with violence. Yet the most surprising contemporary outcome in these depictions and understandings of homophobia and sexual prejudice is a discursive shift that reflects contemporary public education, consciousness and debate about HIV and generalised same-sex desire. This shift also reflects some of the new citizenship status of gay men and lesbians. It was noted in the previous chapter that this has occurred as courts have accepted the possibility of same-sex activity by perpetrators and reconfigured it as a form of irresponsible male risk. This is done in ways that have appeared to eschew sexual essentialism but actually have emphasised a far-reaching cultural gulf between heterosexuals and homosexuals.

As a consequence of the more frequent media and public depictions of homosexuality in liberal nations that include a mix of both deviant and less threatening imagery, it is now marginal sexualities outside of the heterosexual/homosexual dyad that are viewed as particularly disturbing. This means victims who cannot be readily classified with any fixed identity are now more effectively demonised in criminal trials and media accounts. A further example of a form of minoritising discourse about human sexuality is the more legitimate victimhood that may now be accorded to those deceased who are assumed to have had an unambiguous and homogenised 'gay' cultural identity. Of course, this is greatly ironic in view of the historical oppression of homosexuals in the criminal law. With far more subtlety than obvious anti-gay stereotyping, some victims have been depicted as marginal and even dangerous outsiders to newly respectable notions of gay, lesbian or queer identity. A more complex process of devaluation that contrasts individual sexual oddity with a publicly known and partly tolerated gay culture may unfold. Victims with more fluid or mysterious and unknown sexualities and identities are then readily stigmatised in courtroom discourse (George, 2005).

A frequent aspect of this has been the understanding of 'non-gay' victims of anti-homosexual violence as probable paedophiles. A portrayal of a victim as both sexually predatory, non-gay and having likely paedophiliac desires characterised the trial of the killer of Kevin Marsh (see Chapter 6). Despite the gravity of the crime, press reports quickly looked for the lighter side of the death of the eccentric 'bachelor recluse' ('Killed by a gnome', *Sydney Morning Herald*, 2 July 1993). At the hearing, a court accepted the allegation of a forceful homosexual assault by the deceased who had an 'adverse reputation' in his local community. This relied on snippets of evidence given by a variety of witnesses about his past behaviour and sexual leanings. For example, two men related how six or seven years prior to the killing, they and another teenage male friend visited 'old Kev' to drink some of his homemade beer. When they did this,

> he brought out these porno books and because we were only young blokes we grabbed them and started having a look and that's when he started talking about masturbation. . . . (*R v. T*, 11 April 1994, p. 105)

Another witness told the court that when he was a homeless teenager, Marsh had allowed him to reside in his flat. While sleeping on the lounge he was allegedly woken one night to find 'Mr. Marsh touching my body and masturbating over my face' (11 April 1994, p. 106). These accounts would have seemed very bothersome to the court. They touched on social and legal anxieties about the heightened and fluid sexual desire of adolescent males that is believed to render them most vulnerable to sexual corruption. But the youth who had stayed with Marsh had no trouble packing up and leaving the day *after* the alleged advance. Similarly, the two friends easily dismissed Marsh's antics and felt unthreatened by them. They 'just laughed at him and said, "don't be silly" and walked out' and also visited a few times later as 'he cooked really nice chips and good pizza' (11 April 1994, p. 103).

These statements certainly depicted Marsh as a sexual nuisance. Other evidence may have seemed more disturbing as it suggested that the deceased was driven by diffuse and dangerous sexual aims. This included further suggestions of a preoccupation with pornography. In the general male population, this is not uncommon. Yet the alleged subject matter of the material would have been construed as quite unsettling. A woman secretary at a local sports club related how the deceased had once requested to photocopy pages from a book that catered to an unusually broad range of sexual tastes including anal intercourse (11 April 1994, p. 112). The picture of sexual depravity which this sketched also seemed to fit with the courtroom reference to how, after the death, police found 'numerous sex magazines of a hetero and a homosexual nature' in the victim's flat (7 April 1994, p. 72). The earlier suspicions about paedophilia also overlapped with a final courtroom anecdote. The court heard from a neighbour who had an argument with Marsh about the behaviour of her oldest son. The encounter reached the stage where the victim unsettled the woman by suggesting that he might 'fuck him up the arse' (11 April 1994, p. 109).

If read together, these accounts suggested that the victim had a keen interest in erotica and a surprisingly strong libido for his age and he was less discreet about sexual matters than members of the suburban community he lived in could cope with. The evidence also suggested that he had in the past made unwanted advances on other males. However, the direct relevance of this material to the killing, the alleged violent sexual attack and the issue of the perpetrator's guilt were not obvious. The deceased did not make persistent and forceful sexual advances on those men who interested him. He was no trouble to the young men who voiced their lack of interest.

The courtroom portrayal of a sexual pest appeared to corroborate some of the story about the killing given by the accused, though this was centrally focused more around establishing an entire negative sexuality more than any pattern of annoying behaviour. The negative sketch went far beyond suggesting that he had an interest in younger partners. The unclassifiable nature of his pornography, his position in a suburban community as a social outsider and his alleged remarks concerning the neighbour's boy (if taken literally rather than as a very effective bit of needling in a heated argument) were all construed as meaning that he was a likely paedophile. He therefore occupied a place on the lowest moral rung on a sexual hierarchy where the openly homosexual were only very recently and tentatively promoted to a higher level.

The pathologising discourse of the 'non-gay' and even the 'non-homosexual' victim has also been evident in cases involving men with histories of public sexual cruising and activity with heterosexually identified men. In a similar fashion in the trial of the killer of Maurice McCarty, details about the victim's regular casual sex encounters with a range of different men and his ostensible isolation from the mainstream gay and lesbian subculture were raised in a way that served to pathologise him as a sexual predator. A key element of this process was the impact of detailed statements about the victim's sexual habits. These were made by an air steward who was a flatmate and former lover of the deceased, during early police investigations. In the trial of the accused these were entered into evidence. In the first of these F stated:

> I have known Maurice McCarty for about 22 years . . . in fact I had a relationship with Maurice from 1971 until 1978. . . . Maurice was a homosexual who I would describe as a person not openly involved in the 'gay' scene. By that I mean he would never frequent the bars, nor would he dress or act in a 'gay' manner. In fact if [you] weren't aware of his homosexuality you wouldn't know it. From what I know of Maurice's habits he would frequent places like the 'Pleasure Chest' at Kings Cross or the cinema in Goulburn Street [the scene of meeting with his

killer] . . . in my opinion Maurice would get satisfaction from going to places like that. They are normally frequented by so-called 'straights', that is males who considered themselves to be heterosexuals, but who go there knowing that they will get satisfaction from a male, as no women ever go there.

Maurice was into what I would call anonymous sex, that is once the act was over both parties could go their separate ways and never see each other again. Maurice was known to attend various public toilets. . . . To my knowledge Maurice didn't have a lasting relationship. . . . I believe that you can't find a lasting relationship frequenting the places Maurice did. During the time he stayed with me he never brought anyone home. . . . Maurice did mention to me that he liked a young guy that works at the pizza shop. . . . Maurice and the friend of the guy from the pizza shop had a couple of beers with the security guard who works on the building site opposite. . . . I know Maurice had casual sex with this person once . . . his name is S . . . and he is married and his wife has just had a baby. (Police statement, 8 April 1991)

F made another statement a few days later which related more information about the victim's sexual partners and practices. One day, he had approached a younger man on the street and took him to a secluded part of a building site to have casual sex (police statement, 10 April 1991). Provision of this sort of information and comment to police might strike some as a disloyal act from a close friend. However, other records indicate that this is not uncommon in the investigation of such killings. F provided these statements in good faith to assist detection of a perpetrator. He also made his own moral distinction between different sorts of homosexual activity that reflect a new respectability for men seeking committed and monogamous relationships in an open gay subculture.

Two different views of the deceased could be drawn from this sketch. From a sexually liberal perspective, he engaged in sexual cruising in a responsible way. He did not take undue risks with regard to violence by leaving his phone number on public display in any beat or usually take strangers home. In these situations of casual sex he did not engage in behaviour which carried the highest risk of HIV infection, preferring oral sex instead. Given his apparent success with cruising considerably younger and also straight-identified partners, it seems likely that he was quite skilled in the latter practice. In a more negative light, these revelations suggested that he was a regular user of beats for anonymous public sex. This is an activity that has generally breached laws regarding public decency and is often even stigmatised in gay male circles.

Sex with men who regard themselves as heterosexual is also an activity that produces mixed responses among gay men. To some it is a mild source of pride due to its apparent subversive qualities. It also reflects the ongoing status of many heterosexual males as hegemonically masculine and therefore highly desired objects (Bersani, 1988). To others, this is a waste of time that will never produce the more valued 'lasting relationship' of the sort that F favoured. General observers might even have regarded this sexual behaviour as alarming in view of the political and medical imperative about disease containment within the gay male community which has underlain much recent discourse about HIV in Western nations. At least from the viewpoint of many heterosexuals, it would have been directly unsettling that the victim appeared to have initiated this sort of activity by taking advantage of sexual frustration and a lack of restraint among men.

Beyond his representation as being promiscuous, immoral and predatory, a further stage in the negative depiction of this victim was his implausible construction in trial evidence as a 'non-gay' or 'non-homosexual'. The springboard for this may have been a statement by a second flatmate. W admitted that he barely knew McCarty, but recalled a conversation in which 'he said words to the effect that he didn't go to gay bars, or places where homosexuals usually went looking for sexual partners'; W concluded 'I do not know if "M" is a homosexual man' (police statement, 10 April 1991). It may have been this subcultural view of both gay and homosexual identity, and the curious possibility of identifying a person's sexuality according to where they meet their partners, which suggested a creative courtroom approach for defence counsel.

An openly gay male couple who were neighbours of the deceased were called to give testimony. They described how they heard the sounds of a fight, a door slamming and a call for help on the night of the killing. One of these men, D, was asked questions which gave him the impromptu status of an expert witness on men's sexual habits and venues. In response to defence questioning, D assured the court that he was knowledgeable about gay venues in Sydney, especially the better-known ones on Oxford Street. He knew of the Eros theatre where the victim and accused first met and also knew 'of gay people that have gone there' but stated that 'I would just class it as a sex shop' (*R v. McKinnon*, NSWSC, 15–24 November 1993, Studdert J, p. 62). He did not recall that the outside advertising of the Eros included a naked woman's figure but when finally pressed to ascribe a sexual label to the building itself, he agreed that it was 'a heterosexual establishment' (*R v. McKinnon*, 16 November 1993, pp. 62, 61).

Another witness with a greater knowledge of the Eros and who gave a human face to its clientele was a man who knew McCarty and greeted him as a fellow regular at the venue. S visited the cinema on the night of the killing and saw the deceased parked outside. He described this place as being a typical sex-on-premises venue:

I think it is—how would I classify that—I think it is a place where they have cubicles where people go and watch movies, porno movies, and they also have a theatre, a gay theatre, on the second floor. (*R v. McKinnon*, 16 November 1993, p. 73)

He eventually agreed to the defence proposition that 'gay men who do not particularly want to mix in openly gay scenes . . . might go to the Eros' (*R v. McKinnon*, 16 November 1993, p. 76). But he also observed that the Eros was advertised in gay papers, and added that 'generally whenever people go to those sex shops there is always something gay going on anyway' (*R v. McKinnon*, 16 November 1993, p. 76).

Defence questioning had a second line of purpose in addition to suggesting the marginality of the victim in the gay subculture. In contradiction to having elicited from D a view that the theatre was really 'a heterosexual establishment', the defence asked S if a visitor might enter the Eros without knowing the 'gay connotation' of the premises. He responded with apparent honesty:

> I don't know. I think if somebody walks by and does not know what goes on, and probably goes up, they might not know what it is. I don't think it is quite open as such like Newtown or Oxford Street, probably yes. (*R v. McKinnon*, 16 November 1993, p. 75)

These questions about hypothetical and accidental visits to the Eros by sexually aroused males did not arise from a general concern for protecting the sensibilities of heterosexual men. They appeared to have been necessary to explain away any suspicion that the accused killer was inside a venue which he knew or realised had a significant homosexual clientele that might include a likely victim for a planned assault and robbery. If a juror thought the accused had really been inside the theatre, they might then have believed this was a mistake reflecting his naïveté or enticement by the very erotic image of a naked woman on the outside advertising.

Most importantly, this courtroom discussion played on the uncertainty about the identity of the clients of the sex-cinema. To the extent that it was a 'heterosexual establishment' the deceased was present as a sexual misfit. In as much as it had a 'gay connotation' the accused did not consciously belong in or near it. The image of the venue that was presented to the court was of a place that attracted men who were non-gay and seeking impersonal sex from others. This was contradicted by the facts that the gay witness had gay friends who went there, the venue advertised in the gay men's press and the possibility that gay friendships might emerge among clients like S and McCarty. Depiction of the victim as a non-gay and non-homosexual also sat oddly with alleged or admitted references by the accused and his friends to the 'gay killing', having 'rolled a fag' and the disposal of the stolen 'fag's car' (Tomsen, 2002: 62).

Sexual identities are not socially fixed categories. Yet on reflection, there was a surreal quality to this process of casting doubt on the sexual identity of a known homosexual professional ballet employee with marginal but obvious links to a gay male lifestyle. The victim resided with a male ex-lover and a third gay man in a gay area of inner Sydney from where openly gay neighbours travelled to the witness box for the trial of his killer. The unlikely success of this 'non-gay' or 'non-homosexual' depiction relied heavily on the subjectivism of a cultural understanding of contemporary sexual categories. A pencil sketch of the accused as utterly naïve about the sexualised elements of following a male stranger home from a sex-cinema and the claim of an unwanted advance, were accepted by the court. The killer was fully acquitted of any culpability for a brutal slaying in the victim's home.

MORAL HIERARCHIES AND IDENTITIES

In a well-known piece of writing, Rubin (1993) argued that modern history has been characterised by a series of 'sex panics', such as the late 1800s campaign over prostitution and the 1950s scare about homosexuality coinciding with McCarthyism and the anti-Communist drive in the United States. A later panic dates from the 1980s. This was said to be a generalised panic over forms of 'deviant' sexuality that included concerns about HIV/AIDS, same-sex rights, public sex education, pornography and intergenerational sex. It resulted in the stigmatising, vilifying and criminalising of target groups by conservative lobby groups, media, politicians and criminal justice officials. In the United States these issues had become a field of much conflict about sex and sexual morality. This was especially so with the neoconservative fundamentalist backlash that aimed to reimpose traditional ideas about appropriate gender patterns and sexual practices (see also Herman, 1997).

More broadly, these panics also reflected the ongoing 'sex negativity' of the Western view of sex. This regards sex as danger, sin or pathology, is hostile to sexual variation and places great weight on small differences in desire or behaviour to produce different sexual classes with wide implications for social, medical and legal responses (Rubin, 1993). An imaginary line between good and bad sex has been drawn and enforced by powerful groups and moral entrepreneurs, and often results in repressive use of 'sex law'. As a result of this line a narrow range of sexual acts and identities are privileged and many others are stigmatised:

> Most of the discourses on sex, be they religious, psychiatric, popular, or political, delimit a very small portion of human sexual capacity as sanctifiable, safe, healthy, mature, legal, or politically correct. The 'line' distinguishes these from all other erotic behaviors, which are understood to be the work of the devil, dangerous, psychopathological, infantile, or politically reprehensible. Arguments are then conducted over 'where to draw the line' and to determine what other activities, if any, may be permitted to cross over into acceptability. All of these

models assume a domino theory of sexual peril. The line appears to stand between sexual order and chaos. It expresses the fear that if anything is permitted to cross this erotic DMZ, the barrier against scary sex will crumble and something unspeakable will skitter across. (Rubin, 1993: 14)

In the 1980s and 1990s some new respectability was won by unmarried but committed heterosexual and homosexual couples in liberal democratic systems. But other categories still featured low down in the moral order. This reinforced a dominant sexual hierarchy and criticisms of 'sexual minorities' such as unattached or promiscuous homosexuals, transsexuals, bisexuals, fetishists and sex workers.

These decades also witnessed splits between feminists over sexuality, particularly in relation to sex work, erotica and SM/BD as forms of sexual practice (Segal & McIntosh, 1992; Chancer, 1993). The early feminist optimism about sexuality had reflected a view that liberated women could enjoy sexuality on an equal footing with men (Segal, 1994). This was displaced by a sense of pessimism about sexual equality and a view that sexuality (particularly heterosexuality) was typically an arena of exploitation and even closely linked with violence against women. In the so-called 'sex wars', radicals disrupted sanctified views about women's sexuality as naturally founded in emotional care and selflessness (SAMOIS, 1982; Vance, 1989a). For Rubin and her allies, 'sex-negative' feminism merely reinforced the impact of these panics. Conservatives in the contemporary United States had learnt to appropriate the puritanical elements of feminism—such as respect and esteem for sexually restrained women—into their own position. This merely reinforced a dominant sexual hierarchy and attacks on sexual minorities.

The unfolding of these conflicts spread well beyond American borders and was closely watched by many gay men and directly involved many lesbians as combatants and commentators (Jackson & Scott, 1996; Matthews, 1997). A much smaller amount of gay male writing openly incorporates the puritanical feminist stance in relation to such matters as pornography and graphic depictions of casual and impersonal sex between gay and apparently 'straight' men (see Kendall, 2002). Yet a covert and modified version of sexual moralism is not uncommon among gay men who disapprove of homosexual practices other than their own. It is also evident from the courtroom depictions and evidence discussed earlier that both these social panics and activist debates about sexuality have impacted on legal discourse and the views that gay men and lesbians hold about themselves and others. Inside gay and lesbian communities, people may be regarded as holding inferior moral status by virtue of regular engagements in disreputable sexual activities that could include promiscuous, public, or intergenerational sex and regular homo/hetero same-sex forms of contact.

There can be no doubt that in a range of jurisdictions there has been a contemporary shift in the status of male homosexuals from criminal deviants to legal subjects whose sexual identity accords rights of citizenship that include a legitimate claim on victimhood from violence. This has been more evident in improved relations with police than elsewhere in the legal system. And this development may have resulted in a further pressure for change as an increased number of accused killers have been arrested and tried for their crimes. The mixed outcomes of these trials suggest that the courts have become more responsive to the demands of a newly mobilised pressure group demanding equality in the courts. However, the traditional masculinism of the law which is inscribed in legal doctrines regarding male violence has still meant dubious outcomes among the substantial number of cases in which perpetrators allege a sexual advance by a homosexual victim.

It is these cases which are more often marked by the negative depictions of the deceased and their sexual histories that run in tandem with sanitised accounts of the actions and character of perpetrators. This can take the more expected form of reinforcing essentialist views of sexuality and negative stereotypes of homosexual men as being without sexual restraint. The trials discussed earlier indicate that a new pattern of negative depiction of victims reflected heightened concerns and new discourses about other sexual groupings such as paedophiles. Consequently, the resulting focus on the 'dangerous' sexuality of some deceased victims can even sometimes seem like near appropriations of the notions of fluidity that derive from a constructionist view of human sexuality, though with a sense of great dread rather than tolerance about it.

The growing number of cases in which accused killers sought to vindicate fatal attacks by suggesting that the victim was a probable paedophile reflected a new panic over this sexual identity.[2] The word 'paedophile' has passed from sexology and psychological discourse into the media and popular language and is now known to, and invoked by, a broad range of people. In fact, this has become both a floating signifier of moral degeneracy and a form of cheap abuse directed at targets that include an expanding number of homicide victims. The extended demonisation of this category with an alien and monstrous nature accorded to its entire membership has alleviated some of the social anxiety that resulted from awareness of high levels of sexual abuse of children in respectable family contexts. It is apparent that this also mirrored widespread levels of sexual guilt in the male population who engaged in a shifting pattern of same-sex activities, especially while teenagers and young men. The distancing from same-sex partners that the frayed stereotyping of homosexual men as weak and effeminate had formerly enacted was now less significant than the protection of heterosexual identity with an exaggerated fear of paedophile molestation as a key driver of same-sex experimentation.

Gay and lesbian activism and successful claims on citizen rights have also inadvertently driven these shifts. The pattern of negative depiction of the victims in some of these trials exemplified the lowered status that had resulted from ascribing an outsider label in relation to the mainstream urban gay and lesbian subculture that developed in cities like Sydney since the 1970s. This was a historically remarkable phenomenon if it is considered that only a few decades earlier a thorough emphasis on the homosexuality and gay community links of a victim would have been deemed to be the most powerful negative sketch that could be drawn. It is also likely that the portrayal of McCarty and his sex life as 'non-gay' may even have reflected a growing self-consciousness in the criminal courts about the new and critical external scrutiny of such trials by the gay and lesbian media and community. The assertion of respectable homosexual citizenship resulted in a historical irony that might dismay some older gay men and lesbians. It certain contexts, it had became easier to enact an injustice on a 'non-gay' victim.

The depiction of victims as culturally and sexually marginal potentially undermined a wider interest in these trials and any political agency taken on behalf of victims. Worst of all, it might also have led some observers into a glib belief that these victims were so culturally and morally dissimilar from homosexual or gay men that these attacks were not in reality 'anti-homosexual' and that any activist concerns about police investigations and trial outcomes in such cases were misplaced.

VICTIMS, MOBILISATION AND GOVERNMENTALITY

This moral element of gay and lesbian gains in social and political status converged with the persistent though evolving influence of sexual essentialism in social-movement discourse about violence, victims and the necessary measures to be taken to avoid attacks. This was particularly so with campaigns that emphasised a shared victimhood and the fundamental importance of effective 'risk management' to the actual identity of urban gay men and lesbians.

In and since the 1990s, violence and safety issues have drawn a much wider level of interest and sympathy, in the general and specific media. Locally, safety became a major theme in gay and lesbian press items running in tandem with a conscious creation of a united readership. A survey of such key local print media as the *Sydney Star Observer*, *Capital Q* and *Lesbians on the Loose* revealed the extent to which issues of safety and violence had taken prominence in that decade (see George, 2005). The experience and fear of violence and harassment became key discursive elements of the affirmation of a collective identity and a shared sense of community. The same issues were a key means of petitioning for state recognition, influence and resources and had a new importance among previously uninterested politicians, police officials, researchers and bureaucrats, and they put activist concerns and achievements in a national spotlight.

Much of this was real change and not a merely cosmetic involvement in political decision making. This local shift also consolidated the new political clout of urban gay men and lesbians. In the 1990s this came mostly through the structure and activities of the Lesbian and Gay Anti-Violence

Project. This was a pivotal organisation that significantly focused on victim advocacy (rather than direct support), sponsored research on violence, engaged in law reform lobbying and also generated innovative public education campaigns. The anti-violence issue and its rhetoric, strategies and symbolism have reflected obvious American borrowings. But a high level of integration at official levels followed on from the historically unfolding pattern of HIV/AIDS policy in Australia (see Ballard, 1992). In the 1990s, it could also be compared to the Social Democratic scenarios of the Netherlands where police had an early involvement in anti-violence measures and research in the 1980s, or to the United Kingdom where violence and safety became a critical means of suddenly shifting away from a history of overwhelmingly hostile relations between homosexuals and police (Moran et al., 2004).

In these shifts, inner-city gay men and lesbians were given a far more legitimate group status in policing and legal matters. Having pushed reforms enacting anti-vilification laws and anti-violence monitoring, lobby groups voiced concerns regarding the general rights of crime victims and accused offenders. Local government bodies began to consult with activists over aspects of street planning and design and the use of public space, sometimes through their own specific gay and lesbian liaison staff. The greatly expanded size of the openly gay and lesbian population since the 1980s, a more obvious commercial subculture and an increasingly mainstream popularity and tourist-dollar value of gay and lesbian public events, were all elements of this change. The intricate organisation of the Mardi Gras parade and its related dance parties became closely watched and emulated models of successful event management achieved by an elaborate process of police–community consultation and joint planning. At the same time, police actions directed at men cruising for public sex outside the confines of the inner city persisted and combined with a use of new technologies of surveillance and changes to the design of public space, by local councils, businesses and transport authorities (Swivel, 1991; Tomsen, 1993; Dowsett, 1996a).

These shifts in the formal relationship that gay men and lesbians had to legal and official bodies could be partly understood in old Left terms as an exemplary case of the state incorporation of dissent and the qualified tolerance that can be attained within the framework of liberal discourses of equality and justice. Moving beyond the consideration of such institutional effects alone, the issue of safety and violence also had a deeper significance that could be understood in relation to changes around cultural identity. Foucault's legacy now includes scholars interested in patterns of 'governmentality' and the often veiled exercising and internalisation of power in both expert (medical, psychiatric and legal) and liberatory understandings of human identity which have prevailed in the modern West (see Rose, 1999). Sexual categories and in particular the importance of the contemporary homo/hetero divide, which gay and lesbian politics presupposes, comprise key elements of these processes. The relevance of these notions of governance and theorising about the implications of the definition and management of risk in the control of groups and populations in contemporary societies has been most obvious in the HIV/AIDS example.

In some locations AIDS strategies have been a historically remarkable instance of collective education, community building and mobilisation, especially evident in gay male enclaves in Greenwich Village, San Francisco and inner Sydney. This has been much concerned about inculcating a capacity for individuals (particularly sexually active gay and bisexual men) to regulate their own desire and assume responsibility for avoiding sexual practices that are designated as 'unsafe' or 'high risk'. With this, an urbanised gay identity has been vitally reconfigured to include elements of self-discipline and risk control. Gay men and lesbians increasingly have learnt about safety strategies, violence avoidance and their enhanced vulnerability from undisciplined drinking and drug use.

Critiques of the impact of this reconfigured gay male citizenship in the HIV field have suggested that the ubiquitous pressure to self-regulate was always resisted by some gay and bisexual men who experience an instructive safe-sex regime as the very opposite of the free expression of sexual desire (Bartos, 1996). The alleged new spread of 'bare-backing' and the official concerns about this signalled this opposition between self-regulation and pleasurable risk-taking. HIV activists and organisations internationally resisted the stigmatising of specific infected groups including gay men, sex workers and IV drug users as morally blameworthy victims of the epidemic. Yet a dubious distinction between good and bad victims may have been implied in discourse about violence and resulted from the stress on self-responsibility and management of personal risks that characterised community campaigns against 'homophobic' violence.

British scholars have produced important Foucauldian critiques of gay and lesbian safety campaigns in the United Kingdom (Stanko & Curry, 1997; Moran et al., 2004). This research, and the parallel with HIV politics and prevention, suggests a pattern of self-regulation in the field of violence that has drawn little comment, though it applied even more broadly throughout the 'homosexual community'. In fact, it was likely that the real significance of the violence issue in reconstructing notions of identity concerned its more plausible inclusion of lesbians and many less sexually active gay and bisexual men into the fears and warnings that characterised it. Whereas AIDS/HIV prevention and advocacy or lobbying against anti-sodomy and public indecency laws have been more pressing to the interests of homosexual men in Western nations, in the 1990s the issue of violence appeared to be valued by activists for its more obvious implication of a shared interest between lesbians and gay men.

An apparently self-defined and autonomous understanding of chic gay and lesbian identities as safe from violence was the intended outcome of certain activist and specific police campaigns. For example, well-publicised posters and press materials about the threat of violence followed on the

Figure 8.1 'Violence can happen. Just be aware'. ACON Anti-Violence Project Poster 1995. Photography: C. Moore Hardy, Design: DesignNation, Words: Greg Logan.

'real scenarios—real choices' style of the safe-sex advertisements pioneered among Sydney's gay men in the 1980s. These showed an attractive gym-pumped gay man choosing to avoid danger by crossing a city street (Figure 8.1), and an attractive and partnered young lesbian evading menacing thugs on a railway station with her decision to take a taxi (Figure 8.2).

Figure 8.2 'Violence can happen. Just be aware'. ACON Anti-Violence Project Poster 1995. Photography: C. Moore Hardy, Design: DesignNation, Words: Greg Logan.

In another, a man in a city gay bar wisely ignores the blunt over-tures of the 'rough trade' he suspected was a mercenary criminal trying to victimise him (Figure 8.3). The fair hair and masculine square jaw were recognisably attractive to the intended audience of gay men. The

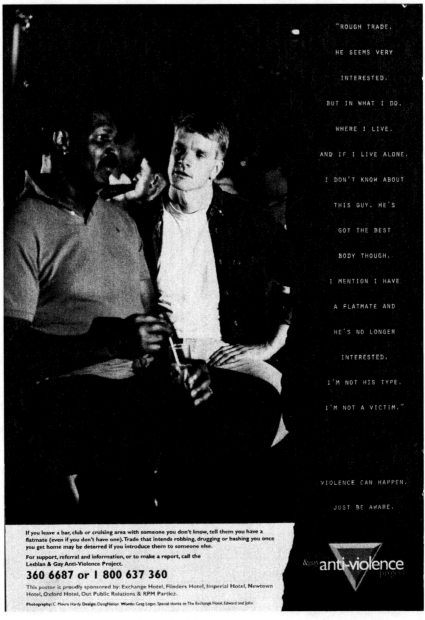

"ROUGH TRADE.

HE SEEMS VERY

INTERESTED.

BUT IN WHAT I DO.

WHERE I LIVE.

AND IF I LIVE ALONE.

I DON'T KNOW ABOUT

THIS GUY. HE'S

GOT THE BEST

BODY THOUGH.

I MENTION I HAVE

A FLATMATE AND

HE'S NO LONGER

INTERESTED.

I'M NOT HIS TYPE.

I'M NOT A VICTIM."

VIOLENCE CAN HAPPEN.

JUST BE AWARE.

If you leave a bar, club or cruising area with someone you don't know, tell them you have a flatmate (even if you don't have one). Trade that intends robbing, drugging or bashing you once you get home may be deterred if you introduce them to someone else.

For support, referral and information, or to make a report, call the Lesbian & Gay Anti-Violence Project.

360 6687 or 1 800 637 360

This poster is proudly sponsored by: Exchange Hotel, Flinders Hotel, Imperial Hotel, Newtown Hotel, Oxford Hotel, Out Public Relations & RPM Partiez.

Photography: C. Moore Hardy. Design: DesignNation. Words: Greg Logan. Special thanks to The Exchange Hotel, Edward and John.

&gay anti-violence project

Figure 8.3 'Violence can happen. Just be aware'. ACON Anti-Violence Project Poster 1995. Photography: C. Moore Hardy, Design: DesignNation, Words: Greg Logan.

seductive 'straightness' and criminality of the would-be perpetrator were also visually signalled by an appearance and attire associated with the disrespectable working class: a heavy build, well-worn jeans and denim shirt. The implicit message was about the danger of desire that selects an

Figure 8.4 'Violence can happen. Just be aware'. ACON Anti-Violence Project Poster 1995. Photography: C. Moore Hardy, Design: DesignNation, Words: Greg Logan.

inappropriate partner. Considerable didacticism lurked behind this offer of smart choices about safety, yet this was not always delivered in a wholly effective way and produced unexpected resistance from the intended audience. The least successful poster in this series specifically concerned violence against transsexual/transgendered people. It drew transsexual/transgender community ire as a poster supposedly representing the issue of violence against this whole group as it offered an unflattering and clumsy portrayal of a pale and exhausted transsexual complaining about customer harassment while engaged in sex work in a darkened street (Figure 8.4).

Gay and lesbian media accounts of many violent incidents from this key period were also often essentialist in their imagery and pattern of framing this issue. These relied on the dichotomy between homosexual/victims and heterosexual/assailants through reports in which violence was principally interpreted as the acts of hateful homophobes. This opposition further induced a collective fear of physical danger and bigotry. Assailants who engaged in same-sex activity generally threatened this dichotomy, and in gay and lesbian media they were often viewed as even more monstrous and pathological than other perpetrators.

The seemingly equal relevance of concerns about violence and safety to all who identify as non-heterosexual coincided with a period of renewed debates about the nature and meaning of the local gay and lesbian communities. In various nations, the expansion and consolidation of the inner-city culture of more privileged upwardly mobile homosexuals, and an uneven tendency towards the desexualisation of identity in the era of HIV/AIDS and moral backlash, appeared to have further fragmented gays and lesbians on the basis of class, race, ethnicity and also by region. Subsequent divisions and misgivings over the issues of leadership, representation and identity were at the heart of debates over the reality or meaning of any 'community' and the critiques of the processes of mainstream homosexual politics in the 1990s.

A growing awareness of the gap between sexual behaviour and sexual identity meant a reconfiguring of gay and lesbian status built around a shared form of urban cultural identity rather than sexual activity. The surprising evolution of the meaning of 'queer' from an inclusive vision of a diverse sexual community, to a subcultural label for a distinctively consumerist urban homosexual lifestyle, seemed to encapsulate these issues rather than offer an analytical tool to decipher them (Hennessy, 1995). Evidence about shared actual or potential victimisation and fear of violence proved to be ideologically inviting and symbolically important in a period of uncertainty about what homosexual identity actually comprised in an erotic, cultural or political sense, and the multiple divisions within communities that are fractured by divisions of locality, social class, health status, race, ethnicity and age, as well as gender (Jackson & Sullivan, 1999b).

It is evident that the issues of safety, violence and 'homophobia' became key discursive elements of the affirmation of a collective identity and a shared sense of community. It is most likely that the campaigns and publicity had success by a reduction in the level of opportunities for victimisation. Nevertheless, they also sparked intended and unintended secondary political and cultural effects. The more urgent sharing of fear can be personally debilitating, especially if it is exaggerated by the misleading notion of equally shared risk. In some community-based research with specific young urban sample groups, the rate of violence directed against gay men and lesbians was found to be extraordinarily high by comparison with the level of assaults experienced in the wider community.[3] It was unsurprising that levels of fear were also very high in these groups.

Most open lesbians or gay men have experienced some episode of harassment or assault they credibly believe was related to their sexual identity. Harassment and violence have intruded sharply on homosexual lives in many times and places and many gay men, transsexuals and lesbians have become self-taught practitioners in the basics of what experts call situational crime prevention (Clarke, 2003).[4] This could be especially the case with those whose attire, self-presentation or gender nonconformity draws a quick public scrutiny. Nevertheless, there are uneven patterns of real risk. This fact is the result of the considerable diversity in lifestyles and localities belied by the homogenised images of gay and lesbian identity that have been offered up in the media and sometimes replicated in well-intentioned activist work focused on community building.

When coupled with the emphasis on a responsibility for the self, this generalised fear has been potentially divisive. The seductiveness of new notions of citizenship and the respectability which the stress on violence and safety gave also invite moral judgments about a range of different victims. Some failed the tests of proper self-management in their use of illicit drugs and drink, or their sexual lusting and interest in 'non-gay', rough or young partners. 'Bad victims', who favoured anonymous sex with pick-ups and may have frequented beats or sex clubs, appeared to have problems with their own identity. As sexual outsiders, they may also have been unfashionably oblivious to risk. These outcomes of the campaigns about safety and their new link to the construction of 'gentrified homosexual identities' (Tomsen, 2001b) not only mould the judgments about crime victims that were beginning to prevail in gay and lesbian circles. They could reverberate back onto legal deliberations which also signalled the importance of these discursive shifts in understanding particular identities, including criminal trials featuring the unsubtle sketching of sexually irresponsible and risk-taking victims.

Conclusion
Essentialism, Activism and Citizenship

Despite research that has stressed the openness of human sexual capacity and erotic desire, the belief that sexuality is a key means for dividing people into fully coherent groups with their own separate forms of desire, practices and collective identities still persists. Contemporary concern about 'homophobia' has meant resistance to the repression of stigmatised sexual groupings. Yet the view that hostility and violence stem from a pathology founded on the repression of desire in a specific minority group of homophobes does not move beyond the notion that such violence is a minor group matter where the repressed victimise the sexually open.

This binary division in thinking about sexuality and violence is belied by the actual levels of same-sex activity and desire between perpetrators and victims. Some of the very worst incidents of violence occur in settings that arise because of a mutual search for contact and pleasure between homosexual and heterosexual men. This no longer justifies convoluted inquiry and explanation via a discourse of pathology. The occasions in which killers have both pleasurable and profitable casual sexual relations with their eventual victims give a dangerous half-truth to courtroom claims about the sexual interest and advances of the homosexual deceased. These cases challenge us to awaken to the underlying unstable quality of all sexual identities and broad evidence of the wide occurrence of such same-sex behaviour. Law and legal discourse reinforce this same narrow binary when they judge the masculine violence of different perpetrators and condemn, excuse or exonerate acts of abuse, assault and killing. The dead end reached by the notion of 'homosexual panic' in the Anglo-American legal world has now more problematically been re-formed in the 'homosexual advance' allegation that normalises masculine violence targeting sexually marginalised individuals and groups.

The relationship and ranking between regimes of sexuality and gender as distinct, parallel or overlapping modes of oppression have been increasingly vexed matters for social movements in the last four decades. Activists and community leaders have often understood 'homophobia' as describing a needless bias or prejudice held by unenlightened individuals, bigots and backward social groups with outmoded views and values. The focus on this has been thought to offer the most likely basis for a link between the separate forms of violence and harassment that homosexual/gay men and lesbians experience. Gendered social practice must now be understood as shaping much of the commonality of violence in relation to offending as well as victimisation. This book has drawn out the contradictory but mainstream and fundamentally gendered basis of sexual prejudice and the masculinity of the violence that it reflects. The analysis of the actual violence inflicted on victims reflects how perpetrators both police and punish sexual deviance and enforce conventional gender identity. In effect, they seek to socially impose closed sexual and gender categories by their very actions.

Additionally, this book has demonstrated the significance of many attacks for the attainment and protection of a valued masculine status and the validation of a gender conformity that is linked to a social system of heterosexual privilege. Different scenarios of killing signal the deeply rooted tie with masculine concerns. This includes the establishment of group status among marginalised youths and the protection of honour and bodily sanctity of perpetrators responding to a real or projected homosexual advance. Despite popular expectations, most such crimes of masculine violence are not done by disturbed or pathological assailants.

Nevertheless, the unconscious and corporeal features of this violence are of paramount importance. These should not be theoretically erased by a displacement of essentialism with a view of sexuality as a bodiless field of discursive signs. Such a 'dethroning' (Vance, 1989b: 23) of the body in relation to gender and sexuality would hastily discount the very possibility of any inherent human sexual impulse that is shaped socially and in line with corporeal difference. In human cultures that force the ascription of sexual labels, all people are significantly burdened by the unbounded and openly erotic aspects of the human unconscious, and the lingering shadows of this in everyday consciousness, bodily awareness and social practice. The recognition of this is vital in light of the significance of a relatively stable (though hardly uniform) male somatic experience of homo-desire as a threat compelling violence.

The attraction of such violence to many young men who are not regularly criminal or psychologically disturbed begs further explanation of this phenomenon as it is tied to more ubiquitous and culturally esteemed models of masculinity. The social backdrop to these attacks also includes elements of a possible crisis regarding representations of masculinity linked to the objectification of male sexuality in the homoerotic gaze or 'queering' of some contemporary cultures. For this reason anti-homosexual violence and the response to it can be likened to a microcosm of wider social conflicts over sexual and gender identity.[1]

The tensions between the unstable forms of sexual prejudice and the social categories that these are based upon, and real and compelling gay and lesbian fears of violence, were evident in the author's study of safety at public events. This indicated a substantial concern about harassment and safety in public space, a mainstream attraction towards participation in gay and lesbian festivals and events and situational and varied forms of sexual prejudice. These findings have contradicted the model of fixed prejudiced personality types which mirror a simple division between human sexual categories. Even among most sexually liberal self-identified heterosexuals, there is a spectre of bodily wariness and disgust lurking behind support for social tolerance and legal equality for sexual minorities.

Globally, violence has become a key platform of gay and lesbian politics. References to these incidents as 'hate crimes' has usefully assisted the mobilisation of a gay and lesbian community response to such forms of victimisation. Claiming a legitimate victimhood in regard to the experience of violence has become an important element of associated political action in many nations. The violence and hate crime issue is a cogent example of how new social movements focus on building and asserting a particular collective identity, rather than just engaging in conventional political lobbying to alter state practices. This collective action is driven by and takes place against the backdrop of an evident contemporary uncertainty regarding social identity. Conflicts over gender, sexuality and nationality, and the exclusive assertion of religious, racial/ethnic identities in violence and revived fundamentalism, have all reflected the post-industrial situation of people experiencing uncertainty about fading social forms and patterns of living (Beck et al., 1994; Bauman, 2007).

Official and community responses to violence reflect contradictions and shifts in perceived and projected sexual identity at the social-movement and subcultural levels. Most gay men and lesbians are aware that in various ways they both belong to and feel outside the community or identity shaped for their own sexual minorities late in the last millennium. For each individual this contradictory sense of self-understanding or group belonging will shift during a life course. This process can be acutely painful, seem to not matter, feel closer to a situation of free choice or even seem liberating. This is the everyday experience of the constructed and multifaceted aspects of sexual identity. The notion that sexual communities are necessary fictions that people need and value at many points in their lives, but also have a contingent and negotiated relation with, is subjectively understood by most of their members (Weeks, 1995). The paradox of identity politics is the way that this is premised on the fixed existence of minority categories that are known to be socially constructed and historically and culturally varied.

Inequality is both contested and reproduced in discourse about individual and collective difference. In these circumstances, new social movements have asserted difference to build an empowering and resistant collective identity in shifting strategies of recruitment and mobilisation as strategic 'identity deployment' (Bernstein, 2005). This focused pursuit of limited essentialism for particular gains can be both 'enabling and constraining' (Stein 1992: 52) according to different circumstances where the opening and closing of boundaries is needed to recruit, build and mobilise around new issues (Gamson, 1995). Some have cautioned that repeated attacks on fixed identity may romanticise deconstruction in a way that undercuts more successful struggles for recognition (Weeks, 1998; Gamson & Moon, 2004). Furthermore, what matters most is not the actual existence of boundaries around collective identity, but the extent to which these have excluded and marginalised some people and not others (Plummer, 2007).

Where does an awareness of the constructed form of identity leave anti-violence activism? Activists and others involved in anti-violence organisations and lobbying were not just confronted by these issues but they also shaped and consolidated a particular collective identity for themselves. The 'gay and lesbian victim' of violence is not a discursive fiction but is nonetheless a concept shaped by these social-movement forces. Many activists and commentators have felt troubled with any view of sexuality that has appeared to undermine the possibilities of effective mobilisation around relatively fixed notions of identity. For this reason, contemporary gay and lesbian politics has frequently incorporated elements of a commonsense use of categories in viewpoints that stress a fundamental dichotomy between heterosexuals and homosexuals and a view of perpetrators and victims as two distinct groups: dangerous heterosexuals and vulnerable 'sexual minorities'.

This sort of approach to understanding oppression has a more obvious fit with social-movement demands built on liberal models of justice and minority rights. It has also seemed to be ready-made for the most effective mobilisation against violence, harassment and discrimination. Recent successes in attaining a more legitimate victim status in some jurisdictions have meant that the legal response to anti-homosexual killings and associated violence is evolving but ambiguous. Police consciousness has shifted in many locations (see Jenness & Grattet, 2001), and more courts appear willing to denounce and seriously punish openly prejudice-driven attacks. This new official resolve has been undermined in cases characterised by allegations about a homosexual advance from the deceased, especially when perpetrators have been very young. This has reflected the masculine model of violence, honour and bodily integrity inscribed into the law of provocation, in addition to ongoing concerns and anxieties about the need for the criminal law to protect the sexuality of young men.

The activism around these killings and similar violence was a direct consequence of justifiable gay and lesbian furore about frequent victimisation and media, political and legal disinterest or even some condoning of such acts. It also reflected significant recent shifts in culture and politics that created a tenuous new respectability and wider support for claims of equal citizenship. These developments ran alongside internal differences of social status and the queer emphasis on diversity and critiques of any artificial depiction of sexual groups with unified identities. The politicisation of violence and safety has had an extended and contradictory relation to notions of sexual identity, community and citizenship and the power relations that are inscribed in these. Most significantly, a sense of threat from violence now intricately shapes understanding of the social self and how different groups are conceived.

Community and identity will remain as key terms in the mobilisation against the harassment and brutality that many victims still incur. But evidence about trial patterns and movement activism in this field has suggested that the very success of this strategy requires taking a reflexive view of the altered ways in which victims and perpetrators are seen. Tight distinctions between victims and offenders may be a politically advantageous stance for groups and movements in oppressive conditions to assume. A galvanising symbolism in which heterosexuals and homosexuals are recast as divided species of 'perpetrators' and 'victims' then emerges in discourse about these issues (Tomsen, 2006). Nevertheless, this symbolism and its associated community activism may also neatly match with conservative social and legal trends that must be questioned. The avid pursuit of safety and security 'is one context in which a progressive and emancipatory politics of sexual violence may in fact reinforce modalities of subordination and exclusion' (Moran et al., 2004: 3). A paradox of the police and official protection of certain specific groups in designated urban spaces is that by implication victims do not belong and should more readily expect harassment and attacks in other locations.

The contemporary metropolitan tolerance of some previously deviant lifestyles and behaviours has now coincided with moral panics about such matters as pornography, prostitution, promiscuity and intergenerational sex. In these circumstances, the promise of an increased social respectability may attract many to participate in the reproduction of new boundaries between acceptable and non-acceptable identities, possibly by disowning or stigmatising the 'minorities within'. In this respect it is interesting to reflect on the negative depiction of some homicide victims as outsiders to the gay and lesbian community and the exclusion that this entailed. This same cultural dynamic and moral binary also potentially stigmatises victims who engage in apparent risk behaviour that leads to violence and even fatal attacks. These include beat-users, those who are promiscuous and have sex with non-homosexually identified partners, sex workers, youths or 'rough trade'. Such victim-blaming ignores the socially and materially constrained circumstances of the experience of same-sex pleasure in the life histories of different men, and how this is delimited by current cultural representations of desirable masculinity.

Openly gay men have been a key force in the patterns of 'urban renaissance', transforming less desirable spaces into tourist sites and giving an aura of cosmopolitan diversity alongside the attainment of more respectable identities in the social and political life of inner cities (Rushbrook, 2002; Bell & Binnie, 2004). Many lesbians have not had the wealth to make an identical social impact, yet they may instead be drawn to a form of familial ideology that is tied to the attainment of domestic respectability and affirms a need for social order. Consequently, an unintended outcome of campaigns about violence and safety and their link to the construction of newly respected and gentrified homosexual identities is the ongoing likelihood of moral division (Tomsen, 2001b). The stress on violence can raise fear to debilitating levels. This has also given prominence to notions of self-regulation and personal 'responsibilisation' for crime that further invite damning judgments and impose blame on a range of different victims (Stanko & Curry, 1997; Moran, 2001).

Some of these consequences of the anti-violence issue have diverged sharply from what can be drawn from research evidence. A sharpened fear of the fully irrational homophobic stranger retains its potency in most gay and lesbian communities around the globe. Yet appreciation of the everyday qualities of this violence and its perpetrators may only serve to further exacerbate feelings of loathing regarding a broader range of people and social locations as either potential assailants or danger spots. With a general activist emphasis on street-based violence these could include most men or groups of youth, and all social spaces and activities outside a narrow range of inner-urban queer locales.

In reality, widespread violence is not the same as constant and ubiquitous violence. Certain victims have much higher or lower levels of overall risk than other groups of homosexual men and women. Moreover, the recent emphasis on the recognition of the everyday forms of this violence suggests a need to more adequately explain occasions of contradiction and tolerance as a social backdrop to prejudice and hostility. Conflation of homosexual and victim identities and a social-movement stress on the shared danger of victimisation can easily emphasise the general risks of violence in ways that can reinforce static and divisive understandings of sexual prejudice.

In recent decades there has been a major global swing to a more punitive response to crime and delinquency (Garland, 2002). This was usually linked to the general revival of neo-liberal ideas stressing individual self-reliance and discipline. Nation-states moved resources away from the welfare sector and towards the legal system, criminal justice, policing and military. A return to mass imprisonment has gathered strength and been accompanied by an ongoing law and order politics stressing rational individual causes and punishment for crime (Christie, 1994). In particular, there has been a notable revival of older liberal ideas of the personal responsibility of offenders and lowered interest in deep explanations of motive due to extra-individual and social structural factors.[2]

Offender differences and social determination are eschewed for the stress on criminal voluntarism, a more narrow focus on crime prevention in specific events or spaces and reshaping of social environments to become crime free. In the criminological imagination, the calculating and conscience-free eighteenth-century individual transgressor has been transported to a new social landscape of wide spatial surveillance, tracking, hot spots and target hardening. As most offenders are presumed to engage in a free and rational choice to commit crime, there has been support for harsh and ostensibly more uniform punishments directed less at rehabilitation and more at retribution or the simple incapacitation of offenders (Feeley & Simon, 1996). In these circumstances, future relations with homosexual men and lesbians may be negatively impacted by a technocratic shift in policing and inflated public fear about serious crimes and terrorism that encourage command-led rather than community-based approaches.

There has been an evident price to pay for the enthusiastic petitioning of public authorities that has been pursued by activist groups in recent decades, including those which had become dependent on police goodwill and local state funding. An apparent drop in the locally recorded anti-homosexual killings in recent years may reflect anti-violence education campaigns and some heightened victim awareness. Yet this also appears to mirror a lower priority within the police bureaucracy and the waxing and waning of public concern about these crimes. Sociologists studying patterns of rise, growth and decline in social movements view such changes as inevitable. There have been historical signs from muted concerns about violence in localities such as San Francisco, Amsterdam and Sydney that movement bureaucratisation and the incorporation of activists into official processes or their displacement by official agencies can all serve to ossify and erode grassroots involvement around violence issues. Particular victim groups can fall away from interest. In some locations there is now less publicity, discussion and dedication of resources alongside a possible new laxity in monitoring violent incidents that have a likely anti-homosexual motive.[3]

Activist groups which call for greater responsiveness to the needs of a widening array of victims in the operation of the law have grown and spread dramatically in recent decades (Elias, 1993; Stanko, 2000). The contemporary rise of these political lobby groups has coincided with a populist critique of judges, courts and crime experts as too removed from the presumed commonsense and single worldview of ordinary people in relation to crime and punishment. Such groups are quite varied in form, but they often articulate a worldview that marginalises the interests of the poor, young and racial minorities who experience police harassment and are still clearly stigmatised within justice systems.

The activism against anti-homosexual violence can be seen as analogous to the rise of such groups. The creative borrowing of the victim mantle by sexually marginalised groups has signalled that this victim-centred politics is not inherently conservative. Projecting a new public image in debates about violence has served to rupture the traditional view of these marginal groups as deviants deserving the harsh repression by the police and courts they experienced in the past. It is unsurprising that some commentators have even advocated a mainstream stance on moral and social issues for homosexual activists as a key platform for future political acceptance.

Responding to the negative courtroom characterisation of some victims by means of a further demonisation of perpetrators may seem like a tempting path to follow. Queer loathing and fear are an unsurprising but restrictive reply to heterosexual disgust. Commentators must also acknowledge the outer limits of the usefulness of this politics and any uncritical duplication of a law and order stance from other victim groups (Moran, 2001). Claims of a legal right to protection and a newly respectable citizen status raise hard questions about understandings of shared identity and community. Furthermore, the political dilemmas faced by those countering violence have dovetailed with disquiet regarding the appropriate position to be assumed by gay men and lesbians in criminal justice politics. A focus on punishment and retribution would derive from an almost exclusive concern and anger with the brutality of assailants and an absolute belief in individual choice and responsibility in crime causation. The abhorrent quality of the actions of the perpetrators who have been tried and prosecuted for attacking and killing homosexual victims is obvious. These are actions that reflect real decisions to offend, but the freedom to do so is exaggerated in the neo-liberal stress on rational choice. Such attacks are not the mere consequence of quick estimations about the limited chances of detection, or occasions of criminal opportunism from a random assortment of potential perpetrators. Agency and voluntarism are framed within the strict limits of gendered social structures and patterns of social disadvantage that may then also relate to matters of social class, race, ethnicity, age and region (Messerschmidt, 1997).

As extreme forms of violent crime, homicides evoke emotional and simplified reactions from politicians, media commentators and members of the public. These emotions often configure around evil archetypes of offenders and a heroic imagery of most victims as survivors (Rock, 1998). Vicious killings of the sort that the murders of homosexual men in public space typify have full salience as moments of horror and atrocity. The 'moral shock' (Jasper, 1997: 106) of such events has a vital impact on the affective dimension of social-movement recruitment and mobilisation (Goodwin et al., 2001). In so doing, they have inverted the more usual emotionality of moral panics about sexuality directed at gay men and lesbians (Irvine, 2007). The global publicity surrounding the torture and grisly death of Mathew Shephard in the 1990s (Loffreda, 2001), or the general revulsion felt about a nail bomb attack which killed three people and injured dozens of others in a London gay bar in the same decade and was described by onlookers as an act of terror, barbarism and a 'war scene' (BBC News, *On This Day*, 'Dozens injured in Soho nail bomb', 30 April 1999), both attest to this. Underneath the understandable outrage about these crimes, such attacks offered political opportunities with a high level of resonance for victim claims. In fact, these incidents comprised some of the key international moments in the recent public struggle over crimes of 'sexual hatred' via what political sociologists would see as an adversarial 'framing process' with a binary moral contrast between supporters and opponents (Benford & Snow, 2000: 616).

Alongside this drama of public representation and imagery, the research discussed in this book suggests the everyday circumstances of most violent incidents and the unexceptional qualities of most perpetrators. In the case of anti-homosexual killings, it is apparent that assaults are usually not intended to kill, and it is erroneous to view the bulk of this violence as the result of an exceptional bigotry or phobia. The great majority of bashers of homosexuals do not carry extremist political views and many of them are motivated by concerns other than what can be termed as simple hatred. Most perpetrators of public attacks are psychically ordinary young men, although they often do usually have a marginal social existence that may encourage antisocial and criminal practices.

These young and relatively powerless men have acted out in their violence the prejudiced and masculinist values that have been instilled in them by older and more respectable authority figures. Such attitudes and values have a considerable degree of acceptance in the criminal justice system that requires a continuous challenge. An ignorance of these contradictions in current legal arrangements will only reinforce an uncritical reproduction of law and order rhetoric among sexual groups that in some ways are still subject to repression and disenfranchisement in the criminal law. Previous homosexual activism typically favoured the reduction of the reach of the criminal law and policing in society. From the 1950s in the United Kingdom, and then later in the United States and Australia, there was a concerted drive to decriminalise 'victimless crimes', including some forms of illicit drug use and consenting sexual behaviour such as prostitution and homosexuality. Globally, the long mobilisation against anti-sodomy provisions still has a course to finish and a selective use of public order legislation against male homosexuality persists in many places. Despite what is argued in some caricatured critiques of hate crime activism, most efforts in the criminal justice arena have been concerned with ensuring the investigation and punishment of attacks and violence on an equal footing to similar crimes with other victims.

In itself, this is not a betrayal of the goals of social and legal equality by activists though it suggests a new and more complex political scenario than the more straightforward libertarian opposition to heavy policing of moral behaviours. Overall, gay men and lesbians have a limited meaningful investment in law and order campaigns regarding disorder and violence. An abstract and depoliticised opposition to all violence does not have an obvious relationship to homosexual politics. This also seems ironic if the much-celebrated history of occasions of violence directed against repression and injustice like the New York Stonewall rebellion, the 1978 Sydney Mardi Gras riot and the San Francisco Milk murder trial protests is reflected on. Holding on to a steady view of the social genesis of sexually prejudiced violence and its contradictions can balance the allure of exclusively official solutions and narrowly punitive responses. In this way, the potential gains for victims of harassment and violence and for the wider attainment of the goal of sexual justice for all people will not disappear from sight.

Notes

NOTES TO CHAPTER 1

1. 'Sexual prejudice refers to negative attitudes toward an individual because of her or his sexual orientation . . . it conveys no assumptions about the motivations underlying negative attitudes' (Herek, 2000: 19).
2. 'Essentialism can take several forms in the study of sexuality: a belief that human behavior is "natural", predetermined by genetic, biological or physiological mechanisms and thus not subject to change; or the notion that human behaviors which show some similarity in form are the same, an expression of an underlying human drive or tendency. Behaviors that share an outward similarity can be assumed to share an underlying essence and meaning' (Vance, 1989b: 14).
3. Throughout this work the term 'homosexual' refers broadly to same-sex attraction and behaviour. The terms 'gay' and 'lesbian' refer to homosexual social identities evolved in the modern West. In particular, the latter became mass labels in the urban sexual subcultures that developed around the globe in the last four decades.
4. Similar tensions about open boundaries of sexual identity were evident in the research on attitudes to heterosexual attendance at gay and lesbian events that is discussed in Chapter 2.
5. Reservations about the erasure of non-discursive bodily elements in some radical versions of constructionism have been expressed by its sympathetic critics (e.g., Vance, 1989b; Connell, 1995a). In such versions: 'The logical limit of the social constructionist tendency is a purely semiotic view of sexuality, concerning itself only with discourse and subject positions in discourse. . . . Bodies are present as surfaces on which discursive meanings are inscribed. . . . This definition evacuates, rather than resolves, problems about bodies: which are certainly surfaces to be written on, but are also busy growing, aging, reproducing, getting sick, feeding well or badly, getting aroused or turned off, and so on. All of these are social processes, and all are hard to separate from sexual practice and sexual signification' (Connell, 1995a: 387).

NOTES TO CHAPTER 2

1. In a 1990s interview Weinberg discussed the personal and professional circumstances behind his generation of this new term: 'After seeing in the 1950's and 1960's the enormous brutality against gays and seeing that I myself couldn't introduce known, professed homosexuals even to my friends who were supposedly liberal or psychoanalysts . . . that they always had reasons for avoiding

these people [and] they weren't at all distressed by the worst kinds of brutalities toward gays. I realized that something else was going on—more than simple mis-education. This was some deep emotional misgiving these people had, some phobic dread . . . this was something that had a very deep root, [it was] a classical phobia, but of all the phobias, the most destructive being homophobia. Claustrophobia or agoraphobia—if you can't go to the theater or outside—or you have almost any kind of dread . . . doesn't ordinarily get converted into the violence. These were recognized as phobias, but this—homophobia—was not recognized as one' (G. Weinberg, interview, *Badpuppy Gay Today*, 3 December 1997, retrieved from http://gaytoday.com/garchive/interview/0203397m.htm).

2. 'A tiny number of inconceivably coarse axes of categorization have been painstakingly inscribed in current critical and political thought: gender, race, class, nationality, sexual orientation are pretty much the available distinctions . . . the comparison of different axes of oppression is a crucial task, not for any purpose of ranking oppressions, but to the contrary because each oppression is likely to be in a uniquely indicative relation to certain distinctive nodes of cultural organization' (Sedgwick, 1994: 22–33).

3. The questionnaire gathered information from 332 respondents with open and closed questions concerning gay, lesbian and queer participants' perceptions and experiences of hostility, threats and violence on the basis of their sexuality before, during and after these events.

4. Ages were teens (9), 20s (32), 30s (15), 40s (13), and 50s (3). Stated occupations included unemployed, housewife, student, manual labour, skilled trades, child-care, policing, hospitality, management, law, finance and information technology. Twelve interviewees were from second-generation Mediterranean or East European backgrounds, one from South-East Asia and a further five people were Indigenous Australians. All of these were recruited as self-describing 'heterosexuals' although during the interviews a few discussed their own same-sex experiences.

5. 'I need not spell out just how contaminating, how disgusting, the anus is. It is the essence of lowness, of untouchability, and so it must be hemmed in with prohibitions. The anus is to be properly only an exit for foodstuffs that first entered via the mouth. Of course it can be penetrated and therein lies the danger. Even those penetrations consented to and not forced lower the status of the person so penetrated' (Miller, 1997: 100).

6. '"Reaming" is typical of the way Gilbert and George make a kind of contemporary history painting. Their subject matter is drawn from the streets of London but the youths they feature take on the mantle of the heroic male model of European traditions. Gilbert and George confronted the gay sexual issues of their world in public when these subjects were usually private acts and seldom spoken of except as scandal. They aimed to "unshock" the public by confronting people with their images while making them as seductive as possible' (*Art Gallery of New South Wales Contemporary Collection Handbook, 2006*; retrieved from the Art Gallery of New South Wales web site: http://www.artgallery.nsw.gov.au/collection/browse).

NOTES TO CHAPTER 3

1. Stanko (2001) has offered the interesting suggestion that many of the problems with this term, particularly the confusing definitional barrier around stranger and non-stranger relations, could be overcome with a new emphasis on addressing various forms of 'targeted violence'.

2. 'The perpetrators of hate crimes—against particular racial or sexual minorities, for example—frequently seek to give contemporary violent expression to the discriminatory principles embodied in past laws and official practices. While the laws may have changed, the cultural attitudes they embodied may survive among large sections of the mainstream population. Also, relevant public and private authorities are not necessarily immune from these surviving attitudes, so the boundary between "official" and "hate" violence may on occasions prove to be a very blurred one' (Brown & Hogg, 1998: 67).

3. A New South Wales legislative amendment that is not well known gave judges a direction to consider hate motives when calculating a criminal sentence if the: 'offence was motivated by hatred for or prejudice against a group of people to which the offender believed the victim belonged (such as people of a particular religion, racial or ethnic origin, language, sexual orientation or age; or having a particular disability' (*Crimes [Sentencing Procedure] Act 1999* NSW S. 21A [2] [h]). Interestingly, this enactment coincided with public concern about an alleged deliberate targeting of young Anglo women in 'ethnic gang rapes' in Western Sydney. The irrational responses to these attacks are discussed in Warner (2004).

4. With this shift there had been loss of collective memory about police brutality and the extortion and corruption that characterised the regulation of old gay subcultures (see Wotherspoon, 1991; Johnston, 1999). Those most stunned by the direction of the 1996–1997 New South Wales Royal Commission into Paedophilia—including its underlying fascination with consensual sex between men and adolescent boys and its skimming over evidence of serious police violence and abuse—were those most convinced by the new imagery. On the contemporary revival of social and legal fears of male homosexuality as paedophilia see Dalton (2006a).

5. A double irony can emerge from the uneven subjection of victim claims to this sort of analysis when this comes from a key former interactionist. In the early 1990s the author gave the first ever presentation on anti-homosexual violence at an Australian national crime conference. This outlined new evidence of substantial under-reporting, the significance of the phenomenon and its overall trivialisation by criminologists. As if to reinforce the latter point, this was delivered in a session chaired by Stan Cohen himself and his concluding commentary stressed the charge that the author was mischievously setting off his 'own moral panic' (Tomsen, 1992).

NOTES TO CHAPTER 4

1. In 40 tried matters, 44 perpetrators had been drinking at the time of the fatal attack. A further 11 were influenced by illicit drugs. The frequency of joint drinking and high alcohol consumption also suggested the causal relevance of cognitive impairment with the misreading of social cues, intentions and interactions that characterise heavy drinking sessions by men (Boyatzis, 1974). In 16 of the matters in which a sexual advance was alleged, the victim had been engaged in heavy drinking with the accused. Intoxication of victims was important in only three of the matters concerning group attacks at public locations.

2. The 15 unsuccessful uses of advance claims also arose in killings which mostly occurred in private space. These had six instances of multiple perpetrators. A total of 14 perpetrators and co-perpetrators had an involvement in illicit drug use, and four were involved in homosexual prostitution. Additionally, in six trials with failed allegations the perpetrators were double-killers and

in nine of these the perpetrators were described as mentally disturbed. These personal factors could have undermined the arguments of any accused about a non-criminal nature, or a special sensitivity to homosexual advances.

NOTES TO CHAPTER 5

1. In a more oblique way, an interest in masculinity has long been evident in the discipline's ongoing homoerotic focus on young male perpetrators. To any reader with queer sensibilities, key classic visual depictions of delinquents and tough-guy physiques (see Sheldon et al., 1949) recall aspects of postwar gay male erotica (Tomsen, 1997b).
2. Against the stress on individual free will in classicism and on individual pathology in early criminology, sociologists have studied the relationship between deviance and crime and social structures (Newburn, 2007: chaps. 5–9). Durkheim's explanation concerned shifting levels of social cohesion and 'anomie' in industrialised societies and later researchers in this vein focused on the importance of 'social strain' for offending. Bonger (2003) and his heirs emphasised the class relations of criminality in industrial capitalism and the liberal state's unjust focus on the deviance of the poor and working class. A further strand of postwar sociological research examined delinquency to produce causal models that emphasised the influence of 'differential association' in local communities, subcultures and the role of authorities in producing criminality by official labelling processes (Taylor et al., 1973).
3. For replies to specific critiques in criminology and to a very wide related social science literature, see Connell (2002) and Connell and Messerschmidt (2005).
4. There is an obvious similarity here with the violence that the author has also studied in a variety of urban drinking locations and which may also involve group attacks on vulnerable individuals (Tomsen, 1997a, 2005). Yet this may often require a greater bodily challenge with more risk of failure or retaliation than surprise group attacks on confused and morally compromised victims in frequently dark and isolated settings.

NOTES TO CHAPTER 6

1. For an early example, see *R v. Howe* (1958) *State Reports of South Australia*, p. 95.
2. These criminological accounts appear more credible in the light of historical evidence about the relationship between this aggressive pattern of comportment between men and the evolving modern forms of masculinity emerging in the late 1800s (see McLaren, 1997).

NOTES TO CHAPTER 7

1. The work of Kempf can be seen against the backdrop of the particular professional climate of the birth of American psychiatry and its rival disciplines. The goal of professional respectability and external political pressures including McCarthyism meant studies of homosexuality accentuated social pathology and danger (see Hatheway, 2003: chap. 8, 'America physicians discover the homosexual'; Lewes, 1995; Robinson, 2001). Lewes (1995) offers a lucid account of all aspects of Freud's views of homosexuality and of how the later stress on serious pathology was not warranted by the original psychoanalytic account.

2. In some American cases this evidence of frenzied violence has even been referred to as 'homosexual overkill' (Schmidt, 1994: 85–6).

3. For a contemporary example of such Leftist criticisms of gay/homosexual men emphasising social and sexual privilege see Demetriou (2001). This article suggested that the fictional American film *Cruising*, which was set in the New York gay leather subculture of the early 1980s, was compelling evidence of the reality and forms of a new and growing gay global privilege. The controversy, debate and political demonstrations set off when this film premiered two decades earlier, are never referred to. It is no coincidence that this same film was noted for a crude conflation of homosexuality and violence that appeared to confirm the disavowal of societal blame for anti-homosexual attacks (see Dalton, 2001). Furthermore, it is sobering to reflect on how such a stereotyping and tendentious attack on gay men was published in a leading international journal of social theory (*Theory and Society*).

NOTES TO CHAPTER 8

1. A survey of American cases found a contemporary persistence of depictions of victims as effeminate, sick, predatory and monstrous (Smyth, 2006).

2. In the notorious South Australian Snowtown serial killings, the perpetrators loosely referred to their socially marginal gay, homosexual and transsexual victims as paedophiles. This effectively silenced gay and lesbian observers and removed the discursive possibility of these attacks being viewed as hate crimes as 'victim groups that provoke feelings of contempt or disgust may jeopardize the hate crime cause by "polluting" the moral claims of other, less tainted, victim groups' (Mason, 2007: 266).

3. For example, one key local study in this period reached this conclusion after comparing reports from two quite differently structured samples of homo-sexual and heterosexual respondents (Price Waterhouse, 1995). This also found that 90 per cent of urban gays and lesbians, compared to 56 per cent of the general statewide population, were 'concerned' or 'very concerned' that they or their friends might be assaulted.

4. 'For women and non-heterosexuals who have long been denied State provision of safety and security, the rise of individual and private safety strategies is not so much a new development within the politics of crime control and thereby their social inclusion, but a long established feature of their social exclusion' (Moran, 2001: 337).

NOTES TO THE CONCLUSION

1. The principal focus of the empirical discussion of criminal violence directed at sexual minorities in this book has been on incidents of serious physical violence directed at homosexual/gay men. This violence is ubiquitous in con-temporary societies, closely linked to the history of 'state violence' frequently directed at male homosexuality and of critical interest due to its sharpened significance for masculine identity.

2. These include Rational Choice, Routine Activities and Opportunity theories of crime. See Newburn (2007), Chapter 14, 'Contemporary classicism'.

3. The pattern of decline or issue abeyance may sometimes be reversed by exter-nal events. For example, a widespread gay and lesbian concern about serious attacks associated with a deregulated and expanded night-time economy of aggressive male drinking grew in inner Sydney in 2008. Publicity and debate

about incidents that included a police refusal to assist the gay victim of a serious bashing led to the organisation of a public rally from freshly concerned individuals. Former anti-violence activists and their organisations were taken by surprise and had difficulty reassuming the direction of these events ('Vigil attracts huge crowd', *Sydney Star Observer*, 27 January 2008).

References

Adam, B. (1998) 'Theorizing homophobia'. *Sexualities*, 1 (4): 387–404.
Allport, G. (1999) 'The nature of hatred'. In R. Baird and S. Rosenbaum (eds.) *Hatred, Bigotry, and Prejudice: Definitions, Causes and Solutions*. New York: Prometheus.
Allwood, G. (1998) *French Feminisms: Gender and Violence in Contemporary Theory*. London: UCL Press.
Althusser, L. (1971) *Lenin and Philosophy and Other Essays*. London: NLB.
Altman, D. (1972) *Homosexual: Oppression and Liberation*. Sydney: Angus and Robertson.
———. (1994) *Power and Community: Organisational and Cultural Responses to AIDS*. London: Taylor and Francis.
———. (1998) 'The uses and abuses of queer studies'. In R. Aldrich and G. Wotherspoon (eds.) *Gay and Lesbian Perspectives: Volume Four*. Sydney: University of Sydney.
———. (2001) *Global Sex*. St. Leonards, NSW: Allen and Unwin.
Archer, J. (1994) 'Violence between men'. In J. Archer (ed.) *Male Violence*. London: Routledge.
Baird, B. et al. (1994) *The Police and You*. Adelaide: Lesbian and Gay Community Action.
Bakhtin, M. (1985) *Rabelais and His World*. Bloomington: Indiana University Press.
Ballard, J. (1992) 'Sexuality and the state in time of epidemic'. In R.W. Connell and G. Dowsett (eds.) *Rethinking Sex: Social Theory and Sexuality Research*. Melbourne: Melbourne University Press.
Barker, M., S. Page and D. Meyer. (2003) 'Urban visitor perceptions of safety during a special event'. *Journal of Travel Research*, 41 (May): 355–61.
Bartlett, P. (2007) 'Killing gay men, 1976–2001'. *British Journal of Criminology*, 47: 573–95.
Bartos, M. (1996) 'The queer excess of public health policy'. *Meanjin*, 55 (1): 122–31.
Bauman, Z. (2007) *Liquid Times: Living in an Age of Uncertainty*. Cambridge: Polity.
Beck, U., A. Giddens and S. Lash. (1994) *Reflexive Modernization*. Cambridge: Polity.
Becker, H. (1967) 'Whose side are we on?' *Social Problems*, 14 (3): 239–47.
Bell, D. and J. Binnie. (2004) 'Authenticating queer space: citizenship, urbanism and governance'. *Urban Studies*, 41 (9): 1807–20.
Bell, M.D. and R.I. Vila. (1996) 'Homicide in homosexual victims: a study of 67 cases from the Broward County, Florida, Medical Examiner's Office (1982–

1992) with special emphasis on "overkill"'. *American Journal of Forensic Medicine and Pathology*, 17 (1): 65–9.

Benford, R. and D. Snow. (2000) 'Framing processes and social movements: an overview and assessment'. *Annual Review of Sociology*, 26: 611–39.

Bernstein, M. (2005) 'Identity politics'. *Annual Review of Sociology*, 31: 47–74.

Bernstein, M. and C. Kostelac. (2002) 'Lavender and blue: attitudes about homosexuality and behavior toward lesbians and gay men among police officers'. *Journal of Contemporary Criminal Justice*, 18: 302–28.

Bersani, L. (1988) 'Is the rectum a grave?' In D. Crimp (ed.) *AIDS: Cultural Analysis/Cultural Activism*. Cambridge, MA: MIT Press.

Bland, L. and L. Doan (eds.) (1998) *Sexology in Culture: Labeling Bodies and Desires*. Chicago: University of Chicago Press.

Bonger, W. (2003) 'Criminality and economic conditions'. In E. McLaughlin, J. Muncie and G. Hughes (eds.) *Criminological Perspectives: Essential Readings*. London/Thousand Oaks, CA: Sage; originally published in 1916.

Bourdieu, P. (1997) *Outline of a Theory of Practice*. Cambridge: Cambridge University Press.

Boyatzis, R. (1974) 'The effects of alcohol consumption on the aggressive behaviour of men'. *Quarterly Journal of Studies in Alcohol*, 35: 959.

Bristow, J. (1997) *Sexuality*. London: Routledge.

Brooks, P. (ed.) (1996) *Law's Stories: Narrative and Rhetoric in Law*. New Haven, CT: Yale University Press.

Brown, D. and R. Hogg. (1998) *Rethinking Law and Order*. Sydney: Pluto Press.

Buhle, M.J. (1998) *Feminism and its Discontents: A Century of Struggle with Psychoanalysis*. Cambridge, MA: Harvard University Press.

Buhrke, R.A. (1996) *A Matter of Justice: Lesbians and Gay Men in Law Enforcement*. New York: Routledge.

Burchell, G., C. Gordon and P. Miller. (eds.) (1991) *The Foucault Effect: Studies in Governmentality*. London: Harvester Wheatsheaf.

Burke, M. (1993) *Coming out of the Blue*. London: Cassell.

Burston, P. and C. Richardson. (eds.) (1995) *A Queer Romance: Lesbians, Gay Men and Popular Culture*. New York: Routledge.

Butler, J. (1990) *Gender Trouble: Feminism and the Subversion of Identity*. London: Routledge.

———. (1997) *Excitable Speech: A Politics of the Performative*. New York: Routledge.

Campbell, A. (1986) 'The streets and violence'. In A. Campbell and J. Gibbs (eds.) *Violent Transactions: The Limits of Personality*. Oxford: Blackwell.

Carbery, G. (1995) *A History of the Sydney Gay and Lesbian Mardi Gras*. Melbourne: Australian Gay and Lesbian Archives.

Carr, A. (1997) 'Dead men do tell tales'. *Outrage*, August: 48–53.

Carrigan, T., J. Lee and R.W. Connell. (1985) 'Towards a new sociology of masculinity'. *Theory and Society*, 14 (5): 551–604.

Chan, J. (1997) *Changing Police Culture: Policing in a Multicultural Society*. Cambridge: Cambridge University Press.

Chancer, L. (1993) 'Prostitution, feminist theory and ambivalence'. *Social Text*, 37: 143–71.

Cherney, A. (1999) 'Gay and lesbian issues in policing'. *Current Issues in Criminal Justice*, 11: 35–52.

Chodorow, N. (1994) *Femininities, Masculinities, Sexualities: Freud and Beyond*. Lexington, KY: University of Kentucky Press.

Christie, N. (1994) *Crime Control as Industry: Towards Gulags, Western Style*. New York: Routledge.

Clarke, R. (2003) '"Situational crime prevention": theory and practice'. In E. McLaughlin, J. Muncie and G. Hughes (eds.) *Criminological Perspectives*, 2nd ed. London: Sage.

Clatterbaugh, K. (1990) *Contemporary Perspectives on Masculinity*. Boulder, CA: Westview Press.

Cohen, P. (1979) 'Policing the working-class city'. In B. Fine, R. Kinsey, J. Lea, S. Picciotto and J. Young (eds.) *Capitalism and the Rule of Law*. London: Hutchinson.

Cohen, S. (1972) *Folk Devils and Moral Panics: The Creation of the Mods and Rockers*. Oxford: Martin Robertson.

———. (1985) *Visions of Social Control: Crime, Punishment and Classification*. Cambridge: Polity Press.

Collier, R. (1998) *Masculinities, Crime and Criminology: Men, Heterosexuality and the Criminal(ised) Other*. London: Sage.

Comstock, G. (1991) *Violence against Lesbians and Gay Men*. New York: Columbia.

Comstock, G. (1992) 'Dismantling the homosexual panic defence'. *Law and Sexuality: A Review of Gay and Lesbian Legal Issues*, 2: 81.

Connell, R.W. (1990) 'The state, gender and sexual politics: theory and appraisal'. *Theory and Society*, 19: 507–44.

———. (1992) 'A very straight gay: masculinity, homosexual experience and the dynamics of gender'. *American Sociological Review*, 57 (6): 735–51.

———. (1995a) 'Democracies of pleasure'. In L. Nicholson and S. Seidman (eds.) *Social Postmodernism: Beyond Identity Politics*. Cambridge: Cambridge University Press.

———. (1995b) *Masculinities*. St. Leonards, NSW: Allen and Unwin.

———. (2002) 'On hegemonic masculinity and violence: response to Jefferson and Hall'. *Theoretical Criminology*, 6 (1): 89–99.

Connell, R.W. and G. Dowsett. (eds.) (1992) *Rethinking Sex: Social Theory and Sexuality Research*. Melbourne: Melbourne University Press.

Connell, R.W., M. Kimmel and J. Hearn. (eds.) (2005) *Handbook of Studies on Men and Masculinities*. Thousand Oaks, CA: Sage.

Connell, R.W. and J. Messerschmidt. (2005) 'Hegemonic masculinity—rethinking the concept'. *Gender and Society*, 19 (6): 829–59.

Coss, G. (1998) 'Revisiting lethal violence by men'. *Criminal Law Journal*, 22: 5–9.

Cox, G. (1990) *The Streetwatch Report*. Sydney: Gay and Lesbian Rights Lobby.

———. (1994) *The Count and Counter Report*. Sydney: Lesbian and Gay Anti-Violence Project.

Cunneen, C. (2001) *Conflict, Politics and Crime: Aboriginal Communities and the Police*. Sydney: Allen and Unwin.

Cunneen, C., D. Fraser and S. Tomsen. (eds.) (1997) *Faces of Hate: Hate Crime in Australia*. Sydney: Hawkins Press.

D'Emilio, J. (1983) *Sexual Politics, Sexual Communities: The Making of a Homosexual Minority in the United States, 1940–1970*. Chicago: University of Chicago Press.

Dalton, D. (2001) 'The deviant gaze: imagining the homosexual as criminal through cinematic and legal discourses'. In C. Stychin and D. Herman (eds.) *Law and Sexuality*. Minneapolis: University of Minnesota Press.

———. (2006a) 'The haunting of gay subjectivity: the cases of Oscar Wilde and John Marsden'. *Law Text Culture*, 10: 72–100.

———. (2006b) 'Surveying deviance, figuring disgust: locating the homocriminal body in time and space'. *Social and Legal Studies*, 15 (2): 277–99.

————. (2007) 'Policing outlawed desire: "homocriminality" in beat spaces in Australia'. *Law and Critique*, 18: 375–405.

Davies, M. (2004) 'Correlates of negative attitudes toward gay men: sexism, male role norms, and male sexuality'. *The Journal of Sex Research*, 41 (3): 259–66.

De Cecco, J. and J. Elia. (eds.) (1993) *If You Seduce a Straight Person, Can You Make Them Gay? Issues in Biological Essentialism versus Social Constructionism in Gay and Lesbian Identities*. New York: Haworth Press.

Decker, S. (1993) 'Exploring victim–offender relationships in homicide: the role of individual and event characteristics'. *Justice Quarterly*, 10 (4): 585–612.

Demetriou, D. (2001) 'Connell's concept of hegemonic masculinity: a critique'. *Theory and Society*, 30 (3): 337–61.

'Developments: sexual orientation and the law'. (1989) *Harvard Law Review*, 102: 1511–1620.

Dollimore, J. (1991) *Sexual Dissidence: Augustine to Wilde, Freud to Foucault*. Oxford: Clarendon Press.

Doty, A. (1993) *Making Things Perfectly Queer: Interpreting Mass Culture*. Minneapolis: University of Minnesota Press.

Douglas, J., A. W. Burgess, A. G. Burgess and R. Ressler. (eds.) (2006) *Crime Classification Manual*. San Francisco: Jossey-Bass.

Douglas, M. (1969) *Purity and Danger*. London: Routledge and Kegan Paul.

Dowsett, G.W. (1996a) *Practicing Desire: Homosexual Sex in the Era of AIDS*. Stanford: Stanford University Press.

————. (1996b) 'What is sexuality? A bent answer to a straight question'. In C. Berry and A. Jagose (eds.) Australia Queer [Special issue], *Meanjin*, 55 (l): 16–30.

Dressler, J. (1995) 'When "heterosexual" men kill "homosexual" men: reflections on provocation law, sexual advances, and the "reasonable man" standard'. *The Journal of Criminal Law and Criminology*, 85 (3): 726–63.

Dreyfus, H. and P. Rabinow. (1982) *Michel Foucault: Beyond Structuralism and Hermeneutics*. Chicago: University of Chicago Press.

Duyvendak, J.W. (1996) 'The depoliticization of the Dutch gay identity, or why Dutch gays aren't queer'. In S. Seidman (ed.) *Queer Theory/Sociology*. Cambridge: Blackwell.

Edwards, T. (1994) *Erotics and Politics: Gay Male Sexuality, Masculinity and Feminism*. London: Routledge.

Ehrlich, H. (1992) 'The ecology of anti-gay violence'. In G. Herek and K. Berrill (eds.) *Hate Crimes: Confronting Violence against Lesbians and Gay Men*. Newbury Park, CA: Sage.

Eisenstein, Z. (1996) *Hatreds*. London: Routledge.

Elias, R. (1993) *Victims Still*. Newbury Park, CA: Sage.

Epstein, S. (1987) 'Gay politics, ethnic identity: the limits of social constructionism'. *Socialist Review*, 43/44: 9–49.

Faro, C. and G. Wotherspoon. (2000) *Street Seen: a History of Oxford Street*. Melbourne: Melbourne University Press.

Feeley, M. and J. Simon. (1996) 'The new penology: notes on the emerging strategies of corrections and its implications'. In J. Muncie, E. McLaughlin and M. Langan (eds.) *Criminological Perspectives: A Reader*. London: Sage.

Felson, R. and H. Steadman. (1983) 'Situations and processes leading to criminal violence'. *Criminology*, 21: 59.

Ferber, A. (ed.) (2004) *Home-Grown Hate: Gender and Organized Racism*. New York/London: Routledge.

Foucault, M. (1978) *The History of Sexuality: An Introduction*, vol. 1. Trans. Robert Hurley. New York: Vintage.

Free, M. and J. Hughson. (2003) 'Settling accounts with hooligans: gender blindness in football supporter subculture research'. *Men and Masculinities*, 6 (2): 136–55.

Freud, S. (1977) 'Infantile sexuality' [1905]; 'The transformations of puberty' [1905]; 'The dissolution of the Oedipus Complex' [1924]; 'Some psychical consequences of the anatomical distinction between the sexes' [1925]. In *The Pelican Freud Library: Vol. 7, On Sexuality*; trans. James Strachey. Harmondsworth: Penguin.

Gadd, D. and S. Farrall. (2004) 'Criminal careers, desistance and subjectivity: interpreting men's narratives of change'. *Theoretical Criminology*, 8 (2): 123–56.

Gadd, D. and T. Jefferson. (2007) *Psychosocial Criminology: An Introduction*. London: Sage.

Gagnon, J. (1977) *Human Sexualities*. Glenview, IL: Scott, Foreman & Co.

Gagnon, J. and W. Simon. (1973) *Sexual Conduct: The Social Sources of Human Sexuality*. London: Hutchinson.

Gamson, J. (1995) 'Must identity movements self-destruct? A queer dilemma'. *Social Problems*, 42 (3): 390–407.

Gamson, J. and D. Moon. (2004) 'The sociology of sexualities: queer and beyond'. *Annual Review of Sociology*, 30: 47–4.

Garber, M. (1992) *Vested Interests: Cross-Dressing and Cultural Anxiety*. London: Routledge.

Garland, D. (1985) *Punishment and Welfare: A History of Penal Strategies*. Aldershot: Gower.

———. (2002) *The Culture of Control: Crime and Social Control in Contemporary Society*. Oxford: Oxford University Press.

Gay Men and Lesbians against Discrimination (GLAD). (1994) *Not A Day Goes By: The GLAD Survey into Discrimination and Violence against Lesbians and Gay Men in Victoria*. Melbourne: GLAD.

Gemert, F. van. (1991) 'Noordafrikaanse en turkse homomoordenaars: op zoek naar een culturele verklaring' (North African and Turkish anti-gay killers: looking for a cultural explanation). *Justitiele Verkenningen* (Justice Investigations), 17 (1): 87–106.

———. (1994) 'Chicken kills hawk: gay murders during the eighties in Amsterdam'. *Journal of Homosexuality*, 26 (4): 149–74.

George, A. (2005) 'Anti-gay violence, criminal justice and victimhood in New South Wales'. Unpublished PhD thesis, University of Newcastle.

Glick, B. (1959) 'Homosexual panic: clinical and theoretical considerations'. *Journal of Nervous and Mental Disease*, 129: 20.

Goodey, J. (1997) 'Boys don't cry: masculinities, fear of crime and fearlessness', *The British Journal of Criminology*, 37(3): 401–17.

Goodwin, J., J. Jasper and F. Polletta. (2001) *Passionate Politics: Emotions and Social Movements*. Chicago: University of Chicago Press.

Gould, S.J. (1981) *The Mismeasure of Man*. New York: W.W. Norton & Co.

Greason, D. (1997) 'I was a teenage fascist'. In C. Cunneen, D. Fraser and S. Tomsen (eds.) *Faces of Hate: Hate Crime in Australia*. Sydney: Federation/Hawkins Press.

Green, R. (1992) *Sexual Science and the Law*. Cambridge, MA: Harvard University Press.

Greenberg, D. (1988) *The Construction of Homosexuality*. Chicago: University of Chicago Press.

Grosz, E. (1994) *Volatile Bodies: Towards a Corporeal Feminism*. St. Leonards, NSW: Allen and Unwin.

Grosz, E. and E. Probyn. (eds.) (1995) *Sexy Bodies: The Strange Carnalities of Feminism*. London/New York: Routledge.

Gusfield, J. (1963) *Symbolic Crusade: Status Politics and the American Temperance Movement*. Urbana, IL: University of Illinois Press.

Habermas, J. (1976) *Legitimation Crisis*. London: Heinemann.

Haeberle, E. (1989) 'Swastika, pink triangle and yellow star: the destruction of sexology and the persecution of homosexuals in Nazi Germany'. In M. Duberman, M. Vicinus and G. Chauncey (eds.) *Hidden From History: Reclaiming the Gay and Lesbian Past*. London: Penguin.

Hage, G. (1998) *White Nation*. Sydney: Pluto Press.

Hall, N. (2005) *Hate Crime*. Cullompton, UK: Willan.

Hall, S. (2002) 'Daubing the drudges of fury: men, violence and the piety of the "hegemonic masculinity" thesis'. *Theoretical Criminology*, 6 (1): 35–61.

Halperin, D. (1989) 'Sex before sexuality: pederasty, politics, and power in classical Athens'. In M. Duberman, M. Vicinus and G. Chauncey (eds.) *Hidden From History: Reclaiming the Gay and Lesbian Past*. Harmondsworth: Penguin.

———. (1990) *One Hundred Years of Homosexuality*. New York: Routledge.

Hamm, M. (1993) *American Skinhead: The Criminology and Control of Hate Crime*. Westport: Praeger.

———. (ed.) (1994) *Hate Crime: International Perspectives on Causes and Control*. Cincinnati: Anderson Publishing.

Harry, J. (1992) 'Conceptualising anti-gay violence'. In G. Herek and K. Berrill (eds.) *Hate Crimes: Confronting Violence against Lesbians and Gay Men*. Newbury Park, CA: Sage.

Hatheway, J. (2003) *The Gilded Age Construction of Modern American Homophobia*. New York: Palgrave.

Hay, D., P. Linebaugh, J. Rule, E.P. Thompson and C. Winstock. (1977) *Albion's Fatal Tree: Crime and Society in Eighteenth-Century England*. Harmondsworth: Penguin.

Heilpern, D. (1998) *Fear or Favour: Sexual Assault of Young Prisoners*. Lismore, NSW: Southern Cross University Press.

Hennessy, R. (1995) 'Queer visibility in commodity culture'. In L. Nicholson and S. Seidman (eds.) *Social Postmodernism*. Cambridge: Cambridge University Press.

Herdt, G. (1981) *Guardians of the Flutes: Idioms of Masculinity*. New York: McGraw Hill.

Herek, G. (1984) 'Beyond homophobia: a social psychological perspective on attitudes towards lesbians and gay men'. *Journal of Homosexuality*, 10 (1/2): 1–21.

———. (1992) 'The social context of hate crimes: notes on cultural heterosexism'. In G. Herek and K. Berrill (eds.) *Hate Crimes: Confronting Violence against Lesbians and Gay Men*. Newbury Park, CA: Sage.

———. (2000) 'The psychology of sexual prejudice'. *Current Directions in Psychological Research*, 9 (1): 19–22.

———. (2007) 'Confronting sexual stigma and prejudice: theory and practice'. *Journal of Social Issues*, 63 (4): 905–25.

Herek, G. and K. Berrill. (eds.) (1992) *Hate Crimes: Confronting Violence against Lesbians and Gay Men*. Newbury Park, CA: Sage.

Herek, G. and J. Capitanio. (1996) '"Some of my best friends": intergroup contact, concealable stigma, and heterosexuals' attitudes towards gay men and lesbians'. *Personality and Social Psychology Bulletin*, 22 (4): 412–24.

Herek, G., J. Cogan and J. Gillis. (2002) 'Victim experiences in hate crimes based on sexual orientation'. *Journal of Social Issues*, 58: 319–39.

Herman, D. (1997) *The Antigay Agenda: Orthodox Vision and the Christian Right*. Chicago: University of Chicago Press.

Hester, M., L. Kelly and J. Radford. (eds.) (1996) *Women, Violence and Male Power*. Buckingham: Open University Press.

Hocquenghem, G. (1978) *Homosexual Desire*. London: Allison & Busby.

Hodge, S. (1995) '"No fags out there": gay men, identity and suburbia'. *Journal of Interdisciplinary Gender Studies*, 1 (1): 41–8.

Howe, A. (2001) 'Homosexual advances in law: murderous, excuse, pluralized ignorance and the privilege of unknowing'. In C. Stychin and D. Herman (eds.) *Law and Sexuality*. Minneapolis: University of Minnesota Press.

Hughes, E. (1962) 'Good people and dirty work'. *Social Problems*, 10 (1): 3–11.

Human Rights and Equal Opportunity Commission. (1991) *Racist Violence: Report of National Inquiry into Racist Violence in Australia*. Canberra: Australian Government Publishing Service.

Humphreys, L. (1970) *Tearoom Trade: Impersonal Sex in Public Places*. Chicago: Aldine.

Irvine, J. (2007) 'Transient feelings: sex panics and the politics of emotions'. *GLQ, A Journal of Gay and Lesbian Studies*, 14 (1): 1–40.

Jackson, P. (1996) 'The persistence of gender'. *Meanjin*, 55 (1): 110–21.

Jackson, P. and G. Sullivan. (eds.) (1999a) *Lady Boys, Tom Boys, Rent Boys: Male and Female Homosexualities in Contemporary Thailand*. New York: Haworth Press.

———. (1999b) *Multicultural Queer: Australian Narratives*. New York: Haworth Press.

Jackson, S. and S. Scott. (eds.) (1996) *Feminism and Sexuality: A Reader*. Edinburgh: Edinburgh University Press.

Jacobs, J. (1996) 'The social construction of a hate crime epidemic'. *Journal of Criminal Law and Criminology*, 86 (2) Winter: 366–91.

Jacobs, J. and K. Potter. (1998) *Hate Crimes: Criminal Law and Identity Politics*. New York: Oxford University Press.

Jagose, A. (1996) *Queer Theory*. Melbourne: Melbourne University Press.

Janoff, D. (2005) *Pink Blood: Homophobic Violence in Canada*. Toronto: University of Toronto Press.

Jasper, J. (1997) *The Art of Moral Protest*. Chicago: University of Chicago Press.

Jefferson, T. (1997) 'Masculinities and crime'. In M. Maguire, R. Morgan and R. Reiner (eds.) *The Oxford Handbook of Criminology*. Oxford: Clarendon Press.

———. (2002) 'Subordinating hegemonic masculinity'. *Theoretical Criminology*, 6 (1): 63–88.

Jeffreys, S. (1990) *Anticlimax: A Feminist Perspective on the Sexual Revolution*. London: Women's Press.

———. (2004) *Unpacking Queer Politics: A Lesbian Feminist Perspective*. Cambridge: Polity Press.

Jenness, V. and K. Broad. (1997) *Hate Crimes: New Social Movements and the Politics of Violence*. New York: Aldine de Gruyter.

Jenness, V. and R. Grattet. (2001) *Making Hate a Crime*. New York: Russell Sage.

Johnston, C. (1999) *A Sydney Gaze: The Making of Gay Liberation*. Sydney: Shiltron Press.

Johnston, L. (2001) '(Other) bodies and tourism studies'. *Annals of Tourism Research*, 28 (1): 180–201.

———. (2005) *Queering Tourism: Paradoxical Performances at Gay Pride Parades*. London: Routledge.

Kantor, M. (1998) *Homophobia: Description, Development and Dynamics of Gay Bashing*. Westport: Praeger.

Katz, J. (1976) *Gay American History: Lesbians and Gay Men in the USA*. New York: Crowell.

———. (1988) *Seductions of Crime: Moral and Sensual Attractions of Doing Evil*. New York: Basic Books.

———. (1995) *The Invention of Heterosexuality*. New York: Plume Books.

Kelley, J. (2001) 'Attitudes towards homosexuality in 29 nations'. *Australian Social Monitor*, 4 (1): 15–22.

Kempf, E. (1920) *Psychopathology*. St. Louis: C.V. Mosby Co.

Kendall, C. (2002) 'The harms of gay male pornography: a sex equality perspective'. *Gay and Lesbian Law Journal*, 10: 43.

Kimmel, M.S. (ed.) (1987) *Changing Men: New Directions in Research on Men and Masculinity*. Newbury Park, CA: Sage.

Kinsey, A., W. B. Pomeroy and C. Martin. (1948) *Sexual Behavior in the Human Male*. Philadelphia: W.B. Saunders.

Kite, M. (2002) 'When perceptions meet reality: individual differences in reactions to lesbians and gay men'. In A. Coyle and C. Kitzinger (eds.) *Lesbian and Gay Psychology: New Perspectives*. Malden: Blackwell Publishers.

Kitzinger, C. (1987) *The Social Construction of Lesbianism*. London: Sage.

Knopp, L. (1998) 'Sexuality and urban space: gay male identity politics in the United States, United Kingdom and Australia'. In R. Fincher and J. Jacobs (eds.) *Cities of Difference*. New York: Guildford Press.

Lane, C. (1997) 'Psychoanalysis and sexual identity'. In A. Medhurst and S. Munt (eds.) *Lesbian and Gay Studies: A Critical Introduction*. London: Cassell.

Laplanche, J. and J.B. Pontalis. (1973) *The Language of Psychoanalysis*. New York: W.W. Norton & Co.

Lauritsen, J. and D. Thorstad. (1974) *The Early Homosexual Rights Movement (1864–1935)*. New York: Times Change Press.

Lee, C. (2003) *Murder and the Reasonable Man: Passion and Fear in the Courtroom*. New York: New York University Press.

Lesbian and Gay Anti-Violence Project. (1995) *'Homosexual Panic Defence' and Other Family Values*. Sydney: Lesbian and Gay Anti-Violence Project.

Lesbian and Gay Community Action. (1994) *The Police and You: A Survey of Lesbians and Gay Men in South Australia*. Adelaide: Lesbian and Gay Community Action.

LeVay, S. (1993) *The Sexual Brain*. London: MIT Press.

LeVay, S. and S. Valente. (2002) *Human Sexuality*. Sunderland, MA: Sinauer Associates.

Levin, J. (2007) *The Violence of Hate*. Boston: Pearson.

Levin, J. and J. MacDevitt. (1993) *Hate Crimes: The Rising Tide of Bigotry and Bloodshed*. New York: Plenum Press.

Levine, M. (1998) *Gay Macho: The Life and Death of the Homosexual Clone*. New York: New York University Press.

Lewes, K. (1995) *Psychoanalysis and Male Homosexuality*. Northvale, NJ: Jason Aronson Inc.

Loffreda, B. (2001) *Losing Mathew Shephard: Life and Politics in the Aftermath of Anti-Gay Murder*. New York: Columbia University Press.

MacKinnon, C. (1983) 'Feminism, Marxism, method and the state: toward feminist jurisprudence'. *Signs*, 8 (4): 635.

Maddison, S. and S. Scalmer. (2006) *Activist Wisdom: Practical Knowledge and Creative Tension in Social Movements*. Sydney: UNSW Press.

Manderson, L. and M. Jolly. (eds.) (1997) *Sites of Desire, Economies of Pleasure: Sexualities in Asia and the Pacific*. Chicago: University of Chicago Press.

Marcuse, H. (1966) *Eros and Civilization: A Philosophical Inquiry into Freud*. Boston: Beacon Press.

Markwell, K. (2002) 'Mardi Gras tourism and the construction of Sydney as an international gay and lesbian city'. *GLQ, A Journal of Gay and Lesbian Studies*, 8 (1): 83–102.

Mason, A. and A. Palmer. (1996) *Queer Bashing: A National Survey of Hate Crimes against Lesbians and Gay Men*. London: Stonewall.

Mason, G. (1997) 'Heterosexed violence: typicality and ambiguity'. In G. Mason and S. Tomsen (eds.) *Homophobic Violence*. Sydney: Hawkins Press.

———. (2001a) 'Not our kind of hate crime'. *Law and Critique*, 12: 253–78.

———. (2001b) *The Spectacle of Violence: Homophobia, Gender and Knowledge*. London: Routledge.

———. (2007) 'Hate crime as a moral category: lessons from the Snowtown case'. *Australian and New Zealand Journal of Criminology*, 40 (3): 240–71.

Matthews, J. (ed.) (1997) *Sex in Public: Australian Sexual Cultures*. Sydney: Allen and Unwin.

McKintosh, M. (1968) 'The homosexual role'. *Social Problems*, 16: 182–92.

McLaren, A. (1997) *The Trials of Masculinity: Policing Sexual Boundaries, 1870–1930*. Chicago: University of Chicago Press.

McNamara, L. (2002) *Regulating Racism*. Sydney: Sydney Institute of Criminology.

McPhail, B. (2002) 'Gender-bias hate crimes'. *Trauma, Violence and Abuse*, 3 (2): 125.

Messerschmidt, J. (1993) *Masculinities and Crime: Critique and Reconceptualization of Theory*. Lanham, MD: Rowman & Littlefield.

———. (1997) *Crime as Structured Action: Gender, Race, Class, and Crime in the Making*. Thousand Oaks, CA: Sage.

———. (1998) 'Men victimizing men: the case of lynching, 1865–1900'. In L. Bowker (ed.) *Masculinities and Violence*. Thousand Oaks, CA: Sage.

———. (1999) 'Making bodies matter: adolescent masculinities, the body, and varieties of violence'. *Theoretical Criminology*, 3 (2): 197–220.

Miller, B. and L. Humphreys. (1980) 'Lifestyles and violence: homosexual victims of assault and murder'. *Qualitative Sociology*, 3: 169–85.

Miller, W. (1997) *The Anatomy of Disgust*. Cambridge, MA: Harvard University Press.

Mison, R. (1992) 'Homophobia in manslaughter: the homosexual advance as insufficient provocation'. *California Law Review*, 80: 133–78.

Mitchell, J. (1974) *Psychoanalysis and Feminism*. London: Allen Lane.

Moran, L. (1995) 'Violence and the law: the case of sado-masochism'. *Social and Legal Studies*, 4 (2): 225.

———. (1996) *The Homosexuality of Law*. London: Routledge.

———. (2001) 'Affairs of the heart: hate crime and the politics of crime control'. *Law and Critique*, 12: 331–34.

Moran, L. and A. Sharpe. (2004) 'Violence, identity and policing: the case of violence against transgender people'. *Criminal Justice*, 4 (4): 395–417.

Moran, L. and B. Skeggs, with P. Tyrer and K. Corteen. (2004) *Sexuality and the Politics of Violence and Safety*. London/New York: Routledge.

Morgan, J. (2002) 'US hate crime legislation: a legal model to avoid in Australia'. *Journal of Sociology*, 38 (1): 25–48.

Mort, F. (1987) *Dangerous Sexualities: Medico-Moral Politics in England since 1830*. London: Routledge and Kegan Paul.

Mott, L. (1996) *Epidemic of Hate: Violations of the Human Rights of Gay Men, Lesbians and Transvestites in Brazil*. San Francisco: Grupo Gay da Bahia/International Gay and Lesbian Human Rights Commission.

Mullins, C. (2006) *Holding Your Square: Masculinities, Streetlife and Violence*. Cullompton, UK: Willan.

Murray, C. (2003) 'The underclass'. In E. McLaughlin, J. Muncie and G. Hughes (eds.) *Criminological Perspectives: Essential Reading*. London: Sage.

Nardi, P. (ed.) (2000) *Gay Masculinities*. Thousand Oaks, CA: Sage.

Newburn, T. (2007) *Criminology*. Cullompton, UK: Willan.

Newburn, T. and E. Stanko. (eds.) (1994) *Just Boys Doing Business? Men, Masculinities and Crime*. London: Routledge.

O'Sullivan, K. (1997) 'Dangerous desire: lesbianism as sex or politics'. In J. Matthews (ed.) *Sex in Public: Australian Sexual Cultures*. St. Leonards, NSW: Allen and Unwin.

Ordonez, J. (1995) *No Human Being is Disposable—Social Cleansing, Human Rights, and Sexual Orientation in Colombia*. San Francisco: Colombia Human Rights Committee/International Gay and Lesbian Human Rights Commission.

Parker, R. (1991) *Bodies, Pleasures and Passions: Sexual Culture in Contemporary Brazil*. Boston: Beacon Press.

Perry, B. (ed.) (2003) *Hate and Bias Crime: A Reader*. New York: Routledge.

Petrosino, C. (1999) 'Connecting the past to the future: hate crime in America'. *Journal of Contemporary Criminal Justice*, 5 (1): 22–47.

Pharr, S. (1998) *Homophobia: A Weapon of Sexism*. Little Rock, AR: Chardon Press.

Phillips, K. and B. Reay. (eds.) (2002) *Sexualities in History: A Reader*. New York: Routledge.

Plant, R. (1986) *The Pink Triangle*. New York: Holt.

Plummer, D. (1999) *One of the Boys: Masculinity, Homophobia and Modern Manhood*. Binghamton, NY: Harrington Park Press.

Plummer, K. (1975) *Sexual Stigma: An Interactionist Account*. London: Routledge and Kegan Paul.

———. (1995) *Telling Sexual Stories: Power, Change and Social Worlds*. London: Routledge.

———. (2007) 'The flow of boundaries: gays, queers and intimate citizenship'. In D. Downes, P. Rock, C. Chinkin and C. Gearty (eds.) *Crime, Social Control and Human Rights*. Cullompton, UK: Willan.

Polk, K. (1994) *When Men Kill: Scenarios of Masculine Violence*. Melbourne: Cambridge University Press.

Porter, S. and M. Woodworth. (2007) '"I'm sorry I did it . . . but he started it": a comparison of the official and self-reported homicide descriptions of psychopaths and non-psychopaths'. *Law and Human Behaviour*, 31: 91–107.

Price Waterhouse. (1995) *Out of the Blue: A Police Survey of Violence and Harassment against Gay Men and Lesbians*. Sydney: Price Waterhouse.

Ravenscroft, N. and X. Matteucci. (2003) 'The festival as carnivalesque: social governance and control at Pamplona's San Fermin fiesta'. *Tourism, Culture and Communication*, 4: 1–15.

Reich, W. (1975) *The Mass Psychology of Fascism*. Harmondsworth: Penguin.

Robinson, P. (2001) 'Freud and homosexuality'. In T. Dean and C. Lane (eds.) *Homosexuality and Psychoanalysis*. Chicago: University of Chicago Press.

Robson, R. (1992) *Lesbian (Out)Law: Surviving Under the Rule of Law*. New York: Firebrand Books.

Rock, P. (1998) 'Murderers, victims and "survivors"'. *The British Journal of Criminology*, 38: 185–200.

Rose, N. (1999) *Powers of Freedom: Reframing Political Thought*. Cambridge: Cambridge University Press.

Rothenberg, P. (1999) 'Construction, deconstruction, and reconstruction of difference'. In M. Baird and S. Rosenbaum (eds.) *Hatred, Bigotry and Prejudice*. New York: Prometheus Books.

Rubin, G. (1993) 'Thinking sex: notes for a radical theory of the politics of sexuality'. In H. Abelove, M. Barale and D. Halperin (eds.) *The Lesbian and Gay Studies Reader*. New York: Routledge.

Rushbrook, D. (2002) 'Cities, queer space, and the cosmopolitan tourist'. *GLQ, A Journal of Gay and Lesbian Studies*, 8 (1/2): 183–206.

Sabo, D., T. Kupers and W. London. (eds.) (2001) *Prison Masculinities*. Philadelphia: Temple University Press.

SAMOIS. (eds.) (1982) *Coming to Power: Writings and Graphics on Lesbian S/M*. Boston: Allyson Publications.

Sandroussi, J. and S. Thompson. (1995) *Out of the Blue: A Survey of Violence and Harassment against Gay Men and Lesbians*. Sydney: New South Wales Police Service.

Sarat, A. (ed.) (2005) *The Death Penalty: Influences and Outcomes*. Aldershot: Ashgate.

Sarre, R. (1996) 'The state of community policing in Australia: some emerging themes'. In D. Chappell and P. Wilson (eds.) *Australian Policing: Contemporary Issues*. North Ryde: Butterworths.

Schembri, A. (1992) *The Off Our Backs Report*. Sydney: Gay and Lesbian Rights Lobby.

———. (1995) 'Beaten black and blue: naming AIDS hate crime'. *National AIDS Bulletin*, 9 (6): 26–8.

Schmidt, M. (1994) 'Dahmer discourse and gay identity: the paradox of queer politics'. *Critical Sociology*, 20 (3): 81–105.

Scutt, J. (1991) 'The domestic paradigm: violence, nurturance and stereotyping of the sexes'. *Women's Studies International Forum*, 14 (3): 163–72.

Sedgwick, E.K. (1994) *Epistemology of the Closet*. London: Penguin.

Segal, L. (1990) *Slow Motion: Changing Masculinities, Changing Men*. London: Virago.

———. (1994) *Straight Sex: Rethinking the Politics of Pleasure*. Berkeley: University of California Press.

Segal, L. and M. McIntosh. (eds.) (1992) *Sex Exposed: Sexuality and the Pornography Debate*. London: Virago.

Seidman, S. (1997) *Difference Troubles: Queering Social Theory and Sexual Politics*. Cambridge: Cambridge University Press.

Sheldon, W.H., with E. Hartl and E. McDermott. (1949) *Varieties of Delinquent Youth*. New York: Harper.

Shilts, R. (1982) *The Mayor of Castro Street: The Life and Times of Harvey Milk*. New York: St. Martin's Press.

Silver, A. (1967) 'The demand for order in civil society: a review of some themes in the history of urban crime, police and riot'. In D. Bordua (ed.) *The Police: Six Sociological Essays*. New York: John Wiley.

Simpson, M. (1994) *Male Impersonators: Men Performing Masculinity*. London: Cassell.

Smart, B. (2002) *Michel Foucault*. London: Routledge.

Smyth, M. (2006) 'Queers and provocateurs: hegemony, ideology, and the "homosexual advance" defense'. *Law and Society Review*, 40 (4): 903–30.

Snow, D., E. Rochford, S. Worden and R. Benford. (1986) 'Frame alignment processes, micromobilization, and movement participation'. *American Sociological Review*, 51 (4): 464–81.

Spargo, T. (1999) *Foucault and Queer Theory*. Cambridge: Icon Books.

Stanko, E. (1990) *Everyday Violence: How Men and Women Experience Sexual and Physical Danger*. London: Pandora.

———. (2000) 'Victims R us: the life history of "fear of crime" and the politicisation of violence'. In T. Hope and R. Sparks (eds.) *Crime, Risk and Insecurity*. London: Routledge.

———. (2001) 'Re-conceptualising the policing of hatred: confessions and worrying dilemmas of a consultant'. *Law and Critique*, 12: 309–29.

Stanko, E. and P. Curry. (1997) 'Homophobic violence and the self "at risk": interrogating the boundaries'. *Social and Legal Studies*, 6 (4): 513–32.

Stanko, E. and K. Hobdell. (1993) 'Assault on men: masculinity and male victimization'. *The British Journal of Criminology*, 33 (3): 400–15.

Stein, A. (1992) 'Sisters and queers: the decentering of lesbian feminism'. *Socialist Review*, 22 (1): 33–56.

Stein, E. (ed.) (1990) *Forms of Desire: Sexual Orientation and the Social Constructionist Controversy*. New York: Garland.

———. (1999) *The Mismeasure of Desire: The Science, Theory and Ethics of Sexual Orientation*. Oxford: Oxford University Press.

Stychin, C. (1995) *Law's Desire: Sexuality and the Limits of Justice*. London: Routledge.

Suffredini, K. (2001) 'Pride and prejudice: the homosexual panic defence'. *Boston College Third World Law Journal*, 21: 279–314.

Swigonski, M., R. Mama and K. Ward. (eds.) (2001) *From Hate Crimes to Human Rights: A Tribute to Mathew Shephard*. Binghamton: Harrington Park Press.

Swivel, M. (1991) 'Public convenience, public nuisance: criminological perspectives on the "beat"'. *Current Issues in Criminal Justice*, 3 (2): 237–49.

Taylor, I., P. Walton and J. Young. (1973) *The New Criminology—For a Social Theory of Deviance*. London: Routledge and Kegan Paul.

Terry, J. (1999) *An American Obsession: Science, Medicine and Homosexuality in Modern Society*. Chicago: University of Chicago Press.

Theron, A. (1994) 'Anti-gay violence and discrimination: the need for legislation against anti-gay hate crimes in the sociopolitically changing South Africa'. *Acta Criminologica*, 7 (3): 107–14.

Tomsen, S. (1992) 'The state and homophobic violence'. Paper presented to the annual conference of the Austalian and New Zealand Society of Criminology, University of Melbourne, September.

———. (1993) 'The political contradictions of policing and countering anti-gay violence in New South Wales'. *Current Issues in Criminal Justice*, 5 (2): 209–15.

———. (1997a) 'A top night: social protest, masculinity and the culture of drinking violence'. *The British Journal of Criminology*, 37 (1): 90–103.

———. (1997b) 'Violence, Sexuality and the Heterosexual Imaginary'. In G. Mason and S. Tomsen (eds.) *Homophobic Violence*. Sydney: Hawkins Press.

———. (1997c) 'Was Lombroso a queer? Criminology, criminal justice and the heterosexual imaginary'. In G. Mason and S. Tomsen (eds.) *Homophobic Violence*. Sydney: Hawkins Press.

———. (2001a) 'Hate crimes and masculine offending'. *Gay and Lesbian Law Journal*, 10:26–42.

———. (2001b) 'Queer and safe: combating violence with gentrified sexual identities'. In C. Johnston and P. Van Reyk (eds.) *Queer City*. Sydney: Pluto Press.

———. (2002) *Hatred, Murder and Male Honour: Anti-Homosexual Killings in New South Wales, 1980–2000*. Canberra: Australian Institute of Criminology.

———. (2005) '"Boozers and bouncers": masculine conflict, disengagement and the contemporary governance of drinking-related violence and disorder'. *The Australian and New Zealand Journal of Criminology*, 38 (3): 283–97.

———. (2006) 'Homophobic violence, cultural essentialism and shifting sexual identities'. *Social and Legal Studies*, 15 (3): 389–407.

———. (2008) 'Introduction'. In S. Tomsen (ed.) *Crime, Criminal Justice and Masculinities: A Reader (The International Library of Criminology, Criminal Justice and Penology)*. Aldershot: Ashgate.

Tomsen, S. and K. Markwell. (2007) *When the Glitter Settles: Safety and Hostility at and around Gay and Lesbian Public Events*. Newcastle, NSW: Cultural Industries and Practices Research Centre, University of Newcastle.

Tomsen, S. and G. Mason. (2001) 'Engendering homophobia: violence, sexuality and gender conformity'. *Journal of Sociology*, 37 (3): 265–87.

Turner, V. (1987) *The Anthropology of Performance*. New York: PAJ Publications.

Van den Boogaard, H. (1987) *Flikkers Moeten We Niet: Mannen Als Doelwit Van Antihomoseksueel Geweld (We Don't Like Queers: Men as Targets of Anti-Homosexual Violence)*. Amsterdam: SUA.

Vance, C. (ed.) (1989a) *Pleasure and Danger: Exploring Female Sexuality*. London: Pandora.

———. (1989b) 'Social construction theory: problems in the history of sexuality'. In A. Niekerk and T. van der Meer (eds.) *Homosexuality, Which Homosexuality?* London: GMP.

———. (1994) 'The war on culture'. In T. Gott (ed.) *Don't Leave Me this Way: Art in the Age of Aids*. Canberra: National Gallery of Australia.

von Schulthess, B. (1992) 'Violence in the streets: anti-lesbian assault and harassment in San Francisco'. In G. Herek and K. Berrill (eds.) *Hate Crimes: Confronting Violence against Lesbians and Gay Men*. Newbury Park, CA: Sage.

Waitt, G. and K. Markwell. (2006) *Gay Tourism, Culture and Context*. New York: Haworth Press.

Walby, C. (1995) 'Destruction: boundary erotics and refigurations of the heterosexual male body'. In E. Grosz and E. Probyn (eds.) *Sexy Bodies: The Strange Carnalities of Feminism*. New York: Routledge.

Walters, M. (2005) 'Hate crime laws in Australia: introducing punishment enhancers'. *Criminal Law Journal*, 29: 201.

Warner, K. (2004) 'Gang rape in Sydney: crime, the media, politics, race and sentencing'. *The Australian and New Zealand Journal of Criminology*, 37 (3): 344–61.

Warner, M. (ed.) (1993) *Fear of a Queer Planet*. Minneapolis: University of Minnesota Press.

Watney, S. (1994) 'Queer epistemology: activism, "outing" and the politics of sexual identities'. *Critical Quarterly*, 36 (1): 13–27.

Weber, M. (1970) 'Politics as a vocation'. In H. Gerth and C.W. Mills (eds.) *From Max Weber: Essays in Sociology*. London: Routledge.

Weeks, J. (1985) *Sex, Politics and Society: The Regulation of Sexuality since 180*. Harlow, UK: Longman.

———. (1986) *Sexuality*. London: Routledge.

———. (1991) *Against Nature: Essays on History, Sexuality and Identity*. London: Rivers Oram Press.

———. (1995) *Invented Moralities: Sexual Values in an Age of Uncertainty*. New York: Columbia.

———. (1998) 'The sexual citizen'. *Theory, Culture and Society*, 15 (3/4): 35–52.

———. (2003) *Sexuality*, 2nd ed. London/New York: Routledge.

Weinberg, G. (1972) *Society and the Healthy Homosexual*. New York: St. Martin's Press.

White, R. (2000) 'Hate crime: a review essay'. *Current Issues in Criminal Justice*, 11 (2): 357–61.

———. (2002) 'Hate crime politics'. *Theoretical Criminology*, 6 (4): 499.

Whitehead, A. (2005) 'Man to man violence: how masculinity may work as a dynamic risk factor'. *The Howard Journal*, 44 (4): 411–22.

Wickberg, D. (2000) 'Homophobia: on the cultural history of an idea'. *Critical Inquiry*, 27 (1): 42–57.

Willet, G. (1997) 'The darkest decade: homophobia in Australia in the 1950s'. *Australian Historical Studies*, 28 (109): 120–32.

———. (2000) *Living Out Loud: A History of Gay and Lesbian Activism in Australia*. St. Leonards, NSW: Allen and Unwin.

Williamson, S., R. Hare and S. Wong. (1997) 'Violence: criminal psychopaths and their victims'. *Canadian Journal of Behavioral Science*, 19: 454–62.

Wotherspoon, G. (1991) *City of the Plain: History of a Gay Sub-Culture*. Sydney: Hale & Iremonger.

Young-Bruehl, E. (1996) *The Anatomy of Prejudices*. Cambridge, MA: Harvard University Press.

LEGAL AUTHORITIES

Death of KB (11 September 1996) Coroner's Report, Abernethy J.
Death of WD (12 December 1994) Coroner's Report, Abernethy J.
R v. Bonner (15–18 May 1995) NSWSC, Dowd J.
R v. D (7 August 1992) NSWSC, Wood J.
R v. Dunn (21 September 1995) NSWSC, Ireland J.
R. v. Gellatly (22 December 1995) NSWDC, Wall, J.
R v. Graham (10 November 2000) NSWSC, Whealy J.
R v. Green (7 June 1994) NSWSC, Abadee J.
R v. Green (14 December 1994) NSWCCA.
R v. Hort (13–18 May 1992) NSWSC, Finlay J.
R. v. Howe (1958) *State Reports of South Australia*, p. 95. See also R. v. Howe (1958) 100 CLR 448. (*Commonwealth Law Reports*).
R v. Leonard (10 November 1997) NSWSC, Badgery-Parker J.
R v. MC & AT (2–26 November 1982) NSWSC, Lee J.
R v. McKinnon (15–24 November 1993) NSWSC, Studdert J.
R v. M, H, M & Y (15 April 1991) NSWSC, Badgery-Parker J.
R v. RM (6 February–30 April 1991) NSWSC, Badgery-Parker J.
R v. T (6 April–14 July 1994) NSWSC, Grove J.
R. v. Turner & Nash (14 September 1990) NSWSC, Finlay J.
R v. Valera (Van Krevel) (21 December 2000) NSWSC, Studdert J.

Index